D1496194

THE
MAN WHO FELL
FROM THE SKY

CamCat Publishing, LLC
Brentwood, Tennessee 37027
camcatpublishing.com

Hardcover ISBN 9781931540278
Paperback ISBN 9780744300789
Large-Print Paperback ISBN 9780744300314
eBook ISBN 9780744300796
Audiobook ISBN 978074430xxxx

Library of Congress Control Number: 2020935784

Cover design by Mimi Bark

5 4 3 2 1

THE
MAN WHO FELL
FROM THE SKY

THE BIZARRE LIFE AND DEATH OF
'20S TYCOON ALFRED LOEWENSTEIN

WILLIAM NORRIS

CamCat
Perspectives

BY WILLIAM NORRIS

Fiction

A Grave Too Many

Make Mad the Guilty

The Badger Game

Nonfiction

A Talent to Deceive

Snowbird

The Man Who Fell from the Sky

Willful Misconduct

TABLE OF CONTENTS

1

It was hot enough to make the angels sweat. Their marble faces glistened in the harsh sunlight, sorrowing blindly, as the small cortège made its slow way along the curving path between them to the northeast corner of the vast cemetery of Evere. There were no crowds.

The group of curious villagers who had gathered at the gate to see the wealthy and the great pass by was left in puzzled disappointment. Tongues wagged. Was this the way the rich buried their dead?

The flowers were some small recompense for their long wait in the baking heat: great mounds of wreaths and sprays that filled the motor hearse to overflowing, hiding from sight the expensive coffin. Their embossed cards of condolence read like a page from the *Financial Times*. Bankers and boards of directors from around the world had paid their floral tributes.

But they had not come to say goodbye. Nor had the donor of the huge wreath of orchids, violets, and pansies, which occupied the place of honor on the coffin lid. And she had been his wife.

Captain Alfred Loewenstein, Companion of the Bath, multimillionaire, aviator and sportsman, friend of kings, maker and loser of fortunes, was going to his grave almost alone. He was fifty-one years old.

At least he would rest undisturbed. In the cemetery outside Evere, which serves the city of Brussels, there are three classes of graves. For those of lesser means, plots may be purchased for fifteen or fifty years, at the end of which time the occupants are dug up and the plots resold. It is a practical arrangement. No such indignity awaited Alfred Loewenstein. His tomb, covered with a plain black slab of polished marble and occupying the space of three graves, had been purchased in perpetuity. The cost, and the occupancy, was shared with the Misonne family, into which he had married. Above all else, Alfred Loewenstein was a businessman.

The hearse had driven hard to take the empty coffin to Calais on the French coast, collect its occupant, and return. Now it crunched to a halt beside the open tomb. A motley collection of cars, from limousines to taxis, tagged on behind. The mourners emerged from them like beetles, murmuring to each other with as much solemnity as they could muster. There were just seventeen of them, all men, and they perspired freely in the black constriction of their formal grief. They looked with sympathy at the pallbearers, staggering under their load: The massive oak coffin was lined with lead, which was a thoughtful gesture. Alfred Loewenstein had died two weeks before, falling four thousand feet from his private aircraft, allegedly unseen by any of the six other people on board. His condition was less than fragrant.

To the general relief, it was quickly over. A few perfunctory prayers from the cemetery's resident priest, and the coffin was lowered into the vault. The mourners departed, the slab was replaced, and Madeleine Loewenstein's wreath was laid carefully on top. The remainder of the flowers were heaped haphazardly upon the graves on either side to fade and rot in the sunshine of that spectacular July of 1928.

In the weeks that followed, no mason came to carve the name of the famous man on the marble slab. Nor would they ever come. Alfred Loewenstein had been tidily consigned to the obscurity of an unmarked grave.

If there was little mourning, there was certainly wailing and gnashing of teeth. The death of Loewenstein had brought financial disaster to stockbrokers and small investors across the length and breadth of Europe. Little old ladies and country gentry alike who had clung to his financial coattails in the hope of becoming rich were suddenly poor once more. Dealers in London and Brussels caught on the margins went to the wall as stock in his companies tumbled. In Berlin and Zurich, Paris and Montreal—almost everywhere where men dealt in money —the story was the same. For the best part of a decade, the man they called the Belgian Croesus had commanded the headlines and mesmerized them all with his flamboyance, his daring, and the sheer effrontery of his behavior.

They had danced to his tune, dazzled by his wizardry, hopeful that his Midas touch would transmute their savings into gold. And so it did—while he lived. But the tune was ended, and the melody lingered not. Alfred Loewenstein had wound up bobbing on the cold swell of the English Channel. In a manner as bizarre and strange as the way he lived his life, the third richest man in the world had died and left them holding scraps of paper. They were puzzled, angry, and afraid. And they were much, much poorer.

————

IN THE SPRING OF 1984, I knew nothing of this. Loewenstein had died five years before I was born, and though I had worked in the newspaper game for most of my life, I had never even heard his name. And this was odd. Headlines fade and stories are forgotten, but the truly sensational lingers on in some backwater of the journalistic mind. The unexplained death of one of the greatest financial czars of the century ought to qualify him for some sort of place in the reporters' hall of fame. But not Loewenstein. For me, and for the contemporary world in general, the extraordinary life and death of Alfred Loewenstein might never have happened. Until, that is, I happened to visit New York and took a ride in the elevator to the fifteenth floor of the Pan Am building on Park Avenue.

All things considered, it was an odd place for me to be. I had just finished a book that was far from complimentary to Pan Am (*Willful Misconduct*, CamCat Perspectives 2020) and that had had a few unkind things to say about American aviation lawyers. Yet here I was in the heart of the enemy camp, about to visit a friend who was, of all things, an aviation lawyer.

Stuart Speiser was and is, I hasten to add, a lawyer of a different stamp from those I had been writing about. He is also an unashamed millionaire, a writer and thinker of no mean distinction, and an inveterate collector of strange stories. His generosity in passing these on can sometimes be an embarrassment.

"You might be interested in this," he said as I was about to leave. A brown folder was thrust in my direction. "I came across this story years ago. Always wanted to write it, but never found the time. It might make a book for you. I know you like turning over stones and seeing what crawls out."

I made polite noises. Stuart's idea of a good story and my own did not always coincide. And, truth to tell, I had recently discovered that writing books was a splendid way to live but a lousy way to make a living. I did not need another one. But to refuse would have been impolite, and impecunious writers are not rude to millionaires, even when they happen to be friends. So I thanked him kindly and stuffed the folder in my briefcase. And there it stayed.

My briefcase is a filing system of some sophistication. Papers are added at the top until it is full to the point of bursting—a process that may take weeks or months. Seen in cross-section, the resulting mass of material, when removed, forms a perfect archaeological record of my procrastination. By mere measurement, I can tell almost to the day when I forgot to do something.

The brown folder, when finally excavated, definitely fell into the New York, or "hassle with publishers," period of my life. I frowned at it, vaguely remembering its origin. Should I read the contents? Well, why not? Whatever lay inside would be an improvement on my preoccupation of that moment, which was paying the telephone bill. I put aside my checkbook. I opened the folder.

There was once a lady named Pandora, who regretted similar curiosity. Investigative writers are supposed to scorn such superstitions. Yet here were demons of a sort. What I held in my hand were blackened photostats of cuttings from *The New York Times* more than half a century old. Some were hard to read, and some downright impossible. But there was enough to tell me that here was the story of a remarkable man who met an extraordinary death. More to the point, that death had never been explained. It was a mystery, the sort of convoluted locked-door puzzle beloved by fiction writers of the 1920s—except that it was more curious than any fiction.

The questions crowded in. How could a man so prominent, so rich and famous, die violently without any trace of an official investigation? If he had committed suicide, what had driven him to such desperation? There was nothing in the cuttings to indicate the slightest reason. Could it have been murder? If so, who had means and motive? An accident, then? But how do you step "accidentally" out of an aircraft in mid-flight and do so, moreover, without any of your fellow passengers noticing?

The detached attitude of the police, who hardly figured in the stories at all, was curious to say the least. Nor did it seem that Loewenstein's associates had been anxious to do anything more than staunch the financial bleeding that followed his disappearance. There was certainly no indication that they wanted to find out how he had died. Quite the reverse: Reading between the lines, there was the distinct impression that an embarrassment had been removed from their staid, stiff-collared world of banking. The man had been a bounder. Good riddance to him.

The longer I looked at those faded cuttings, the more convinced I became that they failed to tell the whole story. I had never been an admirer of financiers, and there were clear indications that Loewenstein had not been one of the most attractive of the breed. Yet whatever else one said of him, this had been a man. And no man deserves to die quite so unloved and uncared for, even one as rich, as brash, as arrogant as Alfred Loewenstein.

Yet what good would it do to resurrect it all, even supposing that I could? The man was dead; nothing could change that. And if no one had cared at the time, why should anyone care now to find out how and why he died? Why should I waste my time and money on a wild goose chase after the solution to a mystery more than half a century old?

Fifty-six years is a very long time. Loewenstein's murderer, if there had been such a person, would be long beyond the reach of human justice. And witnesses, if any survived, would be senile at best. Or so I thought at the time. As it turned out, I could not have been more wrong.

In short, I found a dozen reasons to forget the whole damned thing. The trouble was that none of them could override my curiosity. I wanted to know the truth, or at least come as near to it as I could. And for some unaccountable reason I found myself caring about Loewenstein himself. It seemed time that someone did. With a slight sinking feeling, knowing that I was hooked, I turned over the pile of cuttings and began again.

I cannot remember whether I paid the telephone bill.

2

THE LOGICAL PLACE TO start was Loewenstein's obituary. Obituaries seldom tell the truth, the whole truth, and nothing but the truth, but so help me God I couldn't think of anything else. There might at least, I thought, be some names, dates, and places that would help me carry the search further. It so happened that I was doing a freelance stint on the foreign desk of *The Times* when I began researching Loewenstein, so I headed for the library— which is known in that once-splendid establishment as the Information Department.

The obit was there: a full column of tiny type. But I found to my disappointment that it told me very little of Loewenstein's origins. Nor did the obituaries from other papers, which the librarians of 1928 had thoughtfully clipped. While they all agreed that he was born in Belgium of German stock, the son of a banker who lost his fortune before Loewenstein could inherit, all had different dates of birth. They ranged from 1874 (*Le Matin*, Brussels) to 1879 (*The Times*). Only the *Daily Express*, which split the difference at 1877, had—I later discovered—got it right.

Accounts of Loewenstein's early life were sketchy. It appeared that he was almost forty when he came on to the world financial scene from nowhere, a full-fledged millionaire with a passion for ostentation and an apparently inexhaustible supply of ready cash. But millionaires from impoverished backgrounds do not just happen. Somewhere along the line, Loewenstein got rich.

The trouble was, nobody seemed to be sure how he had done it, and this caused me some concern. How could I unravel the story of his death without first knowing how he had lived? The final eight years had been no secret—quite the reverse—but Loewenstein seemed to have drawn a veil behind himself at the end of the First World War, before bursting on to the center of the financial stage. Was there some secret in his past, I wondered? Could it have had any relevance to the way he died?

Some obituarists claimed that he had worked on the Brussels Stock Exchange, placing large quantities of securities in foreign companies. Others romanticized that he had left a cadetship in the Belgian army on the death of his father, and had opened his own small bank with minuscule capital in order to pay off the parental debts. According to this account, business lagged until a mysterious South American businessman appeared and offered him a deal, as a result of which Loewenstein made millions.

It seemed an unlikely story. It was too facile: the sort of thing that Loewenstein, who loved to surround himself with a cloak of mystery in order to gain more publicity, might well feed to some gullible reporter. And yet, the truth, when I finally uncovered it in Canada some twelve months later, was not far removed from this tale.

Bernard Loewenstein had emigrated from Germany to Brussels some seven years before the birth of his son, had married the daughter of a Belgian banker, and had set up business as a dealer in foreign exchange. It was not a great success. Young Alfred, however, was undeterred by his father's example, and soon after his twentieth birthday launched into the financial world himself. In partnership with a man named Edouard Stallaerts, he established a business for stock issues and loan promotions on the Boulevard Bischoffsheim in Brussels.

It was not a good time for that sort of thing. At the turn of the century, just when Loewenstein was getting established, the Brussels Bourse was hit by a series of financial crises. His father was pushed into bankruptcy, and though Alfred survived the slump, he was left with the task of clearing the family debt.

For the first time, but by no means the last, Alfred Loewenstein had his back to the wall. His reaction was typical. There was no consolidation, no cautious move; Loewenstein gathered together the remnants of his capital and plunged heavily into electrical and artificial-silk securities. And the gamble paid off. Even so, his recovery might have been modest, had it not been for a pair of trans-Atlantic fairy godfathers.

They were Frederick S. Pearson, an American, and the Canadian William (later Sir William) Mackenzie. Mackenzie was a builder of railroads, Pearson an electrical engineer. They had teamed up to construct tramways and hydroelectric power stations in Brazil, and they did so with great success. First in São Paulo and then in Rio de Janeiro, they succeeded in establishing a virtual monopoly over the transportation, power, and lighting industries.

Pearson and Mackenzie were no ordinary businessmen. They were entrepreneurs and gamblers on a huge scale, operating multinational companies before such things had been even thought of. But their base was in Canada, and

Canada could not provide them with the vast amounts of capital they needed. And so they turned to Europe where, waiting for them, was a young man with much the same adventurous ideas and a compatible lack of scruples. Alfred Loewenstein was just what their company, soon to become known as Brazilian Traction, needed. Or so they thought. Here was a man with a growing reputation for selling the equivalent, in financial terms, of ice cream to Eskimos. He was just the fellow to market the highly speculative stock in their South American ventures.

At first, the relationship went well. Loewenstein, who was already learning to manipulate the financial press, succeeded in selling the securities by the million—not only in Belgium, but in France and England as well. As an added incentive to investors who disliked paying taxes, he persuaded Brazilian Traction to introduce "bearer" stock certificates, which allowed the identity of the shareholder to be concealed. Pearson and Mackenzie were delighted with the results. So was Loewenstein, who was earning a lucrative commission.

In 1908, when a sudden need for fresh capital coincided with a panic in the financial markets of New York, it was Loewenstein who came to the rescue with a daring scheme to go to the European money market with a second issue of Rio Tramway Bonds, with a nominal value of £3,500,000. It was hardly an altruistic gesture: The company's existence was at stake, and Loewenstein drove a hard bargain. He arranged for the bonds to be underwritten at large discounts, putting them into the hands of brokers on both the English and Continental stock markets for as little as 68.2 percent of their face value.

The scheme worked. The issue was over-subscribed, and Brazilian Traction netted sufficient cash to pay off its debts and start building the Rio Tramway. The price for the company was high. In all, after the discounts, the bonds had brought in £2,240,000, but the five percent interest had to be paid on the full nominal value of £3,500,000. In effect, Brazilian Traction were therefore paying 7.8 percent for their money, which was a high rate in those days. Nevertheless, the tramway scheme had been saved, and Loewenstein became known in the Brazilian Traction boardroom as "our friend." In the light of what was to follow, the appellation was ironic.

I was to learn a lot about those bonds. Whether or not he realized it in 1908, that single transaction was destined to play a major role in the life of Alfred Loewenstein and possibly in his death. But all that came later, much later. For the moment I was stuck with my nose in a file of obituaries, trying to find out more about the manner of the man. It was hard going.

On the subject of Loewenstein's character, *The Times* was tactfully noncommittal. It concentrated on his daring financial exploits, on his extravagant lifestyle and love of display. There were also hints of bitter business rivalries, which I would clearly have to follow up. But what sort of man was he?

"Captain Loewenstein," *The Times'* obituary writer said, "had a very attractive personality, was loyal to his friends and associates, and enjoyed to an exceptional extent the affection of his subordinates."

Did he indeed? It hardly fitted the picture forming in my mind. But in its usual subtle way *The Times* went on to add an anonymous "Character Sketch" from "a friend who knew him well," in order to redress the balance. It seems worth quoting:

Loewenstein was so much a man of impulse that, however close and various his association with others, he remained invariably a rather lonely figure. His astonishing grasp of the minutest details of any enterprise in which he was engaged enabled him to enlist the co-operation of men of the most diverse character. But he was very intolerant of opposition and generally even of criticism, with the result that he quarreled as easily as he made friends, and his likes and dislikes, always violent, were often unreasonable.

His was a nature which flashed from the depths of depression to the heights of optimism, with but short pauses at any intermediate stage, and which gave him no rest from an intense concentration upon the matter in hand. This concentration resulted in many curious personal traits. He never read a book or a newspaper, and seldom wrote a letter where a telegram would serve. He never smoked and never drank, because he declared that tobacco and alcohol impaired the physical fitness which was the buttress of sustained mental effort.

He had no subjects of conversation except his two passions—business and horses. Every moment that he was awake, even when he was boxing with his private instructor, or being massaged, or taking his bath, or being shaved, he would spend in discussing his affairs. He was as unsparing of others as of himself, and combined, in a high degree the qualities of restlessness and tirelessness.

Although extremely sensitive, he knew many of his own defects, and was used to explaining that he needed other minds to act as brakes upon his hastiness, alike of conception and of temper. When he had offended a business associate he generally recognised that he was a difficult person to work with, but found it very hard to forgive the person whom he had offended.

He was, nevertheless, for all a certain flamboyance, a simple and even primitive personality at heart, capable sometimes of inexplicable behaviour, but capable also of great generosity and loyalty.

If a "friend" could write such a valedictory, I wondered what his enemies might have said. Loewenstein had suddenly become a far more interesting man than a mere tycoon: a man capable of exciting love and hatred in equal measure. A man, perhaps, worth killing.

———

NEXT DAY, I headed for the London suburb of Colindale, where, in a building of appalling ugliness, the British Museum houses its newspaper library. Colindale is a town uncertain of its role, where lower-middle-class suburbia rubs uneasy shoulders with light industry, and the Police College at Hendon is the toss of a tear-gas grenade down the road. But in its newspaper library, so unpromising on the outside, it houses one of the treasure stores of the world. Here, in vast unwieldy volumes brought on carts from the dim recesses at the rear, is almost every newspaper ever published. Some few have been reduced to microfilm, but most are the musty yellow originals—the genuine article.

This is history, written as it was, before the politicians and historians move in with their subtle and distorting art. It is a researcher's demi-paradise, a place to visit for the sheer fascination of finding out. Somewhere among these millions of pages, I was sure, would lie the clue about who did what to Alfred Loewenstein, and why.

I ordered a few volumes more or less at random and went to work. As my starting point I chose the editions of July 5, 1928, the day following Loewenstein's death, working forward as the story developed. I began with the "quality" newspapers: *The Times,* the *Daily Telegraph,* and the *Financial Times.* But it soon became evident that the richest sources, and those that had devoted the most intense coverage to the sensational story, were the more popular journals. The *Daily Mail,* the *Daily Mirror,* and in particular the then newly born *Evening Standard* and *Daily Express* had sent reporters far and wide to garner the gruesome details. The foreign press, too, had spared no effort, for Loewenstein's reputation had been worldwide. Day after day the stack of volumes beside my reader's desk grew and multiplied.

There was no shortage of material. The problem was that much of it was contradictory. The names of those involved were spelled in a dozen different ways, and accounts of the same events varied widely. To sort out the true from the false was a matter of constant cross-checking, of weighing one source against another and trying to make objective judgments. On such a story, when competition among reporters is intense and the pressure from news editors for the latest angle becomes stronger by the hour, imagination has been known to overcome regard for truth. At a distance of fifty-six years, the difference between fact and fiction is not easy to spot, but I did my best. What follows is what one might call the "authorized version" of the death of Alfred Loewenstein. Some of it may even be true.

———

ON ONE POINT there is no dispute: Alfred Loewenstein's last journey began at Croydon Airport, on the southern outskirts of London, on the early evening of July 4, 1928. Croydon Airport today is a sad relic, a patchwork of playing fields and scattered factories, long made useless for aviation by the relentless growth of the city. But in 1928 it was the hub of British commercial aviation, home of British Imperial Airways and the fashionable place from which to fly. The once splendid art-deco terminal still stands forlornly, a forgotten gateway to nowhere. For one man that day it was the gateway to death.

Loewenstein's latest toy, a Fokker F.VIIa/3m monoplane, was already warming up on the tarmac outside the terminal when the two black limousines came to a smooth halt. In the cockpit, mechanic Robert Little jiggled the throttles and checked the magnetos on the three Armstrong-Siddeley Lynx engines while the pilot, Donald Drew, stood by the doorway to receive his passengers. It was a fine evening for flying, warm and still, with hardly a cloud in the sky. Drew was looking forward to a smooth trip to their destination: Haren Airport, Brussels.

Ray Foster, Loewenstein's liveried chauffeur, climbed from the open driving seat of the first Hispano-Suiza to open the rear door. The man who emerged was of medium height, stockily built, with slicked-down greying hair. His features were powerful rather than handsome: thick lips, a heavy nose, and dark eyes deep-set in a swarthy face. Not an attractive man, but a personality to be reckoned with. With a brief wave to Drew, Alfred Loewenstein turned on his heel and strode into the terminal building.

Four people emerged from the second limousine and boarded the aircraft. One was a little man, built like a jockey. Fred Baxter was Loewenstein's valet and traveled with him everywhere he went. The second, taller and in his mid-thirties, was Arthur Hodgson. Hodgson was the financier's secretary, perhaps his closest confidant. With his impeccable pinstripe suiting, the inevitable umbrella, neat moustache, and the air of one born to greater things, it was hardly surprising that no one ever seemed to know his Christian name.

The two men stood aside to let the two women in the party board first. Eileen Clarke and Paula Bidalon were stenographers: vital adjuncts to any trip by Loewenstein, who had been known to wake up shorthand typists from their hotel beds in the middle of the night in order to dictate some urgent letter that had just occurred to him. They carried their notebooks in the expectation that Loewenstein would, as usual, have work for them on the journey.

The party was not kept waiting long. Loewenstein had merely stopped by the KLM office in the terminal to make a call to Sir Herbert Holt, a Canadian financial magnate and business ally who was in London at the time. The conversation was overheard by an airline pilot, Captain Bob McIntosh. The two men, he said later, had been arranging a dinner appointment for the following week.

Shortly after six o'clock, with Loewenstein safely on board, the Fokker taxied away from the terminal on to the grass runway and turned its nose into the almost nonexistent wind. A small group of onlookers saw the financier wave through the large glass windows. They said later that he smiled. It was a perfect take-off. Drew set his course to the southeast, directly towards Brussels, as the aircraft climbed steadily into the evening sky.

———

THE FOKKER WAS ALMOST brand new. Loewenstein, who had owned a fleet of smaller aircraft over the years, had long coveted this particular model and had had it fitted out to his own specifications. It was designed as a flying office, with a well-upholstered chair for the owner at the front of the cabin, facing backwards. A glass partition separated the passenger accommodation from the cockpit, making it possible for Drew and Little, if they wished, to see what was going on behind them. Extra soundproofing had been installed; it was an arrangement that, in theory, would allow Loewenstein to give dictation to his stenographers while in the air. In practice, there is reason to think that the noise of the three 225-horsepower engines in close proximity defeated him.

At the back of the cabin was a windowless door leading into a small compartment containing a toilet and washbasin. From this, on the port side of the aircraft, a second door formed the sole means of entrance and exit from the outside. This door was fitted with a small window, and was directly opposite to anyone using the toilet. The door to the cabin would have been on such a person's right hand, and any confusion between them would be unlikely, if not impossible.

By modern aviation standards, the access door to the Fokker was a joke: a light wooden frame sandwiched between two sheets of thin plywood, approximately six feet high and four feet wide. It was attached to the fuselage at the forward edge by two insubstantial hinges on the outside frame, pivoting on a pair of simple bolts dropped in from the top. The rear edge was fastened by a crude spring-loaded catch, controlled by a short metal handle on the inside. It was an arrangement that would have looked more at home in the average kitchen. The only other means of security consisted of two small interior bolts, which were fastened by Drew or Little as part of their duties before take-off. Nevertheless, the door was regarded as adequate by the air-safety authorities of the day for the height and speed at which the Fokker flew. And it probably was. Nobody was ever known to fall out. Nobody, that is, except Alfred Loewenstein.

As Drew had expected, there was no turbulence in the air. The Fokker climbed smoothly and steadily to its cruising altitude of four thousand feet and settled down to a speed of 110 knots. They crossed the coast near Dover and headed out over the Channel.

Loewenstein, according to the reported accounts of those on board, was reading a book. Soon after they crossed the coastline he marked his place, got to his feet, and went to the toilet compartment in the rear. He smiled as he went and exchanged a few words with Hodgson.

Ten minutes later, he had not returned. There was a short conversation between Baxter and Hodgson, and the valet was dispatched to see if Loewenstein was all right. He knocked on the dividing door. There was no reply. Feeling increasingly anxious, Baxter opened the toilet door. But there was no one there. The toilet compartment was empty. Alfred Loewenstein had disappeared.

———

IN THE NOISY confinement of the cabin, there was consternation. Hodgson rushed forward to bawl at the pilot through the partition, but his words were lost in the roar of the engines. Finally he scribbled a note and thrust it in front of him. CAPTAIN'S GONE, it said.

By this time, the aircraft was approaching the French coast, and the nearest airfield was about five minutes flying time away at St. Inglevert, between Calais and Dunkirk. It lay almost exactly on their course and may well have been in sight from the cockpit on that clear summer evening. But for reasons that he chose never to divulge, Drew did not head for St. Inglevert. Instead, he throttled back and pointed the nose of the Fokker towards a beach, backed with steep sand dunes, which lay dead ahead. With considerable skill he brought the heavy aircraft down to a perfect landing on the smooth wet sand below the high-water mark and climbed out with his remaining passengers to wait for someone to arrive.

Unknown to Donald Drew, the beach on which he had chosen to land the Fokker, at St. Pol, near Dunkirk, was military territory. It was under the control of the First Battalion, Artillery Artificers, stationed at Fort Mardyk. From there, the battalion adjutant, a certain Lieutenant Marquailles, saw the machine come down at 7:29 p.m. Marquailles was annoyed. Civilian aircraft were not supposed to land on his beach. He dispatched a party under the command of a sergeant, Albert Bereau, to place the occupants under arrest.

The actual point of touchdown was out of sight behind the sand dunes. When Bereau and his men clambered over the crest, perhaps six minutes after the landing, they found the crew and passengers standing disconsolately beside the Fokker. He took them to the guardroom, where they were closely questioned by Marquailles and later by the police.

By Marquaille's account, given to a *Daily Express* reporter the following day, it was a curious interrogation. Though Drew and the others immediately admitted that they had lost their employer over the Channel, it was at least half an hour before they would reveal his name. Eileen Clarke said they had no authority to do so, and eventually it was the secretary, Hodgson, who told the police what they wanted to know.

"Believe me," said Marquailles, "it could not have been playacting. It would have been impossible for those on the aircraft to have acted as they did if M. Loewenstein had not met with some terrible fate. The two girl typists were in tears, the valet was greatly affected, his teeth chattered with fright and perspiration poured from the brow of the secretary, Hodgson. It was obvious to me that something dreadful had happened."

Something dreadful had indeed happened, but what? Inspector Bonnot of the Sûreté was sent to the scene and said: "This is a most unusual and mysterious case. We have not yet made up our minds to any definite theory, but anything is possible."

Bonnet arrested no one. Drew and Little were permitted to fly the Fokker to St. Inglevert, where common sense said they might have landed in the first place, and thence to Croydon the following day. The rest of the party were driven to Calais, where they stayed overnight at a hotel before going on to Brussels by train.

And within twenty-four hours of Loewenstein's disappearance, all French police enquiries into the case had been abandoned. It was odd, to say the least.

The official explanation from Paris was scarcely credible. Because, it said, the incident appeared to have happened outside the three-mile territorial limit, it was outside French waters and therefore no concern of theirs. The Belgians, in due course, took the same view. So did the British. According to legal custom, it seemed, anything that happened on board an aircraft over international waters was nobody's affair.

Alfred Loewenstein, financier extraordinary, had fallen to his death through a crack in the law, and no one cared enough to find out how or why.

3

BUT WAS HE DEAD? In the darkness of absent fact, the rumors grew like mushrooms. With hindsight, most were patently absurd, but Loewenstein's extravagant lifestyle and unpredictable personality made anything seem possible.

The *Exchange Telegraph* news agency found a French fisherman from the nearby village of Bray-Dunes who had been out in the Channel that evening. He swore he saw a parachute descend, and a yacht sailing towards the spot where it had hit the water.

The London correspondent of *The New York Times* was told by one source that Loewenstein was driven off in a car when the aircraft landed on the beach, and by another that he had never been on the plane at all. To do the New York paper credit, it did not believe a word of it, describing such stories as concocted by "daring applicants for honors in imaginative fiction."

"Although he loved to live spectacularly," the editorial writer pointed out, "Captain Loewenstein had nothing to gain and everything to lose by such folly. He could never reappear in financial circles, and for him the financial game was the whole pleasure and absorption of his life."

One of the applicants for fictional honors, however, turned out to be *The New York Times'* own man in Calais, who next day filed the following story:

> No definite information can be obtained tonight on reports in circulation that Captain Loewenstein's plane, before it made a landing on the beach at Mardyk, was seen by persons in the locality to make a brief landing on a deserted beach some distance from the village of Bray-Dunes on the Channel coast. These reports give color to one hypothesis that the banker, desiring to make his disappearance from the financial world after reaching an understanding with his personnel, had himself landed and instructed those employees to tell the story of his plunge to death. Other reports say a plane was seen flying along the coast beyond Dunkirk almost as far as the Belgian frontier, and that it turned at Teteghem to land at last at Mardyk where the tragedy was first recounted.

Credence was given to these stories by the apparent reluctance of those on board to name Loewenstein when questioned at Mardyk, and by the account of an Imperial Airways pilot, a Major Rogers, who was flying only eight hundred yards behind Loewenstein's aircraft as it crossed the Channel. Rogers was quoted by the Paris newspaper *L'Oeuvre* as saying that he was in a position to see whether a body fell from the plane, and he did not.

The rumors went on. A "mysterious passenger" was seen to get off the cross-channel ferry *Flamande*, which had left Dunkirk at midnight on the night of Loewenstein's disappearance and docked at Tilbury at six-thirty the following morning. And Loewenstein was said to have drawn $500,000 from his bank before leaving London. One of the most elaborate tales came from a French newspaper that claimed to have discovered that Loewenstein was having an illicit affair with a young female inmate at a local insane asylum and that the two had eloped together.

It was entertaining nonsense for the readers, but for many people, the question of whether Loewenstein was alive or dead was a matter of crucial importance. Not the least of these was Mme. Madeleine Loewenstein, his wife.

Her concern was not merely emotional: There was little emotion in the marriage of Alfred and Madeleine Loewenstein. For his part, he only had time for business and his beloved horses. For Madeleine it seems to have been enough that she should be seen, superbly dressed, in the right places at the right time. They occupied separate bedrooms and lived separate lives. Madeleine, according to one who knew her well, was lacking in emotion and uninterested in sex. She rarely joined her husband on his business travels, preferring, according to the time of year, to stay in Brussels, Biarritz, or Thorpe Satcheville with her unmarried sister Didi.

They were a strangely matched pair. Didi was as ugly as her sister was beautiful—as volatile as Madeleine was calm and remote. "Just like night and day," I was told by a friend who knew them both. Yet they were inseparable. A more cynical age might have wondered at the nature of their relationship, but I encountered no suggestion that it was anything other than sisterly.

As a couple, the Loewensteins were not on bad terms. They were not really on any terms at all. At least they appear to have had a mutual respect for each other, and in that sense it was not a disastrous marriage. Alfred was said to adore his wife and to be proud of her beauty, though it is impossible to escape the feeling that it was much the same pride as he would have felt in owning a thoroughbred mare.

Madeleine was indeed a thoroughbred, one of four daughters of the socially prominent Misonne family of Brussels, who had married Alfred, some years her senior, in 1908. They had one son, Robert, who was eighteen at the time of his father's death. The Loewensteins' marriage seems to have been a marriage of convenience: She provided him with social cachet and the distinction of having an extremely beautiful woman on his arm. He indulged her expensive tastes.

This was no small task, even for someone as wealthy as Alfred Loewenstein. Madeleine was rated as one of the best-dressed women around the most fashionable racecourses of Europe. She maintained lavish homes in England, France, and Belgium, where the housekeeping bills alone were estimated at $100,000 a week, and owned jewellery which, at today's values, was worth about $24 million.

The pride of Madeleine's collection was a necklace. Perfectly matched natural pearls, 177 of them, were strung with diamonds set in platinum. It was insured for a quarter of a million dollars, which translates to about $10 million in today's devalued currency.

On the night of October 16, 1926, this necklace vanished. That day the Loewensteins had been together, for once. They were staying at their summer place in Biarritz, the Villa Begonia (though to call it a villa would be roughly analogous to describing Buckingham Palace as a cottage), and they were doing a little entertaining. Some sixty guests were in the house, including minor European royalty and a host of celebrities, all enjoying the famous Loewenstein hospitality. The staff, as was usual on such occasions, was mostly housed in the seven other villas that Loewenstein owned or rented in Biarritz.

The financier, at the time, was licking his wounds after a business reverse (of which more later) and was pursuing a scheme to recover a few million. The party seems to have been in aid of public relations, but it turned sour overnight when a thief crept into Madeleine's bedroom and stole the necklace. At least, that was Loewenstein's story, and he stuck to it.

By the Belgian's account, given to the police, the burglar had entered the house from the beach, forced the window of the Chinese room, and had gone straight to his wife's bedroom where she lay asleep. There he had taken the key of the safe from beneath a pile of handkerchiefs in her dressing-table drawer, unlocked it, and removed the necklace. For good measure, he had then gone into Loewenstein's own bedroom and that of a guest, stealing cufflinks and other items of jewelery. In support of the story, grains of sand from the beach were found on the carpet in the bedroom corridor and in the bedrooms themselves.

The insurance company was dubious. It sent an assessor from London, a man named John William Bell, to investigate the claim. In the best tradition of the private detective he set out to re-enact the crime. He went down to the beach and tramped around until his shoes were covered in sand. Then he followed the supposed route of the thief. He did it again, and again. But each time he found that the sand had fallen off his shoes long before he reached the bedroom corridor.

That was not the only problem. The Loewensteins were both known to be light sleepers, and that night they had not gone to their separate beds until 2:30 a.m. The theft had been discovered when the masseur woke them at six-thirty.

Between those hours, if Loewenstein's account was true, the thief had not only made his entry, located the key, and opened the safe, but had also paused to remove the jewel from a dress stud and leave the setting, and steal the links from Loewenstein's discarded dress shirt. All without disturbing a soul. He had ignored an imitation-pearl necklace.

Bell, who had contacts in criminal circles (he later served a prison sentence himself), went to a man whom he knew led a gang of Continental jewel thieves. "Swell mobsmen," as they were called in the slang of 1926. But this real-life Raffles denied being involved. His intelligence department, he said, had not told him there was so much valuable property in the Villa Begonia, otherwise he might have done something about it.

Frustrated, Bell pursued enquiries in Belgium, Canada, and the United States. He got nowhere. Nor did the French police, who in December 1926 sent a team to New York after a tip-off that a gang of international crooks had smuggled the loot to America. A reward of ten thousand pounds for the recovery of the necklace went unclaimed. And in the end the Geneth Insurance Company of Paris paid up.

Madeleine Loewenstein never saw her necklace again. Now, almost two years later, she had a greater financial problem. Her husband was missing and, under Belgian law, if the body was not found the liquidation of his estate would be delayed for at least four years. There could be no death certificate, and the will could not be read until he was proven dead. Meanwhile, the household bills were mounting.

It seems that from the very first moment, Madeleine Loewenstein had no doubt that her husband was, in fact, dead. She was in Brussels at the palatial family home on the Rue de la Science when she was told of his disappearance, and she immediately changed into full mourning. Accompanied by Colonel Daufresne, who had traveled with the couple to New York three months previously, she drove through the night to Calais, arriving at the Hôtel Metropole, where Drew and his passengers were staying, at about 5 a.m. According to the hotel proprietor, interviewed later, she presented a forlorn, distraught figure, dressed entirely in black.

However, she was not too distressed to attend to the essential details. Drew and Little were ordered to take the aircraft back to England, and then to charter a tug from Dover to search for her husband's body. On the French side, she let it be known that she would give a reward to whoever found it. The fishermen went quickly into their boats.

Then she went to St. Inglevert to inspect the Fokker, searching, it was said, for some message from her husband. But the only things she found on board were his collar and tie. Madame Loewenstein looked at the aircraft in disgust. "Let it be sold," she said. "I don't ever wish to see it again."

Two hours after she had arrived, Madeleine was back in her car and being driven home to Brussels, leaving Hodgson, Baxter, and the two girls to follow on by train with Loewenstein's four suitcases. There she retired to her room, with a doctor in frequent attendance.

Drew and Little did as they were told and flew back to Croydon. The French police appeared to have lost all interest in the case and no examining magistrate had been appointed, so they were free to go. When they arrived in London, however, the aircraft was immediately impounded by the Ministry of Aviation accident inspectors. This process was somewhat delayed because the crew, whose evidence was needed, had left at once for Dover, where they chartered the harbor tug *Lady Brassey* and set sail in search of the body.

They quartered the Channel for two miserable days. The weather had turned foul and the sea was high, and they found nothing. When they returned to London, they received fresh instructions from Madame Loewenstein. They were to proceed at once to Brussels, where an inquiry into Captain Loewenstein's death was to be held at the Palais de Justice.

This inquiry, which occupied three and a half hours on the morning of July 9, was less than impressive. For a start, it was not an official inquiry at all, but merely a hearing summoned at the request of Madame Loewenstein with the object of obtaining a death certificate. It was conducted by Judge de la Ruwiere, the local magistrate for the district of Brussels where Loewenstein had his home, at the Première Chambre de Tribunal Civile. No records were kept, and no one was asked to give evidence under oath. However, all the leading players in the drama were present, and all told their stories once again.

This time there was a significant addition. Donald Drew and Robert Little, who had brought with them drawings of the Fokker F.VIIa/3m and charts of their route, told the judge that while on their way back to England from St. Inglevert four days before, they had tried an experiment. They had each in turn gone to the rear of the aircraft when it was at full cruising speed and had attempted to open the door. It had, they said, opened easily. And they explained that this was because the fuselage narrowed at that point.

The judge was not an aviation expert, and there was no other qualified witness in court. Though the two men were not under oath, he had little option but to take their evidence at face value. "I consider it proved," he said at the end of the brief inquiry, "that Captain Loewenstein was in the plane, and that he did not get out at some other point, and that the accident theory is probable."

It was a cautious verdict, which seemed to reflect Judge de la Ruwiere's general unhappiness with the way the affair had been conducted. He was especially critical of the French for closing their investigation so quickly and failing to appoint a *juge d'instruction*. Under the French judicial system, this is an examining magistrate responsible for the initial investigation of criminal cases. "If there had been an accident attributable to negligence by the crew, or a crime, the *juge d'instruction* would have had absolute powers," he said. "He could charge everyone, find manslaughter or murder, and be permitted to put all suspects under arrest and hold them incommunicado for three days. In the interests of truth, this would perhaps have been useful."

Le Matin agreed, saying: "Brussels lawyers are a bit astonished at the haste with which the French police have closed their enquiry. For all one knows here, the first statements of the witnesses were very vague, very laconic, and not a little contradictory."

But there was nothing more the Belgian judge could do. If there had been a crime, he said, it had been committed by foreigners, abroad, and it was out of his jurisdiction. The examination of the aircraft, which was of British registration, was up to the English.

Judge de la Ruwiere's doubts were clearly substantial, but he lacked the legal power to do anything about them. There was only one course open to him, and he took it: He refused to grant the death certificate that Madeleine Loewenstein had wanted so badly. The will would remain unopened, and the Loewenstein fortune would remain like a fly trapped in amber. Until they found the body.

ALFRED LOEWENSTEIN, clad in nothing but a pair of silk underpants, silk socks, and shoes, made his reappearance at 4:20 p.m. on Thursday, July 19, 1928. He was floating face downward in a gentle swell, ten miles to the northeast of Cap Gris Nez.

The man who made the discovery was Jean-Marie Beaugrand, skipper of the fishing vessel *Santa Theresa de l'Enfant Jésus*—a craft somewhat less impressive than its name. Beaugrand and his mate, Louis Legris, trawled the body to the side of the boat with an improvised net of sailcloth and hauled it unceremoniously on board with a gaffe. It was abundantly evident that their prize was beyond caring.

The corpse was in an advanced state of decomposition and stank alarmingly, but Beaugrand knew all about the promised reward for finding Loewenstein and steeled himself to examine the watch strap on the man's wrist. There, on a metal plate, were engraved the words "Alfred Loewenstein, 35 Rue de la Science, Brussels." It was the end of fishing for the day.

Because the smell was offending his crew, who were threatening to mutiny if he kept the corpse on board, Beaugrand wrapped it in a sail, attached it to the end of a line, and dropped it back overboard. Then they towed it slowly back to Calais, reaching port at 6:40 p.m. and mooring beside the steps at the Port de la Colonne. The port commandant, Captain Gréquer, recovered the body and had it taken to the local morgue, where Dr. Poulsey, a police surgeon, started an examination. Captain Gréquer lost no time in telephoning Brussels.

Within hours, representatives of the Loewenstein family had arrived in Calais. They were Madeleine's brother, Lieutenant Misonne, and her sister's husband, a lawyer named Convert. They promptly paid Beaugrand his reward of ten thousand francs—about $320 in the exchange rate of the day. It probably seemed a lot of money to the fisherman, though it left a fair bit of change from the fortune of $55 million that his discovery had liberated.

It might have been supposed that officialdom would now take over and go through the formal procedures of autopsy and inquest. It did not happen that way. Though an autopsy was performed, it was done privately and solely at the request of the Loewenstein family. They summoned a Dr. Paul from Paris, who examined the body and took away various organs for further tests by himself and a fellow pathologist, Dr. Kohn Abrest. Without further ado, what was left of Alfred Loewenstein was then put in the coffin brought from Brussels and taken away to its lonely burial at Evere.

With the authorities showing no interest, and with the death certificate now firmly in their hands, it was perhaps surprising that the family bothered with an autopsy. Convert explained, in a statement made in Paris on July 20, that they wanted to dispel the rumors of murder or suicide that were then circulating. Since Loewenstein's brother-in-law knew of no apparent motive for the latter, and there had been no evidence of a fight on board the aircraft, his own explanation was that Loewenstein had taken ill and fallen overboard accidentally. There remained, however, the possibility of poison.

The press pricked up its ears. "We consider that a crime is not impossible," Convert said. "We do not suspect anyone. We do not wish ill on anyone. But we do not wish that in fifteen days, three weeks or a month or more later, when the body of Captain Loewenstein has been buried, some newspaper or financial correspondent will tell us that he could have been poisoned before being pushed out. That is why we have asked Dr. Paul to perform an autopsy."

In the weeks that followed, a steady dribble of information flowed from the Paris laboratory where the two doctors seemed to be spending an unconscionable amount of time on the study of Alfred's entrails. They announced at an early stage that they had found a massive wound in his stomach, probably caused by contact with a rock, and that every bone in his body was broken by the force of the impact. Neither of these findings was surprising or particularly interesting.

Then, on August 14, the Boulogne correspondent of *The Times* reported tersely that Dr. Paul had found "toxic matter" in the organs being examined.

The news went round the world, only to be denied the following day in a report from Paris. The postmortem examination, it was said, was not yet complete. The results would not be forwarded to "the competent authorities" for at least a week.

In fact, it took a good deal longer. On August 28, Dr. Kohn Abrest traveled from Paris to Boulogne, where he conferred with the local *juge d'instruction,* a M. Monmessin. It seemed that at long last the authorities might be taking an interest. For some undisclosed reason, the doctor took back with him to Paris a bottle of seawater collected from the Channel in the area where the body was found. Speculation was renewed.

It was certainly turning out to be an unusual, as well as a prolonged, autopsy. On September 2, *The New York Times* reported that Dr. Kohn Abrest was trying to discover the state of Loewenstein's nerves in the hours before his death. To which end, apparently, he was going to use the quart of seawater—though he never explained how. Wisely, the doctor emphasized that he could not perform miracles, and in the event nothing more was heard of this original line of research.

Finally, on September 10, 1928, the autopsy report was released. *The New York Times* of the following day carried this story:

> All doubt as to the cause of the death of Captain Alfred Loewenstein was set at rest today by the official report of Dr. Paul and Dr. Kohn Abrest, who have just completed a detailed autopsy. Not a single trace of poison was found in his body, they declared, and all the evidence was conclusive that death was due to the fall of 4,000 feet.
>
> The investigation of the physicians disclosed nothing that would support the theory that the financier sought his own death, and the doctors are of the opinion that the fall was accidental. The quantity of alcohol found is regarded as normal.
>
> Sensational rumors of violence are also rejected with emphasis, no indication of this character having been discovered by the doctors in the course of their exhaustive investigation. The report adds that Captain Loewenstein was still alive when he struck the water.

The *Associated Press* correspondent embellished this report by added that the postmortem had discovered "lesions" on Loewenstein's heart and kidneys that would have made him subject to fits of giddiness, amounting possibly to loss of consciousness.

———

IN THE QUIET of the Colindale library, I read these reports through several times. Something jarred, but I could not quite put my finger on it. And then I remembered: The "friend" who had written Loewenstein's obituary report in *The Times* had made a particular point of the fact that the financier neither smoked nor drank. He had been a fitness fanatic, outspoken against both tobacco and alcohol.

So how was it that the autopsy report said that "the quantity of alcohol found is regarded as normal"? For Loewenstein, the only *normal* quantity of alcohol in his body would be zero. Zilch. Yet there had been alcohol there; the two good doctors, who had been so emphatic about the absence of any toxic substance, had said so. And nobody, so far as I could see, had noticed the discrepancy. His family, who had ordered the autopsy, must have seen it instantly. But they had said nothing.

It was too soon to say what it meant, but it had to mean something. I had found a clue.

4

IN THE DAYS that followed the disappearance of Loewenstein, those who had been on board the aircraft were tracked down, one by one, by assiduous reporters. The stories they told were basically the same, with both Hodgson and Baxter claiming that Loewenstein had been reading a book before he made his fatal visit to the toilet. This struck me as odd, because one of his obituary notices had made a specific point of the fact that the financier never, but never, read books. It was a small point—perhaps it meant nothing, for why should the witnesses lie about such a thing? Unless, of course, Loewenstein had actually been doing something else on that flight that they wished to conceal. And I wondered what that might have been.

Paula Bidalon, the French stenographer, was interviewed in Calais on the day following the incident and appeared a different woman from the tear-stained wreck who had been questioned by Lt. Marquailles. She professed herself horrified by what had happened. Loewenstein, said Mlle. Bidalon, had seemed a little tired but was otherwise in apparent good health.

"We were all completely stupefied and at an absolute loss to know how the tragedy could have occurred," Bidalon told a reporter. "It was too terrible for words. Mr. Loewenstein was a wonderful man and a most considerate employer. It does not seem possible that his life has been snuffed out like this, just when he was at the peak of his career."

But the chief target for the reporters was the pilot, Donald Drew, and his interviews showed an intriguing disparity. On July 5, on his arrival at Croydon from St. Inglevert, he described to a reporter from *The New York Times* his reactions on being told that Loewenstein had disappeared. "My first impulse," Drew said, "was to swing the plan around. But I realized the futility of it. Within a second, I had lost my employer somehow—I did not know how. I had never heard of such a thing before. I was almost across the Channel and could see the Dunkirk sands below. I came down and made an easy landing, and went and informed the police. There would have been no use searching. We had been 4,000 feet up, so the body would have been badly broken up by hitting the surface of the water, and death would have been immediate."

However, Drew then gave an interview to *The Times*. This is what he said:

We left Croydon on Wednesday, shortly after six, and were flying towards Brussels when five or six miles before reaching the French coast one of Captain Loewenstein's secretaries came into my cabin and handed me a piece of paper on which I read 'Mr. Loewenstein has fallen out of the plane.'

I immediately changed my course and searched for a time the spot where Captain Loewenstein might have fallen. The machine was 4,000 feet high when I heard of the accident. Nothing could be seen, so I made for Dunkirk, where we landed at 7:29, and reported the accident. As it was impossible for me to make a search, I proceeded to the nearest aerodrome, St. Inglevert, between Boulogne and Calais, where we landed at 9:50 p.m. (Italics mine.)

Had Drew turned back to search, or had he not? The two interviews were given to highly responsible newspapers on the same day, and both statements were given in direct quotes. Yet they contained a complete contradiction. I checked subsequent editions: There was no indication that a correction had been sought.

It was hardly a point on which the pilot could have made a mistake. Either he turned around to search the area, or he did not, and there could be no blame attached to him for either course of action. So why did he lie?

Neither reporter seems to have asked him why he landed on the beach instead of going straight to St. Inglevert, where there would certainly have been an official to whom to report the incident. From this altitude and in clear visibility, the airport must have been in plain view. Nor why, when his aircraft was equipped with two-way voice radio and was within easy range of the transmitter at Lympne on the English coast, he did not use it to send a distress signal. His answers to these questions would have been illuminating, but the questions were not put.

Two days later, on the morning of July 7, Drew gave another interview, this time to the *London Evening Standard*. This must have been given when he returned from his abortive sea search and before he left to give evidence to the Brussels inquiry.

After denying the rumors that Loewenstein might have left the machine on the Dunkirk sands and still be alive,

Drew said, "I don't think for one moment that it is a case of suicide; it is something that just happened. The most extraordinary things happen in the air. A hundred and one things might have occurred in this instance. Captain Loewenstein may have fainted or had a fit, or he might have opened the wrong door. Everything is possible."

He was then asked if Loewenstein was heavy enough, if he fell against the door, to open it. "Well, he may have been, but I cannot definitely say so," Drew replied. *"It would need someone very strong to open the entrance door."* (Italics mine.)

But according to the evidence that Drew gave to the Brussels inquiry two days after giving that interview, he and Little had found no difficulty whatever in opening the entrance door on their flight back from England. It had been that evidence, and that evidence alone, which had swung the court, and thereafter public opinion, to the view that Loewenstein had died accidentally. Again, the pilot had contradicted himself. It seemed to me that Mr. Donald Drew was going to require closer attention.

———

IT WAS the time of the Paris Air Show. Anyone who was anyone in the world of aviation was at Le Bourget airfield when the news of Loewenstein's disappearance broke. They received it oddly. In this company, it was not surprising that there should be little shock and horror; fatal accidents were very much a normal part of flying in the 1920s. All the same, the reaction was unusual enough to impress the correspondent of the weekly magazine *The Aeroplane.* He wrote:

> The curious thing about this was that nobody took it seriously. One had never met Mr. Loewenstein, but one

hears from those who have done so that he, besides being an extraordinarily able financier, was a reckless sportsman. People who have done business with him say that he was a straightforward businessman whose word was a good as his writing.

But somehow none of the aviation community in any country took him seriously. The humor of aviators, living constantly on the brink of breaking their necks, is always apt to be a little grim, but the disaster of the lamented Loewenstein certainly produced more humor, or at any rate, jests of a tough kind, among the international aviators at the Paris show than one has ever heard over anyone else's disaster.

Everyone who knew the machine agreed that the door never opened by accident.

That door again. In its way, it was the most mystifying part of the puzzle. "Naturally," the correspondent of *The Aeroplane* went on, "all kinds of theories have been put forward as to how he left the machine. There seems no good reason why he should have committed suicide. There is a theory that on coming out of the lavatory he lurched against the door and fell out. That seems unlikely, because experiments tried in the machine have shown that although the door could be opened a few inches with an ordinary push, the force of air was such that a very considerable effort would be necessary to open it sufficiently for anybody to fall out."

Was it possible for the door to have been opened by accident? There was certainly no lack of volunteers eager and willing to find out for themselves. In the week that followed Loewenstein's disappearance, the skies seemed to be filled with young men trying to throw themselves out of Fokker airplanes. It must be remembered that these were the free and easy days of flying. (Today, the National Transportation Safety Board in the United States or the Civil Aviation Authority in Britain would take over the whole investigation from the first moment. Freelance efforts to uncover the cause of a disaster would be out of the question. But in 1928, no such organizations existed, although the British Air Ministry did have an Accidents Branch, which appears to have consisted of one inspector.) If anyone wanted to put his life at risk in the air to prove a theory, or just for the hell of it, he was perfectly free to do so. And in those early days of July, many did.

The crux of the problem was best expressed by an RAF pilot, Flying Officer George Terrell, who gave an interview to the *Toronto Daily Mail and Empire* on July 5:

Any person wishing to get out of the door, which opens towards the motors, would have to push a piece of woodwork roughly ten square feet in area, against a slipstream of 120 miles an hour, assisted by the backwash of two 150 horsepower motors. The backwash of these alone is enough to knock a man down when standing on the ground.

Even if a man could get it open—a super-strong man—as soon as the pressure was released, the door would slam shut. His body would be caught and held fast in the closing door.

Furthermore, as soon as the outside door was opened the slightest bit, everyone inside would be aware of it. A blast of wind would blow through the cabin. It is impossible, supposing a man did leap from the machine, that the passengers in the inside cabin should not know something had happened.

In that last sentence, Flying Officer Terrell had put his finger on a vital point. How was it conceivable that someone could leave unnoticed from such a small aircraft in mid-air, even supposing they could open the door? Yet none of those on board, according to their stories, had heard any noise or noticed any wind or anything whatever out of the ordinary until they found the empty toilet compartment.

As the Toronto paper commented: "If Loewenstein could not get out by accident or design without the persons inside feeling the blast of air, their accounts of what happened become interesting."

Interesting indeed, especially when viewed in the light of the experiments that followed.

At Le Bourget, the Dutch Fokker Aircraft Company had their latest products on display for the air show, and the pride of their fleet was the F.VIIa/3m—the same type of aircraft from which Loewenstein fell to his death. The company was naturally concerned: Airplanes that permit passengers to fall out are bad for business. On July 6, less than thirty-six hours after the incident, two mechanics were sent up to test the door. Using their combined strength, they finally managed to open it sufficiently for one to squeeze through the opening. They concluded that it would be an impossible feat for one man acting alone.

A company official who watched the experiment ruled out flatly the possibility that Loewenstein had opened the door by mistake.

One enterprising reporter for the *Evening Standard* had already reached the same conclusion. Crossing the Channel in a Vickers Vulcan on a commercial flight, heading for an interview with the survivors of the Loewenstein incident, he had got up from his seat and tried to open the outside door. He, too, found it could not be done. Which was possibly just as well for the state of mind of his fellow passengers.

The name of the *Evening Standard* reporter was Norman W. Rae. He seems to have been a young man of considerable resource. On his return from France he went to Croydon Airport, where he managed to hire an aircraft closely resembling Loewenstein's and to persuade the pilot to let him try to jump out of it.

Rae's is the only first-hand account of this exercise that I was able to find.

The object, he said, was threefold: to ascertain how far the door could deliberately be opened against the pressure of the wind outside; how far it would yield to a man who might grip the handle accidentally and turn it; and whether it would open to the weight of a heavy man lurching against it sufficiently to let his body drop into the sea.

"The result of the experiment," wrote Rae,

left no doubt that in all three situations it is impossible in an aircraft flying at a speed of about ninety miles an hour to get the door open wide enough to let oneself slip through. My own weight is just over twelve stones [168 pounds, and similar to that of Loewenstein]. But even when I lurched heavily against the door of my machine, I failed to move it, even with the catch withdrawn.

I then proceeded to use the maximum force possible to my strength. I braced one foot against a projection, found a buttress for my right arm, and then thrust against the door with my entire weight. This opened the door about three inches.

But immediately I released my foot the door was banged back by the enormous pressure of the wind. Had I been anxious to jump from the machine, I must have released my foot.

"The door in the interior of the machine," he went on,

is so arranged that it normally closes off the passenger compartment while the lavatory is being used; when it is swung round to cut off the lavatory cabin itself. The outside door on Mr. Loewenstein's machine is held closed normally by two slip catches, and in many respects it differs entirely from the one to the lavatory. For one thing, half of the outside door is glass-paneled, while that of the lavatory is timbered its full length.

Mr. Leleu of Imperial Airways [the pilot] told me at the end of the test that he had distinctly felt an effect on the machine while I was endeavoring to force the door open. He told me that it caused the aircraft to swerve a little.

It is worth recalling that neither Drew nor Little mentioned anything unusual about the behavior of the Fokker at the time of Loewenstein's disappearance.

But despite the evidence of these tests, and others that were carried out in England, France, and Holland, with the same result, there were many who persisted in the belief that Loewenstein had opened the door of that airplane in a fit of absentmindedness. Others blamed air turbulence at a moment when he was off balance, and still others claimed that he suffered from airsickness and had opened the door to get some air. One businessman, who claimed to be a close associate who had often flown with Loewenstein, was quoted as saying that the financier habitually stood at the open door of his aircraft to gaze down at the water below. It was a patent absurdity.

At this point, none of the tests had been official. Loewenstein's Fokker G-EBYI still sat in the hangar at Croydon, waiting for Donald Drew and Robert Little to return from their appearance before the Brussels "inquiry." The airframe had, however, been inspected. The only fault found was a splintering of the wood on the *inner* side of the door frame, at the point where the tongue of the lock was embedded. No significance appears to have been attached to this damage, for it was doubtless argued that if the door had been burst open from the inside, the woodwork would have been torn away on the *outer* edge.

If the Air Ministry's chief inspector, Major J.P.C. Cooper, wondered what had caused it, he kept his thoughts to himself.

Major Cooper's own aerial test was carried out on July 12, using Loewenstein's machine, piloted by Donald Drew. Robert Little was also on board, as was a Captain Jeffs, the control officer at Croydon Airport. Cooper used the same technique as Rae a few days before. He first threw himself violently against the door, which budged about six inches and then closed again, thrusting him back into the cabin. According to *The Times*, "a rope was then tied around Major Cooper's shoulders and held by the other occupants of the airliner, and Major Cooper attempted to open the door and climb out on to the strut. This was accomplished only with great effort and after several abortive attempts, and even when he was on the strut, the pressure of the door wedged him tightly against the machine."

Cooper was insistent that the purpose of his investigation was not to find out how Loewenstein met his death, but to ascertain whether any modification should be made to the passenger door on the Fokker. He decided that none was necessary—which was tantamount to saying that Loewenstein could not have fallen out accidentally.

By this time, of course, Judge de la Ruwiere had already completed his inquiry in Brussels and had decided—on the evidence of Drew and Little—that an accident *was* the most likely cause. Major Cooper was clearly not happy about this. Despite the official ruling that he was not supposed to be concerning himself with the death of Alfred Loewenstein, he flew to Brussels the day after his investigation was completed and tried to have the inquiry reopened on the basis of what he had discovered.

His plea was rejected by the Belgian authorities. It was another indication that someone, somewhere, did not wish the matter looked at too closely. And in this instance it may well have been the Loewenstein family, who were not without influence in Brussels. It had been reported in *The New York Times* in a story datelined Brussels, July 9, that "The family is anxious to avoid a British investigation, owing to the uncertainty of what such an investigation might lead to."

They got their wish. Major Cooper returned from Brussels empty-handed, and all attempts at investigating the death of Alfred Loewenstein ended at that point.

5
_____

IN THE ORDER of social precedence in the United Kingdom, a Companion of the Bath ranks above the eldest son of the younger son of a peer, but below the Master in Lunacy. Alfred Loewenstein was a Companion of the Bath. He was given the award for "services to the Allied cause" during the First World War—a phrase that grossly flattered his contribution to the war effort.

It was not a great honor, but neither was it inconsiderable for a man in his early forties who had spent the war sitting behind a desk in Whitehall and who had risen no higher than the humble rank of captain. It gave Loewenstein the privilege of putting the letters "C.B." after his name, conferring a cachet of respectability that he hoped might prove a passport into the social circle whose membership he craved.

The nuclear device that was Alfred Loewenstein seemed to reach critical mass at the end of the First World War. It was as if sufficient money had now accumulated in his coffers to enable him to explode in public. In financial circles, he had long been known for his ruthless unorthodoxy in business, but his activities had been mainly surreptitious and there was no indication of eccentricity, social climbing, or conspicuous consumption in his life in those earlier years.

All this now changed with a vengeance, which was odd. It was odd because the war had completely shattered the securities network on which Loewenstein depended for his livelihood. He was force to abandon his home and his brokerage business as the invading German armies swept across Belgium, and to take refuge in London with his wife and their young son. There he became attached to the remnants of the Belgian army, and was given the rank of Captain, beyond which he never rose.

But it was not the rank that counted; it was the job that went with it. Loewenstein had become a quartermaster working for the Inter-Allied Board of Control. In this capacity, he was responsible for the provisioning of the Belgian forces, and he bought and sold vast quantities of foodstuffs.

Loewenstein's war service had one distinguishing feature: It left him immeasurably richer at the conclusion of hostilities. He was not the first Army quartermaster to become rich, nor the last. In 1917, however, his activities drew the attention of the Belgian authorities, and he was quietly asked to resign his commission. Loewenstein was completely unperturbed. By this time he had been in London long enough to acquire some influential contacts, and he was back at his desk the very next day with a *British* captain's commission in his briefcase. Business carried on as usual.

After the war, his actions were the subject of discreet inquiries by Belgian officialdom, but by this time Loewenstein was a rich and prominent citizen and the whole affair was quietly hushed up.

Such things happened. Even so, it was a touch unusual for conduct of this kind to be rewarded in the Honours List. But then this was the time of the Lloyd George government in Britain, when it was widely—and rightly—held that rich men could purchase honors for the price of a discreet donation to party funds. The system fell into such disrepute that a Royal Commission was appointed to look into it. Lloyd George was called to give evidence and denied all knowledge of such a practice. So did Lord Balfour, Asquith, and Bonar Law—former prime ministers all. Nobody believed a word. The Royal Commission declared that there had for some time been "touts" who claimed to be able to secure honors in return for specific payments, and in 1923 the system was reformed. But by then Loewenstein was safely ensconced in his Companionship of the Bath.

It seems to have done very little to enhance his social status. Though he also enjoyed the title of Lord of the Manor of Thorpe Satcheville in the county of Leicestershire—a distinction that could be bought quite legitimately—Loewenstein had too many strikes against him to stand a hope of social acceptance at the highest level.

For a start, although a devout Roman Catholic, he was of Jewish descent. Some unflattering press accounts of the day referred to him as "the Israelite." It is not known whether this change of religion was made in an effort to avoid the anti-Semitism prevalent in that era. If so, Loewenstein made an unwise choice, for in English social circles of the day, Catholicism was reckoned to be not much of an improvement. Then there was the question of his money. It was not that polite society disapproved of money; quite the reverse. Many, though not all, of its members in the 1920s were almost as rich as Loewenstein. Nor would they have cared too much where the money came from, for few of England's baronial fortunes would bear too close an examination.

No, it was the fact that Loewenstein had made his fortune, rather than inheriting it, which debarred him from the recognition he sought. He was *nouveau riche*. And he was a damned foreigner to boot.

It was said in the Canadian press, though the story may be apocryphal, that Loewenstein once offered to donate $2 million to charity if he and his wife could be presented at court. But George V's Lord Chamberlain rejected the approach. It is certainly a fact that despite his wealth Loewenstein never even rated an entry in *Who's Who*, the bible of the establishment.

Whatever the extent of Loewenstein's Whitehall profiteering, it was not his sole source of income during the war years. He remained in touch with the world of finance and maintained a close friendship with James Dunn, the piratical Canadian-born financier who had been at the English end of many of his pre-war coups. And though he may have lost his business and failed to carry a field marshal's baton in his knapsack, Loewenstein had saved something rather more valuable: Brazilian Traction bonds.

They were the same bonds that he had touted for the company in 1908, with a second issue in 1911, and they were of two kinds: one to be sold in England at a face value of £100, and the other on the Continent (mainly in Belgium) for five hundred French francs each. They carried an interest rate of five percent, paid twice yearly, and in theory were of equal rank. But there was one major difference: The French-currency bonds carried the endorsement "Obligation de cinq cents francs 5% *or* [my emphasis]."

That one two-letter word, implying that the company had an obligation to pay out in gold, was later to lead Loewenstein to the brink of a gigantic business coup.

Though whether he had that in mind when he slipped it in, unnoticed by the directors of the Brazilian company—who were too desperate for money at that time to care—is a moot point. For the moment those bonds were serving Alfred Loewenstein well for another reason.

A commercial depression in 1913, followed by the deteriorating situation as the First World War loomed closer, was causing a slump in the Belgian currency. In early 1914, in response to the country's worsening financial situation, the government began to impose restrictions on foreign exchange transactions. This had the immediate effect of slashing the value of the Rio Tramway bonds sold on the Continent, most of which had been bought by Belgian investors, but which had to be paid for in French francs. F.S. Pearson reported from London: "The drastic law recently passed in Belgium has practically ruined that market, and those holders of the Rio Second Mortgage Bonds who now desire to sell can find no market, which is seriously depressing these bonds and reflecting discredit on the Rio enterprises and on the securities here in the London market."

Loewenstein promptly came to the rescue. It was something he did throughout his career, and his selfless generosity was invariably profitable for Alfred Loewenstein. This time, in association with James Dunn, he bought up large quantities of the French bonds and brought them to England. As his reward, he demanded that the Brazilian Traction company pay a fixed dividend of nine shillings and eleven pence in English currency on every 12.50 French franc dividend coupon tendered in London. With remarkable lack of foresight, the Brazilian board agreed.

The result was that by 1919, with French francs sinking through the floor, the company found itself paying out more than face value on the 12.50 French franc coupons presented in London. And much of it was going to Alfred Loewenstein. The board woke up to the realization that their Belgian friend and benefactor was not in the habit of giving free lunches.

By this time, the character of Brazilian Traction was changing. F.S. Pearson was dead, drowned when the *Lusitania* was torpedoed in 1915. William Mackenzie was nearing the end of his life. The company's board was becoming more orthodox, and it promptly rescinded its 1914 decision and instructed its London bankers to pay out on the French coupons at "the current rate of exchange."

Loewenstein was furious. He was already annoyed by the persistent refusal of Sir Alexander Mackenzie, the company's president, to grant him a seat on the Brazilian Traction board. (Sir Alexander, an upright Presbyterian lawyer from Toronto, never really trusted him.) Now Loewenstein decided to strike back. The use of the word "gold" (*or*) on the company's bonds, he told them, left no doubt that the French and Belgian bond-holders could not be refused payment in British currency, which was still backed by gold at this time. The board's new decision would mean that the 113,000 French series bonds issued would collect annual interest equivalent to only £55,000, whereas the 30,000 bonds originally sold in England would earn £110,000 annually. Loewenstein accused Sir Alexander of gross injustice to the Belgian and French bondholders. Not to mention Alfred Loewenstein himself.

It was a typical piece of Loewenstein audacity. He himself had been responsible for inserting the word *or* on to the disputed bonds. Now he was insisting that the company stick to a policy it had never intended to follow in the first place. What was more, he went public with his demands, drawing instant sympathy from European bondholders who had not had Loewenstein's advantage of drawing a high rate of interest on their investments for the past five years. Letters of protest began to flood in to Brazilian Traction's main office in Toronto.

In panic, the company rushed to its lawyers, who were the Toronto firm of Blake, Lash, Anglin, and Cassels. It was not merely the prospect of paying more interest to the European bondholders that scared them; the word *gold* cropped up in many of their concessionary agreements with the Brazilian government, and they did not want it too closely defined.

Walter Gow, the partner in the law firm assigned to the case, pondered his opinion. "The prospectus," he reported encouragingly, "imposes no obligation on the company to pay otherwise than in the legal tender of the place where payment is made. The contract is not to discharge the obligation in weight of gold, but in the country where the obligation is to be discharged."

The directors heaved a sigh of relief. Then they read the next paragraph. "It is idle, however," Gow went on, "to shut one's eyes to the fact that the court might easily convince itself that the prominent use of the word '*or*' was an invitation to a prospective purchaser to treat the bonds as payment in gold or on a gold basis."

It was a splendid piece of legal equivocation, and it did little to strengthen the nerves of Sir Alexander and his colleagues. They did not want to take the risk of going to court, and they had few illusions about Alfred Loewenstein's willingness to fight the battle or his ability to blacken their reputation among European investors. In October 1920, they caved in and struck a deal. They would, they said, resume the sterling interest payments on French bonds, but only on those that had crossed the Channel in 1914.

Loewenstein claimed that there were fifteen thousand of these. It was quite unprovable. The directors' avid acceptance of his 1908 proposal that these should be "bearer" bonds had neatly hoisted them with their own petard, for the securities were unidentifiable. They tried to limit the potential damage by agreeing that Loewenstein should have an option to purchase the fifteen thousand bonds, which the company would buy back from him at an agreed price over a ten-year period. But in the meantime, they would honor any dividend coupons he presented at the rate of nine shillings and eleven pence sterling.

There were a lot of bonds out there, and nothing to prevent Alfred Loewenstein from skipping across the Channel, buying them up cheaply, and returning to London to collect a very high rate of interest. By their initial combination of greed and carelessness, and their later stubbornness in refusing to allow Loewenstein to join them, the directors of Brazilian Traction had made a costly mistake. They had been happy enough to employ Loewenstein's peculiar talents when the company was young and hungry for growth. Now, in their post-war respectability, they disdained his methods and despised the man. He represented the sort of reckless financial capitalism that symbolized a past they were anxious to forget.

For his part, Loewenstein had won the battle and grown a little richer. But he was not about to forget the insult. One day, he was going to get control of Brazilian Traction. Or die in the attempt.

6

BUT LIFE for Loewenstein was not all business conflict in the early post-war years. If he had one characteristic that did endear him to the English gentry among whom he had chosen to make his home, it was his love of horses. Horses and money were the two great passions of his life.

Loewenstein brought them together in pursuit of his unattainable ambition to achieve social acceptance. With the single-minded purpose and remarkable energy that were his especial hallmarks, he determined that he would excel in all that his self-styled social superiors admired. He would own the finest bloodstock, he would ride bravely to hounds, and he would tackle the highest fences in the show ring. Nothing was beyond his grasp. The orange and black colors of Alfred Loewenstein would enter the sport of kings at the topmost level, and he would win. For winning was important, though for Loewenstein it was possibly less important than the sheer joy of battle.

In deciding to set up his English estate in Thorpe Satcheville, a few miles south of Melton Mowbray in Leicestershire. Loewenstein had chosen well, for this was the center of fox hunting country, and for half the year fox hunting was the fulcrum of the social scene.

The 1920s were a wild and wonderful era in Melton Mowbray and the surrounding villages, a mad whirl of hunting by day and partying by night, with a good deal of high-stakes gambling and discreet adultery on the side. It had been fashionable fox hunting country since the eighteenth century, but the real attraction for the crowds who now streamed north from London in the autumn was the presence of the royal princes.

There were three of them: Edward, Prince of Wales (later, and briefly, King Edward VIII); George, Duke of York (later to become King George VI); and Henry, Duke of Gloucester. Three bachelor magnets for every woman in England who was eligible—and quite a few who were not. It was at a country house two miles from Thorpe Satcheville that Edward was first introduced to Mrs. Wallis Simpson.

With the coming of the princes, prosperity engulfed Melton Mowbray like a tidal wave of honey. The hunting "boxes" (large country houses with stables) were rented solid for the season. So was every hotel and guest house for miles around.

The royal group, with the Prince of Wales the most diligent reveler, established themselves in a house called Craven Lodge on the western side of town. Rumor has it that Edward had the building altered so that his lady friends, of whom there were many, could visit his apartments unseen. It is still standing, now used as a home for troubled adolescents, and the more cynical might say that it has not greatly changed its purpose.

At Craven Lodge, the princes held a constant succession of dinners and fancy dress parties, with male guests frequently in drag and many of the women dressed as animals or children. The ladies of society vied for invitations like pigs at a short trough. It was a paradise for snobs, a feudal fantasy. It was also, according to those few still alive who took part, great fun.

Loewenstein was never invited, which must have rankled, but nothing and no one was going to keep him out of the hunting field. Three famous hunts quartered the well-tended fields around Thorpe Satcheville and Melton Mowbray: the Quorn, the Belvoir (pronounced beaver), and the Cottesmore. They were the hunts of the "right people," and each had its fashionable days. On Mondays and Fridays, it was the done thing to be seen riding with the Quorn; on Tuesday, the Cottesmore; on Wednesdays the Belvoir. Saturdays offered a choice of either Belvoir or Cottesmore for the amateur huntsmen and women who swarmed north from London at the weekend, determined to be part of the social scene, though many had never ridden a horse before. It was a wonder there were sufficient foxes to go round—and sufficient hospital beds for the injured.

Loewenstein rode with them all. As the tide of red coats swept over the hedges and across the stubble and ploughed fields of the English autumn and winter, the chunky Belgian figure was invariably to the fore. For him, the sound of the horn, the baying of hounds, and the cultured cursing of the sweating aristocracy around him were sweet music.

———

WHEN I HEADED NORTH to Leicestershire more than half a century later, in search of the ghost of Alfred Loewenstein, I had no great expectation of success. It had all been so long ago. There might be one or two old ladies who had worked as maids at the big house and could be retentive vessels of ancient gossip, but my hopes went no higher. I was wrong. I had forgotten that people in the quiet English countryside live a long time. What is more, they tend to stay in the place where they were born. Even after fifty-six years, there proved to be plenty of lively old folk who remembered Loewenstein very well indeed.

As all good reporters should, I began at the village pub. The Fox at Thorpe Satcheville is neither old nor quaint. From the outside, with its plain brick façade erected sometime in the 1930s—not a vintage period in English architecture—it must rank as one of the ugliest public houses in Britain. But the interior is warm and friendly, and the beer is good. It is not a pub that Loewenstein would have known, but it was rebuilt on the same site as its predecessor some years after his death. Pictures on the wall show the old building as it was then. It appears to have been every bit as awful. The Fox is and was a working man's pub. In the 1920s, it served the stable lads, the blacksmiths, the house servants, and farm laborers who worked for the rich man in the big house across the road. Today, with that captive custom gone, the landlord struggles to make a living. The carriage trade has never embraced The Fox.

The landlord himself proved to be new to the village and knew nothing of Loewenstein beyond the name. But he knew plenty of people who used to work for him, and that was all I needed. I wandered woozily away from The Fox with more names in my notebook than I could reasonably have hoped for. It was time to suck a peppermint and survey the scene before blasting old ladies from their doorsteps with the aftermath of the local best bitter.

The house that Loewenstein bought in Thorpe Satcheville was known as "The Pinfold." It was not a monument to his architectural taste. A rambling

Edwardian pile greatly lacking in charm, I found it standing on the southern edge of the village at the crest of a hill. An Edwardian pile seems the only fitting description. Though large, it was built only a few yards away from the main road, and when I came upon it, the once-spacious grounds were studded with modern bungalows and one two-storey house.

Loewenstein's old home had been divided into six flats and was looking decidedly run down. I later discovered that it had been bought by its present owners in 1956, complete with five acres of land, for a mere £4,500. I wondered what the financier would have thought if he could have seen it today. Across the road the stable block was still standing and the clock still worked in its little turret. But the old tack rooms, blacksmith's forge, and living quarters for the stable lads had also been converted into apartments. To one side, between the stable block and the pub, stood two vast green buildings that looked like aircraft hangars. One of these had been Loewenstein's indoor riding school and the covered tennis courts where Madeleine entertained her fashionable friends. Now they were warehouses for animal feed.

Of the Olympic jumping course that Loewenstein constructed at the back of the stables, the private horse-racing track, and the nine-hole golf course, no trace remained. Nor was there any sign that the village hockey field, where he had once landed his aircraft before they became too large and he had to build a private aerodrome at Croxton, had ever been used for anything but hockey. Loewenstein had brought his talent for excess to Thorpe Satcheville, but little of it survived him.

I wandered down the road a little sadly, trying to picture the past glory of the place. No horses now; no tide of red coats led by princes of the royal blood, clattering down the

narrow street on their way to pursue the uneatable fox. No
roar of ancient aircraft. No Hispano-Suizas—the cars that
Loewenstein, according to his former chauffeur, Bob
Harris, used to buy by the dozen at a discount, and then sell
off some months later for a profit. No Loewenstein.

Thorpe Satcheville itself had been added to rather than
changed. A rash of small post-war houses, many displaying
FOR SALE signs in mourning for the British economy,
dotted the village with alien red brick, not so much out of
place as out of time. But traces of the Loewenstein era were
still apparent: a house called The Vines, which once
accommodated a dozen secretaries; the small alleys leading
to crumbling stables where his overflow of horses were
kept; the other hunting boxes, now, like The Pinfold,
converted to more plebeian use.

The hunting tradition in Thorpe Satcheville, I
discovered, was not entirely dead. There was still a local
blacksmith, his wife an amateur historian whose help
proved valuable. And there were still horses in the village.
One of them, I found to my surprise, belonged to the
present Prince of Wales, though the inhabitants—
respectful of his privacy—were reluctant to speak of this to
a stranger.

They were not, thank goodness, reluctant to talk about
Loewenstein. The picture that emerged was very different
from that of the hard-driving, fast-living, irascible financier
I had expected. It seemed that when Loewenstein flew into
Thorpe Satcheville to join his beloved horses, he put on a
coat of another color.

"He was a nice little man," said Mrs. Gertie Horwood, as
we sat in the crowded front room of her little cottage
opposite the seventeenth-century sandstone church.
"Everybody respected him." Gertie had been a child then.
Her family, the Underwoods, had lived in Thorpe

Satcheville since the 1700s. There was not much that went on without Gertie Horwood knowing about it.

"There were these rumors," she said darkly. "It was said that young Fred pushed him out of that airplane."

"Fred?" I asked.

"Fred Baxter, the old man's valet."

Mrs. Alice Foxon, eighty-two years old and sharp as a tack, nodded sage agreement. "All Loewenstein's staff loved him," she said. "No one around her ever believed he fell out of that airplane on his own."

———

IT WAS NOT EVIDENCE, but it was interesting. For the first time I had met someone who knew Loewenstein and his entourage personally, and for the first time I had an open suggestion of foul play. Nor had I voiced my own suspicions at this point: The hint of murder was quite unprompted.

I tried to follow it up, but there was nothing more. After Loewenstein's death, Fred Baxter, who was a local boy, had apparently disappeared from the village. He and his brother Jack had played cricket for the local team. Most people, I gathered, had liked Jack better.

Gertie's father had worked for Loewenstein as an outside laborer. Practically everyone in Thorpe Satcheville had worked for him in one capacity or another. He had owned the village "down as far as the telephone box," and four hundred acres of land around it, on which he operated a stud farm for pedigree cattle. There was no doubt that the coming of the Belgian had transformed the place: Not only did he give the villagers employment, but he paid them well.

As a child, Gertie Horwood had often gone up to the big house and seems to have roamed about it freely. She remembered the furniture, "plain and solid," and Loewenstein's heavy brass bed. She remembered, too, his generosity. "We always had a big Christmas tree for the village children. Marvelous presents. One year I had a marvelous baby doll. Another time I had a really big china doll's tea service. All the village children had presents like that."

There had been extravagant parties at The Pinfold with lots of gentry present. And one day, she recalled, the king of Belgium had come to ride Loewenstein's horses. "There were Hispano-Suizas all over the village that day."

And there had, of course, been scandal at the big house. The butler, a Mr. Darby, had made one of the housemaids pregnant. Mrs. Darby had brought up the baby as her own. Gertie Horwood pursed her lips primly at the remembrance. It was the stuff of village life.

Two miles away, just across the rolling hills from Loewenstein's old home, I met Bill Topley. He was eighty-one years old, a plump and sprightly sparrow of a man who in his youth had worked for the financier as a stable lad. On the table in the tiny lounge of the mobile home where Topley and his wife were living while their cottage was rebuilt stood a silver cigarette box and a silver wine-bottle holder. They were mementoes of Loewenstein, bought at auction for a song when the estate was broken up. "I could have bought the Daily Mail Gold Cup for three pounds," Topley said wistfully. He wished now that he had.

Bill Topley had been closer to Loewenstein than anyone I had met at that stage. It was clear that he had admired him.

"I have never seen a man in my life like him," he said. "He wouldn't spend any time at Thorpe Satcheville without he was riding. He'd have to be out all day long one way or another with horses."

Nor did he have any complaints about him as an employer. The stories of Loewenstein's rough treatment of his business staff did not seem to apply when he was off duty: "I always liked Loewenstein. He was always a good chap. He never used to come in the yard bawling or shouting or anything like that. But whatever he wanted to do, it had got to be done. He paid well. It was good pay in those days. You had your own bedrooms and mess rooms at the stables, though some of us lived in the village."

He recalled the way the Belgian rode. "He was absolutely mad," said Bill Topley. "He was always a daredevil when he was out hunting. He wanted to do things that was impossible. He always wanted to try to do the impossible on horses all the time. He never knew when a horse had had enough. He would jump a five-bar gate. Once he jumped the gates at Rissindale railway crossing because they were closed."

Madeleine, Loewenstein's wife, Topley remembered as attractive but reserved. "He would bring her round the stable and she wouldn't speak one word. She would say good morning to you if you spoke first, and then she would answer you. But that's the only thing you would ever get out of her." A married man, Bill Topley clearly liked silence in women. "A very nice person," he said.

His memory of the time was translucent. He could recall the names of every one of the nine other men who had worked with him in the stables almost sixty years before, and even the names of the horses. Incidents and conversations might have taken place the day before. In particular, he remembered a horse called Easter Hero. But then, quite a lot of people remembered Easter Hero.

———

FLAT RACING, as Topley recalled, was about the only form of equestrian activity that had no interest in Alfred Loewenstein. He liked to see his horses jump, and for preference be on their backs when they did it. Had he been younger and lighter, he would almost certainly have ridden in steeplechases himself, but failing that he wanted the next best thing: to have his colors carried to victory in the premier jumping race in all the world. He wanted to win the Grand National at Aintree.

It was a harmless ambition for a very rich man, and Loewenstein went about it in characteristic fashion. Having had little success over the years, and with nothing in his stable that seemed to stand a chance, he looked around the field in 1928 and decided to buy the best horse in the race just before the start. Once again, the difference between Loewenstein and the common herd was being demonstrated. Other men might back their fancy; Loewenstein bought it.

The name of the horse concerned was Easter Hero. Earlier that month, in a Grand National trial at Kempton Park, it had carried top weight and still managed to win by a neck from a horse called Spear o' War. Sporting Life described it as "a sparkling display," and with just over three weeks to go before the big race, Alfred Loewenstein became very interested.

The owner of Easter Hero, a Mr. Frank Barbour, was willing enough to sell—and enough of a sportsman to be persuaded into a gamble. Loewenstein bought the colt for 7,000 guineas, with the promise of a further 5,000 guineas if it won the Grand National. Perhaps he had a premonition.

At this stage, there were still ninety-one of the original 112 entrants left in the race, and Easter Hero was third favorite at a hundred to eight behind Amberware and

Trump Card. On the day of the Grand National, among forty-two starters, he was still third in the reckoning, in spite of having broken a blood vessel in his previous race while leading the field. Master Billie was now favorite at ten to one, with Trump Card at a hundred to eight and Easter Hero at thirteen to one.

It was March 30, 1928. Alfred Loewenstein had ninety-six days to live. If he had lived for ninety-six years he would never have forgotten that day. It was a day when the bookmakers got rich, when the punters erupted in anger, and when one wealthy Belgian gentleman dearly wished that he was somewhere other than Aintree. It was a day of disaster, and a day of pure farce.

The huge field started three times, only to be called back because the starting tape, seventy-five feet long, had broken. It was an ill omen. When they finally breasted the much-knotted tape, Easter Hero was well up in the running, and when Koko and Amberware fell at Beecher's Brook he surged into the lead. Close behind him streamed twenty-three horses, with another two bringing up the rear. All the rest had already fallen.

Loewenstein cheered, as well he might. As the only class horse left in the race, it looked as though Easter Hero had to do no more than stay on his feet and the Belgian's ambition would be achieved.

Then came the Canal Turn. Next to Beecher's, with its precipitous drop, the Canal Turn is probably the most feared fence on the Aintree course. Peter Powell, in Loewenstein's orange and black racing silks, lifted Easter Hero to the jump and sat powerless as the horse came down squarely on top of it. And there they stayed, unable to move either way, while chaos reigned around them. The next three horses—Grokle, Darracq, and Eagle's Tail—were brought down in a sprawling heap. Behind, the next twenty took a hard look at what was happening and wisely refused to jump at all. The entire remaining field of the 1928 Grand National was left milling around in the middle of the racetrack as their swearing jockeys tried unsuccessfully to get past the stranded Easter Hero.

All, that is, bar two. One American entry, Billy Burton, ridden by Jacky H. Bruce, had spotted a gap in the melee and slipped through. Behind him, far, far behind him, trotted a horse called Tipperary Tim.

Tipperary Tim was a hundred to one outsider whose sire had stood stud for three pounds, five shillings. He himself had once changed hands for £50, and had only been entered for the race because, although he was slow, he had one virtue: He never fell over. As it turned out, his lack of speed was his salvation, for when Easter Hero wrecked the rest of the field, he was so far behind that the rest of the jockeys had given up in disgust before he got to the Canal Turn. Tipperary Tim, ridden by W.P. Dutton, a country solicitor—a "gentleman amateur"—plodded on. In the far distance, Bill Burton, the only other horse left in the race, headed for certain victory. Or it would have been certain victory, had not the American horse fallen at the very last fence. Which was how Tipperary Tim became the first and only horse to win the Grand National at a hundred to one, and how Alfred Loewenstein came to hang his head in shame.

Easter Hero was retired in disgrace to The Pinfold. He never raced again, though Loewenstein did ride him in the hunting field. As it turned out, there were not many jumps left for either of them.

Bill Topley recalled that Easter Hero had had an accident when jumping and had had to be put down. But as to how and why Loewenstein died, he could only shrug his shoulders.

He had not, he said, been surprised: "He was always such a madman. He was a very rich man today; tomorrow he might be down . . . and I think that's how . . . That was the end of it, I imagine."

Suicide? Bill Topley thought so. He was the only man I met who did.

—————

7

WE SAT in front of a blazing log fire, sipping tea and eating biscuits, the vastness of the room around us falling into shadowed corners stuffed with antique furniture. Ancestral portraits frowned down as Miss Monica Sheriffe proffered the Georgian silver teapot.

"Of course," she said, "*we* all knew the man had been murdered."

I felt my jaw drop. It was not so much what she had said as the way in which she said it. The tone was completely assured, utterly matter-of-fact. She might have been asking me to pass the sugar. "We all knew the man had been murdered." Just like that. Happens all the time, don't you know.

Miss Monica Sheriffe paused for reflection, or perhaps to enjoy the dramatic effect. "Nobody thought it was suicide," she went on, "and it couldn't possibly have been an accident. So all my friends just assumed it must have been murder."

Why had they not taken their suspicions to the police? Miss Sheriffe shrugged. "People were dying all the time," she said. "Breaking their necks on the hunting field, that sort of thing. It didn't seem very important." I later learned that her own sister had died in this way.

Alfred Loewenstein might not have shared her casual view, but I forbore to say so. Monica Sheriffe was a find, a treasure, and I had no wish to outstay my welcome. Around Melton Mowbray, they had told me she was a complete recluse, that she would never agree to talk to me.

So I had driven up to Goadby Marwood Hall on the off chance that I might get lucky, crunching through the gravel outside the magnificent seventeenth-century façade and waiting in the steady drizzle as the doorbell echoed somewhere in the back of the house.

I think the tiny Irish housekeeper who opened the door was quite pleased to see me. Marooned in that huge mansion, miles from anywhere, she probably would have been pleased to see the devil himself. At any rate, she promised to find out if "Miss Monica" had risen from her afternoon nap. Sounds of ancient plumbing in the distance seemed to indicate that this was likely.

I stood in the stone entrance hall, twiddling my thumbs and wishing I had dressed for the occasion. The figure who greeted me at length was almost six feet tall and ramrod straight, with not a grey hair out of place.

She wore her tweed trouser suit like a colonel in the Grenadier Guards, and her manner had the natural authority of those who have been obeyed for a century or three. But she was courteous to a fault.

If Miss Monica Sheriffe objected to having her solitude disturbed by a nosy author, she was much too well bred to say so. I became acutely aware that the hand I was shaking had shaken the hand of Alfred Loewenstein. And I marveled at my luck. She led me back into a different world: a world of feudal paternalism, where the carelessly rich still cared for their serfs, after a fashion, and the tugged forelock came as naturally as breathing. A world where everyone knew their place, where death duties and taxes had not yet decimated the vast estates, and where, without question, God reigned over an Anglican heaven. A world in which the young were thankful that they lived, grateful that their mouths, unlike the mouths of so many of their friends, were not stuffed full of Flanders mud. If they could afford it—and those who came to Melton could definitely afford it—they were going to live that salvaged life to the fullest.

Monica Sheriffe had been left behind by the twenties like a seashell dropped by the retreating tide. In the dark at the back of her eyes, I could see reflected in that huge room the Bright Young Things who had danced away the night while the Bugattis waited at the door. I tried to picture Miss Sheriffe, stripped of six decades, dancing the Charleston with the Prince of Wales. It was not difficult. They were all gone now, another war and another world away, but for her the fringed skirts and swinging necklaces were here and now.

She remembered the hunting above all, the narrow lanes choked with as many as four hundred huntsmen at a single meet, all in "pink" (scarlet) coats, with perhaps three hundred second horsemen to provide spare mounts. The baying hounds, the followers on foot, the master, and the whippers-in frustrated by the chaos and the amateur riding. It was a highly inefficient way to kill a fox, but that was not the point. The point was to be seen. And the sight was undeniably magnificent.

———

MONICA SHERIFFE WAS SEEN ALL the time. So was Alfred Loewenstein. Both were good and fearless riders—she created a mild sensation by being the first woman in Leicestershire to abandon the side-saddle and ride astride —but there the similarity ended. For after the hunt was over and the partying began, Monica Sheriffe was invited everywhere. She never dined at home, and when she was not cavorting in fancy dress at Craven Lodge, she could be found, as often as not, playing poker.

Loewenstein—she called him "Low"—was invited almost nowhere. Though he was lavish with his own hospitality, few of his guests bothered to return it. Where he was concerned, a regular routine had been established. The "county set"—a term still recognizable today in the snobbish British outback—would go to The Pinfold on a Sunday morning (Sunday being the one day when no hunt was meeting) and ride his superb show jumpers.

They would stay for lunch. They would listen to and act upon his financial advice, and many got richer in consequence. But they would not invite him back to their own homes. Once he was even attacked in the hunting field by a country "gentleman" who lashed Loewenstein with his riding crop because the shares he had tipped had failed to rise that week. As a matter of record, they went up a week later.

It was natural enough that the hunting fraternity should want to visit Loewenstein's stables. There are conflicting reports of the number of horses he actually kept there, with estimates ranging between forty and eighty. It was said that when they rode out to exercise, with Loewenstein and his head groom, Jules Hendrard, keeping a close watch on the turnout of every animal, the last had not left the stables before the first was crossing the bridge at the next village of Twyford. And that bridge is almost a mile away.

There is no argument, however, that his hunters, show jumpers and racehorses, were among the finest in England. And so they should have been. He paid a great deal of money for them, and a number of local horse dealers became rich in consequence—not merely from his purchases, but also from the stock tips he handed out so freely. One dealer, Bert Drage, was said to have made half a million pounds.

With all this expensive horseflesh at his command, shared out so generously on Sunday mornings at Thorpe Satcheville, Loewenstein had become well known in the show jumping rings of Britain and France. He had scored notable victories at Olympia and Richmond, carrying off the Richmond Gold Cup three years in succession, and the harness room at The Pinfold was filled with ribbons and cups. His bravery—some said fool-hardiness in the saddle—became legend.

But although show jumping was a socially acceptable sport, patronized and enjoyed by the class he sought so hard to enter, Loewenstein remained doomed to disappointment if he hoped his success would open the right doors. Once, after winning a major event at Olympia, he tried to engage Lord Lonsdale, a British peer famous for his support of professional boxing, in conversation. As no mean boxer himself—his admirers claimed he could have won championships if he had taken it up professionally— Loewenstein must have fancied his chances of making a useful social contact. He was roundly snubbed for his pains.

The royal family, too, kept their distance. Though they were often seen riding through Thorpe Satcheville (Prince George said "good morning" and was liked; Prince Edward kept his nose in the air and was not), they never accepted a Sunday morning invitation to The Pinfold.

Of course, the princes could not totally avoid Loewenstein while hunting. On December 18, 1926, the financier got his closest involvement with the royals in a way he would rather have avoided: He fell off his horse while hunting with the Cottesmore. The Prince of Wales, following close behind in the company of a former American chorus girl, chased after the bolting horse and stopped it. Loewenstein was left to pick himself up.

Since the lady was fairly notorious, having once sued an American millionaire because she claimed that his grandson was the father of her illegitimate child, the incident made the front page of *The New York Times*. Loewenstein may not have been introduced to royalty, but he shared the headline.

There was one exception to the social ostracism of Alfred Loewenstein. His name was Major Algy Burnaby, and he was master of the Quorn Hunt. Burnaby lived at Baggrave Hall, not far from Melton Mowbray.

There had always been a Burnaby at Baggrave since the family built the magnificent hunting seat in the eighteenth century, and Algy was the archetypal squire. Handsome, debonair, and an inveterate gambler and womanizer, he was just about everything Loewenstein was not. Monica Sheriffe knew him well: "He was a very popular master of the Quorn. Everybody loved him. He was a right old crook."

As a young man in the 1890s, Burnaby had achieved local fame by winning the Moonlight Steeplechase. By all accounts, this was a race with very few rules, run at night over an impromptu course by riders who wore nightshirts over their hunting breeches.

The only other prerequisite was a goodly intake of port, as a result of which casualties were frequent. Burnaby's special achievement was to win the race while wearing a beribboned pink night-dress belonging to Lady Augusta Fane, since he had forgotten to bring his own nightshirt to the start. It was the talk of the hunting set for years. As master of the Quorn, and with such a lengthy pedigree, Burnaby enjoyed a social status around Melton that was at least the equal of a title. Their mutual love of horses would never have been enough to override the social barriers and bring the major and Loewenstein together. But there was another factor: money. In short, Loewenstein had it and Burnaby did not. Years of gambling and splendidly dissolute living had wasted the family fortune. The house and estate were mortgaged, his first wife had left him in disgust, and his son was estranged. Burnaby was not destitute. He had wisely remarried an American heiress, Mina Field, who had sufficient money to keep him in the style to which he was accustomed.

"I think it was a very happy marriage," Monica Sheriffe recalled. "She was always half sloshed. She used to drink port in enormous quantities. They were always playing poker. If they were winning they used to say that Algy had to get up early tomorrow. If they were losing they would make you sit up all night. Both of them cheated. I have never seen anything like it. There would be murder now if they played like that. They used to put ashtrays in the pot when they raised the bid."

Mina does not seem to have minded Algy's woman-chasing. Monica Sheriffe, who presumably had cause to know, described him as "terrific with the ladies," "a great one for the girls," and "a very attractive gangster." But the one thing missing in his life was money of his own, and to have worked for it would never have occurred to him.

Hence the friendship with Loewenstein, who was quite willing to pay his entrance fee by passing on stock-market tips, usually for shares in his own companies. The share register of Loewenstein's major company at the time shows that the Burnabys took his advice to buy and did very well. For this they were perfectly prepared to tolerate his strange habit of eating all three courses of his meal from a single plate—another reason why other members of the hunting set did not return his hospitality.

It was to Baggrave Hall that Loewenstein went on the last weekend of his life. He had been in London on business and was driven up to The Pinfold by his chauffeur, Ray Foster, on the Friday evening. Madeleine Loewenstein was not with him, having stayed at their home in Brussels. Though it was not the hunting season, he could still enjoy his horses. That night, while the village slept, he rode alone over the floodlit jumps in his indoor riding school until the small hours of the morning.

There are conflicting reports of his health at this time. One villager recalled him to me as "a bent and stooping figure," so crippled with rheumatism that he almost had to be lifted off his horse. In the preceding months there had been reports of deals that had to be broken off because he needed treatment at a clinic in Switzerland, and his doctor is alleged to have said after his death that he suffered from high blood pressure.

The last might account for Loewenstein's choleric nature; the first two seem to throw doubt on his ability to force open the door of the Fokker, but none can be confirmed. Certainly nobody else I spoke to in Leicestershire noticed anything wrong with him.

On Sunday morning, July 1, 1928, Loewenstein attended the 8 a.m. mass at St. John's Roman Catholic Church, Melton Mowbray, for the last time. St. John's is a nondescript little brick building just outside the center of town, which has probably changed little in the intervening years. It seems an unlikely choice for a millionaire's place of worship, but since it was the only Catholic church in town, Loewenstein had little option. He attended regularly while in England.

On this occasion, he is said to have arrived a little late for the service and appeared to be deep in thought. So preoccupied was he that the priest, Father Chapman, told reporters later that Loewenstein's attention had to be drawn to the collection plate. It was the sort of thing Father Chapman would notice. When the service was over, Loewenstein remained on his knees in private prayer for some thirty minutes after the rest of the congregation had left.

This act was later seized on as having some deep significance in connection with his death. Was he having a quiet word with the Almighty before taking his own life? In view of what Algy Burnaby had to say later, it seems unlikely.

Loewenstein arrived for dinner at Baggrave Hall that night in what his host described as "a fighting, joyous mood." He was, Burnaby told a local stringer for the *Daily Express*, "more vitally alive and more interested in life, and held higher hopes for the future than ever before." Even allowing for a little hyperbole on the part of Algy Burnaby, who was clearly enjoying the limelight and had probably fortified himself with a little of Mina's port, it hardly sounded like the description of a man about to commit suicide.

It must have been an interesting dinner party. Burnaby claimed that Loewenstein had brought with him all the documents concerning a new financial scheme that was to form the climax of his career. "The relentless work of years had come to a close, and he had prepared plans for the ultimate discomfiture of his bitter financial enemies."

———

READING this interview in the archives of the local press, I found it strange. Loewenstein was certainly in the habit of passing out tips to the Burnabys, and to almost anyone else, but he discussed his future plans with almost no one. His nature was basically secretive, and in spite of his huge entourage, he essentially walked alone. According to the master of the Quorn, however, the millionaire often asked his advice on financial matters, and did so that night. I found that hard to believe. It was roughly analogous to Pete Sampras asking me for advice on how to hit a tennis ball.

Burnaby did not disclose what these plans had been. He wound up instead with a double-edged eulogy, describing Loewenstein as "a grim man in many ways, forceful and belligerent, but also deeply generous and kind-hearted." Burnaby went on: "He had many close friends, but also many violent and bitter enemies. He was as bitter towards these enemies as he was charming towards his friends." He did not name the enemies either. In the circumstances, it seemed to me that I ought to try to find them.

8

I WENT BACK to Colindale and began searching for traces of people who might have hated Loewenstein. Though I knew nothing at that time of the Brazilian Traction imbroglio, I had a suspicion that the list might be long. There were a lot of papers to cover between the years 1919 and 1928, and with the exception of *The Times* and *The New York Times*, virtually no indexes to help me. The volumes piled up, but I had started on the financial journals as being the most likely to contain clues, and it was not long before a name hit me. The name, moreover, was attached to a long-running story that shouted enmity for Loewenstein from every line. The name was Dr. Henri Dreyfus.

Henri Dreyfus was a self-confessed genius and a man of many words. The two talents were complementary: When the world began to doubt the former, he drowned his audience in such a verbal deluge that they were willing to agree to anything. Even the genius of Henri Dreyfus.

Dreyfus hated Alfred Loewenstein with the passion men reserve for those who have done them the greatest favors. And the feeling was fully reciprocated. This was strange, for any objective review of their fortunes would show that each could thank the other in large measure for his prosperity.

Not that either would have admitted to any such thing. Their enmity was a raging battle fought by fair means and foul, in boardrooms, behind the scenes, and in the public prints. Neither would have contemplated the death of the other with the slightest vestige of regret. But it was Alfred Loewenstein who died. And it was Henri Dreyfus who did not mourn.

To understand their conflict, and the complex soul of Henri Dreyfus, it is necessary to go back in time. Dreyfus was Swiss by birth, of French-Alsatian origin, born in 1882 and educated at the universities of Basle and Paris. He had a brother named Camille who, like himself, was a qualified chemist. In 1912, they joined together with a Swiss silk dyer named Alexander Clavel and established a factory to manufacture cellulose acetate.

Cellulose acetate had been discovered back in 1865 and was made by treating cellulose with acetic acid and acetic anhydride. The process was quite complicated and the uses for the stuff fairly limited at that time, so the Dreyfus brothers did not face much competition. In fact, the only other source of supply in 1912 was Germany, where manufacturers marketed it under the trade names of Cellit and Cellon. Henri and Camille, having taken out various patents, promptly named their own company "Le Société de Cellonit Dreyfus et Cie"—which did not please the Germans—and set up a factory in Basle.

The move was well timed. There was a more common name for cellulose acetate; it was called "dope." And dope was what was used to treat the fabric that covered the fragile aircraft of those early days of flying. A clear, sticky liquid, smelling of bitter almonds, it caused the fabric to shrink tightly on to the airframe, made it windproof and, to a large extent, waterproof. Without cellulose acetate, airplanes could not fly. There was one alternative material —nitro-cellulose—but this suffered from the dual drawbacks of being highly flammable and less water-resistant and, therefore, unsuitable for the warplanes that were then taking shape on designers' drawing boards.

By the outbreak of the First World War in 1914, there was one other source of supply for cellulose acetate—in France. The British had nothing. And though the War Office was typically slow to realize the potential value of the aircraft as a fighting machine, they could not ignore it for long. Henri Dreyfus was quick to see the opportunity and went to London in September 1914 to offer supplies of his precious material to the British government.

It took six months for the point to sink home. Then, in March 1915, Camille Dreyfus was called to meet the head of the Contracts Branch of the Aeronautical Department of the War Office.

He was asked if he could manufacture dope in Britain, since the army was not too happy about the fact that the Dreyfus factory was situated only three miles from the German border. The Swiss chemist agreed, provided that he was given a contract for at least one hundred tons. What the War Office did not know, and were only to find out later, was that the Dreyfus brothers, as good neutral businessmen, were merrily selling their cellulose acetate to the German air force at the same time they supplied the British.

As regulations required, the War Office went through the motions of inviting tenders for the supply of dope. The Dreyfus factory was the only contender, and the brothers used their monopoly position to insist that half the contract should be supplied from Basle.

This was extremely convenient, since the Basle factory could be kept running at full capacity, supplying both sides in the war from neutral territory without either getting to know. And whichever air force shot down large numbers of its opponents, the brothers Dreyfus were going to be the winners. Business is business. They were in no hurry to set up their British factory, although they did make one attempt to do so in 1915, and until 1917, the needs of the British Royal Flying Corps were met from Basle.

There were others involved in the war effort to whom business was business. One of them was a Canadian financier named Grant Morden, who was in Britain as a colonel on the staff of the Canadian Expeditionary Force.

Colonel Morden's military duties did not appear to have been arduous. In 1915, he was approached by a Frenchman, a M. Magrier, who tried to sell him a new way of making cellulose acetate. Morden saw the potential and went to Sir Trevor Dawson, head of the giant Vickers armaments firm, for financial support. In the event, the scheme was a failure, but Morden did not abandon the idea. In February 1916, he traveled to Basle to meet the Dreyfus brothers, and made an agreement with them to set up a new British company.

The British Cellulose and Chemical Manufacturing Company was born a month later. It was destined to become a national scandal.

The company, whose stated aim was to produce cellulose acetate and other chemicals, was to be controlled by two groups: the English group, comprising Colonel Morden, Sir Trevor Dawson, and Edward Robson; and the Swiss group, comprising the Dreyfus brothers and Alexander Clavel. Initially, it was to have had capital funding of between £300,000 and £400,000, of which it was estimated that £85,000 would be needed to build the factory.

The English group was to raise £115,000 in cash by the issue of six percent bonds, and the Swiss would be given half the common stock to cover the value of their patents and "secret processes." They were also to be given £30,000 worth of bonds and a cash payment of £10,000. On paper, the Dreyfus brothers had a pretty good deal.

But when British Cellulose was registered as a private company in March 1916, there was an important change. The Swiss group was reluctantly persuaded to agree to a much smaller initial capitalization, and the company was floated with a nominal share capital of £4,000. This was broken down into 160,000 shares of sixpence each, the aim being to attract as little public attention as possible to one of the more enterprising scams of the period.

What appeared on paper to be a tiny concern, for which no prospectus was published and no application made to the Capital Issues Committee of the Treasury, was in fact a sizeable enterprise that would be financed almost entirely by borrowed money. The actual shareholders, who would be dividing the potential profits among them, would have invested practically nothing. The risk would be taken by those who bought the bonds. If the company succeeded, they would get a fixed rate of interest but no share of the profits. If it failed, they could kiss their money goodbye. The foundation of the Great Dope Scandal had been laid.

It was cleverly done. In less turbulent times it would probably not have been possible. But the times were not so much out of joint as out of control, and with men dying by the thousands on the Western Front no one was watching too closely for sticky fingers in the national till.

In practice, the shareholders and the bondholders were often the same people, for the major purpose of having such a small share capital (which avoided awkward regulations), and then dividing it into so many tiny units, was to be able to give them away to those who could be induced to purchase the highly speculative debentures in the Dreyfus company, of which £120,000 worth were on offer. Friends were given four hundred shares for each £1,000 worth of debentures. If the company was successful, they were told, they were going to make an enormous untaxed capital gain on those shares, Britain having no capital gains tax at this time. They were told no lie.

The Dreyfus brothers and Clavel, under the terms of their agreement, received 79,998 of the sixpenny shares, plus £30,000 worth of debentures. Vickers Ltd. had 19,800 shares with debentures valued at £25,000, and Sir Trevor Dawson took 2,104 shares with a thousand debentures. But he was also the beneficial owner of 12,250 shares held in the name of the Prudential Trust of Canada. Col. Morden took up no debentures, but he had 1,705 shares in its own name, plus 12,900 through the Prudential Trust, of which he was a director.

The War Office was by this time extremely anxious to get its hand on more supplies of dope. The number of military aircraft built in Britain was increasing rapidly, from a mere two hundred in 1914 to 2,342 in 1915 and 6,633 in 1916. This figure was to be more than doubled the following year, and in 1918, the last year of the war, 30,782 aircraft were produced. They all had to be covered with cellulose acetate.

Camille Dreyfus promised that the new company's factory, to be built on land purchased from the Derby Corporation at Spondon in Derbyshire, would be in production by the end of August 1916. It was a hopelessly optimistic estimate. In the meantime, the vital material continued to be imported from Basle. But with the French commandeering all the production from the only other manufacturer, the Usines du Rhône, a critical shortage was developing.

To general relief, deliveries from the Spondon factory started on a small scale in April 1917, and the company was rewarded with a government contract for twenty-five tons of acetone. This was rapidly followed by an order for seven hundred tons of cellulose acetate, which at nine shillings per pound was worth £705,000—equivalent to $141 million at today's values. The Dreyfus brothers were in the big time.

But all this required more investment. The original cash had long since run out, and the company had been propped up by loans from Canada arranged by Morden, and from the "gunpowder syndicate" of Vickers, the Nobel Explosives Company, and the Chilworth Gunpowder Company, orchestrated by Dawson. Much of this was intended for expansion of the factory to produce synthetic acetic acid, which was wanted by the War Office for the making of tear gas.

It was still not enough. The British government, which had already had its arm twisted to give tax concessions to the new company, was now persuaded that unless it was prepared to put public money into the venture, it would not get its precious chemicals. The Ministry of Munitions gave in with hardly a word of protest and put up £200,000. This money went primarily towards the 190-acre extension to the factory that was to produce the synthetic acetic acid. For in addition to their worries about aircraft production, the government was concerned about the U-boat threat to supplies of this material from the United States.

Henri Dreyfus must have been delighted. He knew very well, though he probably neglected to mention it, that synthetic acetic acid might well be needed for tear gas at that moment, but it had other valuable properties.

It was a vital ingredient for the manufacture of artificial silk.

————

FINANCIALLY, the company was now in a bizarre state. Vast sums had been borrowed or otherwise acquired, but the whole ownership was still held by the possessors of those original 160,000 sixpenny shares. Some form of restructuring was imperative, and in March 1918, after the shares had begun to change hands at higher and higher prices, the British Cellulose and Chemical Manufacturing (Parent) Company was formed, with a nominal share capital of £3,500,000.

At this point the sixpenny shares were valued at £14 10/- each,[1] a profit for the lucky holders of 58,000 percent. The Dreyfus brothers' and Alexander Clavel's holding was now valued at a staggering £1,159,971, for which they had paid nothing at all. It was a great deal of money in 1918. Dawson, Morden, and the others had also shared in the bonanza.

Such things do not go unnoticed in the commercial world. Courtaulds, the major British chemical and textile company, saw what was going on and tried to breach the Dreyfus monopoly. But the company's own attempts to make cellulose acetate were still in the laboratory stage, and though it offered to put up the necessary capital itself, it was politely shown the door by the Ministry of Munitions. Undeterred, Courtaulds began to lobby members of parliament to prompt an inquiry into the British Cellulose affair, for it too was looking to the future. It strongly suspected that Henri and Camille Dreyfus were going to emerge as major competitors after the war, with a well-equipped chemical works all ready for the manufacture of artificial silk. A factory, moreover,

which had been partly paid for by the taxpayer. And it was right.

Courtaulds got its wish. In June 1918, a subcommittee of the Select Committee on National Expenditure began to probe the Ministry of Munitions and its dealings with the British Cellulose and Chemical Manufacturing Company. It heard evidence from Courtaulds, from officials who disapproved of the Dreyfus project, and from people who felt aggrieved because they had not been among the select band who had made such a killing from the shares. Not surprisingly, in these circumstances the report published on July 26, 1918, was highly critical and recommended that the Spondon works should be taken over by the government.

The affair reached the floor of the House of Commons. "A more disreputable transaction has never been brought to the knowledge of this House," said a Conservative MP, Sir Frederick Banbury. A Liberal, R.D. Holt, said he had "seldom read an account of a more gross scandal," and claimed to have seen a list of the sixpenny shareholders. "When the House sees this list," he went on, "it will be horrified."

The press had a field day. On August 5, the *Daily Chronicle* came out with a banner headline:

The Dope Scandal. A Most Disgraceful Transaction.
£4000 becomes £2,230,000.

The story that followed accused the Dreyfus brothers of playing one government department against another, while the departments failed to cooperate with each other:

The company made promises it did not fulfill, carried on building operations without consent, issued debentures

without the knowledge of the Treasury, and did all sorts of wonderful things. There was no check on its expenditure. The company got relief from income tax, from excess profits tax, and finally got the State to agree to repay all its capital expenditure, even though that expenditure was not economical.

The company presented itself in the guise of a charitable institution, seeking assistance, concessions and special privileges. And in June last, it went on strike for a new agreement under which it secured an absolute monopoly of supply while the Ministry of Munitions "undertook to make loans at interest to the company to cover a proportion of their approved war capital expenditure," and to place contracts with them to the value of three million pounds on the basis of cost, plus a fixed sum of profit and a bonus for economical production.

In the opinion of the select committee, this was a thoroughly bad bargain for the state. The estimates for installing the company's plant were excessive. The government declined to accept competing offers from British firms—the United Alkali Company and Courtaulds —and it stopped buying from the French company.

The many objectionable features of the affair would have been modified if the company had delivered the goods and the dope had been of a good quality. But all through the report were complaints that the dope was much inferior to the cellulose acetate supplied by the company in Lyons. The Admiralty was anxious to support the company supplying the best quality, and to encourage British competing firms, but did not succeed.

The Admiralty records state that Colonel Grant Morden, one of the company's directors, informed the

secretary on November 8, 1916, that the company was in a
position to begin the manufacture of cellulose at a week's
notice. And that on February 15, 1917, another director, Sir
Trevor Dawson, told them that the company was the only
one in England producing cellulose acetate in any quantity;
although it was not until April 17 that any supplies were
manufactured.

The War Office was first promised supplies in
November 1915. In other words, the company was more
than a year behind, in spite of the privileges it received and
the generous support that it got.

"In the meantime," said the *Daily Chronicle* darkly, "the
company has been most successful in manufacturing
money. Powerful influences and astute minds must have
been at work to accomplish these things."

The paper went on to give a list of fortunate
shareholders, among whom, to the intense embarrassment
of the government, was a Mr. Eric Long, who turned out to
be the son of Walter Long, the colonial minister. General
Sir Sam Hughes, the Canadian minister of the militia, who
had been Grant Morden's commanding officer before he
left office in disgrace, was also named as holder of a
thousand shares. And perhaps worst of all, Professor John
Cadman, who was a member of the Chemical Advisory
Committee of the Ministry of Munitions, was found to have
been given 4,350 shares in the newly formed parent
company.

The implication of graft in high places was clear. *The
Saturday Review* came out with an angry editorial, which
blamed the War Office and the Ministry of Munitions "who
seem to have acted with negligence or ignorance which, in
the case of individuals, is called by a harsher name."

"It is essential," the editorial continued, "that somebody
should be made responsible for this, and that the War

Office and the Munitions Ministry should not be allowed to beat the shuttlecock of blame backwards and forwards until it drops from the weariness of the spectators."

The government dithered, uncertain what to do next. Walter Long sent his parliamentary private secretary to the Commons to make a long speech in defense of the company and its directors, and to praise the patriotic zeal of Colonel Grant Morden. He made no mention of the involvement of Long's son.

Then, on August 7, the *Daily Chronicle* dropped its bombshell.

"The more we probe the matter the uglier the sordid story becomes," it said, and proceeded to reveal that the Dreyfus brothers had been doing business with Germany during the war. What was more, it reproduced advertisements from trade papers in both countries to prove the point.

Public opinion was outraged. It was bad enough for a bunch of foreigners to have fleeced the British taxpayer for their personal profit in time of war. That they should have been supporting the enemy war effort at the same time was too much to swallow.

The *Daily Express*, ever a champion of lost causes, did its best to defend the Canadians involved in the scandal. Its owner, Lord Beaverbrook, was a Canadian himself and a close friend of Grant Morden. The *Express* suggested that Morden was no crook, but a hero who had risked his life in defense of the Empire.

The editorial trumpeted: "The personal risks he took, and the business daring he displayed in snatching this process of manufacturing out of the very jaws of the Germans, and establishing it on British soil out of their reach, must remain a part of the secret history of our time. But few deeds better deserve the gratitude of the Empire."

To which the *Daily Chronicle* had a swift answer: "Why wait for peace to reveal the story? The House of Commons and the public want it now. It cannot be possible," sneered the writer, "that Colonel Grant Morden is one of those modest men who would like their stories to remain unknown." The *Chronicle* went on to elaborate in massive detail exactly what Morden and his colleagues had been up to, and the profits they had made. The paper had uncovered the fact that part of the money had been diverted to set up a company in America—a deal that was expected to net the promoters $15 million.

Undeterred, the *Express* responded with a panegyric in praise of Grant Morden, which referred to him as Canada's foremost commercial magnate and compared his skills as a politician to those of Disraeli and Lord Randolph Churchill. It concluded: "Men of his type will be invaluable to the country in the trying and hopeful days to come, where industrial systems must be reconstructed with vigour, and yet with prudence, to make good the ravages of conflict. Col. Grant Morden has done the state no small service in war, and he should increase the debt due to him in the paths of peace."

There was not a dry eye in Fleet Street. In Westminster, however, there was very grave concern.

The British government did what British governments always do under such circumstances: It sought to cover its embarrassment and buy time by appointing a Commission of Inquiry. Bonar Law announced next day that three peers, a judge, a Lord of Appeal, and two prominent industrialists, would investigate the whole matter. It sounded impressive. In fact, since the tribunal was not authorized to take evidence under oath, it was a dead duck from the start.

The company reacted by engaging Sir Edward Carson, the foremost King's Counsel in the land, to represent them.

His junior was Douglas Hogg, later to become Lord Chancellor. At the same time, the Dreyfus brothers announced that they were launching writs for libel against the *Daily Chronicle* and the *Saturday Review*.

It might be thought that whatever else it did, the breaking of the scandal would put paid to the profiteering activities of the British Cellulose and Chemical Manufacturing Company. Not a bit of it. The war was still on, the air force still needed aircraft, and aircraft still needed dope. The tax concessions were canceled, but the government placed new orders worth nearly £3 million. What was more, they continued to pour money into the company.

These new advances had reached £458,000 by the end of August 1918, £900,000 by October 1918, and £1,450,000 by June 1919. In return the government was given preference shares to the same value, though they never received any dividends—largely due to the intervention of Alfred Loewenstein.

————

For Henri Dreyfus, the war ended too soon. His vast factory at Spondon was almost complete, thanks to the unwitting generosity of the public, but it still needed more capital before he could fulfil his ambition of becoming the world's leading manufacturer of artificial silk. With the fighting over, he could no longer squeeze the government purse, and with the dope scandal hanging over his head he was getting a cool response from the banking community. This was despite the fact that the commission of inquiry had finally produced a whitewash report that laid the blame for the affair on administrative chaos rather than criminal intent. The report had been greatly delayed, which was due in no small measure to the problems the commissioners experienced with the evidence of Henri Dreyfus. It was not just the difficulty of getting him to speak to the point, though that was bad enough. But when they did pin him down, they had the greatest trouble in understanding what he meant through the insipient fog of words and technicalities. Henri had used his second great attribute to advantage.

The commissioners had been further delayed by the fact that Henri's brother, Camille, had been attending to business in America and refused to return to give evidence until July 1919. Nevertheless, the commission decided that there was no evidence of exploitation of wartime scarcity, and that the monopoly had been justified.

No one was very surprised. This verdict was convenient for the government, and thus predictable. But it cut no ice with the financial community, to whom the Dreyfus brothers and all who sailed with them were now commercial lepers. The company had gone public in 1920, but the taint lingered and the money failed to materialize. By 1922, bankruptcy beckoned. In mounting desperation, Henri looked around for the capital he needed to complete his dream. What he needed was a fairy godmother. What he found was Alfred Loewenstein.

It was a fortuitous meeting, or so it seemed at the time. The former quartermaster was not the sort to worry about the Dreyfus brothers' scandalous recent past if there was a profit to be made. Furthermore, he already had a keen interest in the artificial silk industry, having acquired control of the Belgian firm of Tubize. He would, he said, be delighted to help.

When supping with Alfred Loewenstein, it was advisable to use a long spoon. Henri Dreyfus got what he wanted most in all the world: his artificial silk factory and a thriving company soon to be renamed British Celanese Ltd.

The price was Faustian. Loewenstein offered to plough £700,000 into the enterprise, which he intended, after his fashion, to borrow from someone else. But for this he wanted two things: debentures paying an interest rate of eight percent—which was extremely high for the period—and a royalty payment on every bolt of artificial silk the company sold. Dreyfus agreed. He really had very little option. But the net result was that for the next four years, every penny of profit made by British Celanese went straight to Alfred Loewenstein's company. For this, and for reasons we shall come to later, it was a very satisfactory deal for the Belgian financier. It marked the beginning of a dazzling career in the public eye.

In so far as any watershed can be marked, it may also have been the first step on the trail that led to his death.

Loewenstein had not, of course, put himself at any great risk in the Dreyfus deal. He floated a company with a registered capital of £55,000, which he split into 1,100,000 one-shilling shares to appeal to the small investor. This new company, which was destined to grow like Jack's beanstalk, was Cellulose Holdings Ltd. Then he issued debentures at seven percent for the full amount of £700,000 that he was lending to the Dreyfus brothers.

It was a simple scheme, and splendidly profitable. Cellulose Holdings was making a marginal one percent return on its debentures, but the royalties provided a dividend equivalent to the total amount of the company's common stock.

When the Holdings company was first floated, Loewenstein himself took only 1,210 shares. He had thus rescued Dreyfus with a loan of £700,000 at a net risk to himself of only £60. However, as soon as the project showed signs of succeeding, the Belgian rapidly increased his holding to more than 67,000 shares and added to it massively over the years. From small beginnings, Cellulose Holdings Ltd. was to become the centerpiece of his fortune.

For Henri Dreyfus, however, disillusion was swift. One condition of the agreement with Loewenstein specified that the Holdings company should have the right to three seats on the board of British Celanese, and Loewenstein lost no time in making the appointments. One of these was a M. Gustave Popelier, who also happened to be on the board of the Belgian Tubize Company, which had itself taken 30,000 shares in Cellulose Holdings.

M. Popelier knew a great deal about the manufacture of artificial silk, and on the face of it, the appointment made good sense. But as Dreyfus was shortly to discover, Alfred Loewenstein never did anything without a purpose.

9

ALFRED LOEWENSTEIN HAD EMBRACED the twentieth century like a lover. His doings may have been ruthless, and occasionally bizarre, but there was no doubting the man's courage or enterprise. Had he been born fifty years later, today might have found him owning most of Silicon Valley and flirting with the higher reaches of biotechnology. As it was, he concentrated on the two things that seemed to him, from the perspective of the first quarter of this century, to offer the richest potential for a bright industrial future: artificial silk and hydroelectric power.

With the blessed benefit of hindsight, the first may seem an unwise choice to have made. Artificial silk has long been one with the dodo and the dinosaur, falling prey to later and better synthetics along the road of textile evolution. But in the flapper era of the 1920s, it possessed enormous promise. Young women throughout the civilized world who could not afford the luxury of real silk clamored to have it next to their skin.

When Loewenstein came on the scene, there were two principal methods of making this revolutionary fabric. The first was the viscose process, adopted by Courtaulds in Britain, Snia Viscose in Italy, and most of the other giant textile concerns, after many years of unsuccessful attempts to duplicate the magic of the silkworm.

The basic raw material for the viscose process was wood pulp or cotton "linters"—the short hairs of the cotton seed that are useless for spinning—which was then treated with caustic soda. After further treatment, both chemical and mechanical, the resultant substance was forced through minute meshes into a bath of dilute sulphuric acid, and the threads collected on glass spools. These could be woven into a brilliant fabric, which had only two drawbacks: It became easily creased, and it reacted unkindly to water. Still, so long as viscose silk was the only game in town, this did not seem to matter too much.

Then along came the Dreyfus brothers and the cellulose acetate process. Whether or not Henri and Camille really invented this process and had a legitimate claim to their patents was a subject of intense dispute. The fact remained that they had it, it worked, and, thanks to their wartime proclivities, they possessed an almost complete factory, which could put the stuff into production as soon as they found a little more money. And theirs was, without doubt, a superior product—far more tolerant of being washed or caught out in the rain.

In the cellulose acetate process, bleached cotton linters were prepared with a mixture of acetic acid and sulphuric acid and placed in refrigerated containers. There, the mixture was agitated for several hours. It was then put into tanks containing water, and the resultant precipitate ended up after separation as a flaky white substance that could be dissolved in acetone and blown through minute orifices in metal sheets. The threads were allowed to solidify and dry before being reeled, and the solvent was recovered to be used again. This was the material that became known in America as "rayon" and in Britain as "Celanese."

Alfred Loewenstein's initial involvement with the artificial silk industry was, as I have said, with the Tubize Company in Belgium. And Tubize, like everyone else at that time, was using the viscose process. So when Henri Dreyfus came knocking at his door in search of money, the financier was not slow to realize the possibilities. Dreyfus got his cash, and the mills at British Celanese began to turn ever faster. But so, too, did those at Tubize, and at all the other companies in which Loewenstein began to buy an interest. And, strange to tell, these companies, one by one, as though by some mysterious osmosis, discovered the secrets of the cellulose acetate process and began producing a better quality of artificial silk.

Henri Dreyfus was not happy.

It was war. By the beginning of 1926, Tubize was not only competing with British Celanese in the European marketplace, but had begun to sell its artificial silk to Britain and the commonwealth. The Dreyfus brothers were stung into belated action and fired Gustave Popelier from the board of directors.

Now it was Loewenstein's turn to be angry. He reacted by calling for an extraordinary general meeting of British Celanese shareholders, at which he announced that he would demand the resignations of Henri and Camille Dreyfus and also of their friend Sir Trevor Dawson, who was the other survivor of the dope scandal to remain on the board. The Dreyfuses at this time were joint managing directors.

The Times for March 1, 1926, strongly advised shareholders not to waste time raking over old history or crying over spilt milk and to reject Loewenstein's plea. "They can hardly be expected," it said, "to approve the nomination to the Board of gentlemen who may have interests that are capable of conflicting with those of the company." The article provoked a rare letter of protest to the editor from Loewenstein himself, which *The Times* duly printed.

However, when the extraordinary general meeting was held on March 9, 1926, at the Cannon Street Hotel, its instigator did not bother to turn up. Instead, Loewenstein had a statement read to the meeting in which he claimed that Popelier had been the only director on the board who knew anything about artificial silk, and that if he had been listened to, British Celanese would now be as profitable as any other company in the field. As he pointed out with mordant satisfaction, not a penny in dividends had yet been paid to anyone—not even the preference shareholders (who were mainly the government)—and the price of ordinary shares had slumped by fifty percent to five shillings and two pence.

"It is impossible to believe," he said, "that there can be any justification for such poor results when the company is producing the best artificial silk on the market, and the industry as a whole is in a period of such high prosperity."

Loewenstein did not mention, of course, that it was the royalty payments to his own company and the high interest payments on his loan that were largely responsible for the nonprofitability of British Celanese. But the shareholders were not deceived and appeared to have been offended by his absence.

Unable to question the financier, they did the next best thing and threw out his motion neck and crop. There were cheers for Henri Dreyfus, but it was a minor victory for the Swiss group. Loewenstein still had three directors on the board, and he still had the royalty agreement. He still had the Dreyfus brothers by the throat.

Loewenstein, however, was so disgusted by his defeat that he decided to throw his entire stock of 750,000 British Celanese preference shares on the market, mostly at prices below their quoted value of eight shillings and two pence. He was asking six shillings and nine pence for the first 250,000, seven shillings and nine pence for the next third, and ten shillings each for the final quarter million. In retrospect, it appeared that this fit of pique cost him dearly, for most of those shares ended up in the hands of the Dreyfus brothers.

Henri seems to have resolved at this time that the only long-term solution to the Belgian monkey on his back was to gain complete personal control of British Celanese. It was to prove an expensive exercise, for as he went in search of sufficient shares to achieve his object, the price soared. The Stock Exchange watched the extraordinary spectacle of shares in a company that had never paid a dividend in its existence rise in price over a short period by 1,565 percent. They went up from five shillings and nine pence to £4 10/-. But Henri achieved his objective. By May 1927, he and his brother Camille, who was by then running the American Celanese company with rather more success, had acquired a voting majority. They lost no time in putting their new power to the test.

They must have felt that the Loewenstein menace was growing, for in October 1926, the Cellulose Holding and Investment Company had changed its name to become the International Holdings and Investment Company and had vastly expanded its capital and scope.

Loewenstein was extending his tentacles into artificial silk companies in France, Holland, Germany, and Poland. His aim was now clear: the creation of a vast cartel that could dominate the world market. One such cartel was already in existence, with Courtaulds, Snia Viscosa, and the German Glanztoff company as the major participants. This cartel controlled ninety percent of English, German, and Dutch production, seventy-five percent of American, and seventy percent of Italian. But they were still producing the old viscose material. With the cellulose acetate process in his pocket, in spite of Dreyfus's claimed patents, Loewenstein was in a good position to challenge these giants and possibly beat them. And if he could not beat them, he was not averse to joining them. International Holdings already had a major stake in Glanztoff, and moves were afoot to buy into Courtaulds.

Only one thing stood in his way: the enmity of Henri Dreyfus and his adamant refusal to have anything to do with cartels. Dreyfus wanted British Celanese to go it alone. Though his attempts to enforce his patents and preserve his manufacturing secrets sounded very much like the slamming of the stable door after the horse had bolted, they may have been sufficient to make Loewenstein appear an unappealing partner.

On May 3, 1927, Henri Dreyfus struck. He wrote to the chairman of British Celanese, Major General Hugh Dawnay, CBE, CMG, DSO, informed him that he had bought control of the company, and demanded his immediate resignation, along with six other members of the board. They included, naturally, all of Alfred Loewenstein's nominees.

As a retired army officer, Dawnay may not have known too much about the production of artificial silk, but he was straight as a die and as English as his name. He had given the company an aura of respectability at a time when it was badly needed. He was gravely offended by Dreyfus's action. The man was a cad. He had never much liked him, and now he resolved that whatever the outcome of this crisis he would never work with the fellow again.

Dawnay called the twelve members of the board together to consider their position. Two whose resignation had not been demanded, Sir Trevor Dawson and a Mr. Murray, decided to resign at once. The remainder resolved to stick it out until the annual meeting of the company. This was due to take place on May 24, and after that they knew there was no way they could withstand the voting power of the Dreyfus brothers. So they put the meeting off.

At this point, Dreyfus lost his cool completely. He would not be denied. On May 23, 1927, he wrote an open letter to the shareholders of British Celanese, which was published in *The Times* two days later. It occupied a full half page of very small print, and rarely can so much dirty linen have been washed in public.

The crux of his tirade was an attack on Loewenstein, accusing him of continued hostility towards British Celanese and constant obstruction of Dreyfus's policies through his nominated directors. He quoted at length a speech made by Loewenstein to the shareholders of Tubize on November 6, 1926, in which the financier was alleged to have said: "In 1922 a certain artificial silk produced by a new process of cellulose acetate made an appearance on the market. As I was in touch with the inventors of the said process, I immediately endeavored to give to the Tubize Company the benefits of this new discovery. It was thus that the Tubize Company was enabled to be today the only one on the Continent to work at the same time with three processes of manufacture.

"We took control of the Tubize Company, and we believed that we should be able to impose our conditions on our enemies." By this, according to Dreyfus, he meant British Celanese.

The fury of Dreyfus burned through the grey columns of *The Times*. The Belgian had not only stolen his secrets;

he had had the effrontery to brag about it in public.
Further, he said, Tubize had just concluded an agreement
with a German company (Glanztoff), under which it agreed
to pass on all the technical information on the
Dreyfus/Clavel processes. Glanztoff was expected to have a
cellulose acetate plant working within six months, which
would mean yet more competition for British Celanese.

Each month, Dreyfus fumed, a detailed report on the
workings of his company was presented to the board,
revealing its innermost financial and technical secrets. And
yet, two of the three members of that board nominated by
Loewenstein were the deputy chairman and the managing
director of International Holdings and Investments, which
in turn controlled Tubize. This was his justification in
demanding their elimination from the board.

The Times, being a fair-minded newspaper, solicited a
reply from Dawnay, which it published on the same page.
Dawnay's response was cool and haughty. If the managing
director had complaints, he said, he should have brought
them to the board.

He had failed to do so. As for the accusations against
Loewenstein's nominees, "there is no ground for suspicion
that they have acted otherwise than with complete
propriety since taking their seats as members of this
Board." The general meeting of the company, Dawnay
promised, would be held "very shortly."

In fact, it took place three weeks later, on June 15, 1927.
The event resembled not so much a company meeting as
the battle of the Little Big Horn, with Dawnay in the
starring role of General George Custer. Faced with Dreyfus
and more than a million proxy votes besides, the
threatened members of the board made speeches of
dignified disgust and were duly mown down by the Swiss
Indians.

Dawnay announced, somewhat superfluously, that he would not be standing for re-election. Two other directors would be resigning in sympathy, and that would leave the Dreyfus brothers, Alexander Clavel, one director nominated by the government, and the three representatives of International Holdings. As for the last, Dawnay's legal advisers had told him that the contract appointing them was valid, and since they had done nothing wrong, it would be asking for trouble to fire them. As owners of the company, Henri and Camille Dreyfus could do what they liked, but he strongly advised them to leave well enough alone.

Dawnay was spitting against the wind, and he knew it. "I stand before you for the last time with nothing to be ashamed of in rendering account of my stewardship," he concluded, "which is perhaps even something to be proud of considering the many years during which, before my advent, the company had labored in the slough of despond. I have received the most able assistance from my colleagues, who have given me unabated support." It was all very gallant and dignified. Useless, of course.

Sir John Raphael, one of Loewenstein's three nominees (the others were Capt. The Rt. Hon. F.E. Guest and a Mr. Chandler), was not prepared to go so quietly. In his view, Dreyfus was in need of a history lesson.

"In 1922," he reminded the shareholders,

the Celanese Company had come to the end of its resources. It was unable to find the necessary money to carry on. Preference shares of the company stood at three shillings and six pence, and the ordinary shares at one shilling and six pence, or thereabouts. At that time, the Holdings Company was formed specifically to come to its assistance, and Dr. Dreyfus was one of the most anxious suppliants for the assistance of the Holdings Company in order to save his company from bankruptcy.

The Holdings Company, on the strength of a favorable report from the Tubize Company, found a large sum of money—some £900,000 in all. Dr. Dreyfus himself signed the agreement, one of the conditions of which was that the Holdings Company would have the right to nominate three directors to the British Celanese Board. And today Dr. Dreyfus, but the majority which he has obtained, is using that majority to repudiate his own signature.

At this point, *The Times* later recorded, there were cries of "Hear, hear" from his audience. Encouraged, Raphael proceeded to deny that Tubize had made any agreement with the Glanztoff company (though it was widely reported that they had), to deny that International Holdings controlled Tubize (though the company's own balance sheet claimed a controlling interest), and to deny that Loewenstein had ever referred to British Celanese as his enemy.

"But his main principal charge," he went on,

is that we, as representatives of the Holding Company, passed on to the Tubize Company information which we have received as directors of the Celanese Company, and in fact that we are working against its real interests. That is wholly untrue. We have never passed on any information whatever.

These imputations are nothing less than an attack on our integrity as businessmen. They are totally unfounded, and we vigorously resent and repudiate them.

Feigned or real, Raphael's indignation was impressive. He went on to praise Dawnay and his colleagues. "Each member of the Board has worked unremittingly and whole-heartedly for the success of the company. For that they have not had a penny of remuneration. And what is to be their recompense? According to Dr Dreyfus, their discredit and their dismissal."

It was strong stuff. Dreyfus was being branded as an ingrate and a liar. On behalf of all three of Loewenstein's directors, Raphael refused to resign. Dreyfus could do what he liked with his votes; the Holdings Company would stand by its legal rights.

Dreyfus was unabashed. He presented himself as a man who had worked his way up from nothing (he did not say how) to a position where he could acquire two and a half million shares "in order to save the company from men who spend their time at Board meetings, simply talking matters over in such a way as to make believe they know the business." His audience laughed. They laughed again when he described the Board as "a sort of mutual admiration syndicate."

But to Raphael's charges, Dreyfus made no reply. He claimed to have built up the factory from a piece of paper to a position where it employed more than seven thousand people, and now he wanted to take control "so that I can use the same measures I have used successfully in my own private business, in order to make money for the shareholders." He did not elaborate on what those measures had been. He had undeniably made money.

Dreyfus moved for the dismissal of the Loewenstein directors, saying he had been assured that this was perfectly legal. In that case, asked one shareholder, would he take personal responsibility for any damages if

Loewenstein sued? But Dreyfus declined to give any such promise.

The vote was a foregone conclusion, with 4,039,689 for Dreyfus and only 633,389 against. And the bulk of the opposition came from the government nominee, who had been instructed to put his 500,000 shares in support of Dawnay.

The Times described it as DREYFUS'S FINAL TRIUMPH. It was not quite that, for there was still the matter of the royalties to be settled before he could be free of Loewenstein. And the Belgian was determined to drive a hard bargain. In the event, it cost Dreyfus almost one and a half million pounds to buy off the royalty agreement and repay Loewenstein's remaining debenture holdings. And to raise the cash, he had to make a private share issue and thus dilute the capital of his company.

Dreyfus had won the battle, but it was a Pyrrhic victory. And the war was not over yet.

10

In September 1926, Alfred Loewenstein needed to improve his public image. The battle with Dreyfus was not going well, and his bear attack to drive down the price of shares in British Celanese was beginning to look like a costly failure. Most important of all, he had decided to launch International Holdings and Investment Ltd. as his new financial flagship, and if shares in the new company were to gain public confidence, and therefore a high price, it was vital that the name of Loewenstein achieve a new and favorable prominence.

And so he came up with an idea. Like most of Loewenstein's ideas, it was strong on panache, a trifle weak on logic, and guaranteed to drive the financial establishment into a fit of near hysteria. To Loewenstein, that mattered not one jot. He had minimal respect for the conventions of the City of London, and as long as he retained the support of his existing backers he was unconcerned at the derision his proposal would bring forth. His target was the stock-exchange gambler, who could be relied upon to follow a buccaneer in the hope of

large profits. Such men shared his contempt for
conservative finance, but they would also need a larger-
than-life figure to lead them, and preferably one who
promised security as well as instant wealth. Loewenstein
set out to give them one.

Patriotism, said Dr. Johnson, is the last refuge of the
scoundrel. Scoundrel or not, Loewenstein decided to hold
the banner high. As a loyal Belgian, he was, he said,
distressed at the sorry state of the Belgian franc—which
was certainly bouncing around the foreign exchange
market like a punctured Ping-Pong ball at that time. In
order to rescue the currency of his homeland, he offered to
lend the Belgian government $50 million for two years,
completely free of interest. Once that deal had been
concluded, he proposed to do the same thing for the
French.

It sounded too good to be true. And it was.

As a venue for this momentous announcement,
Loewenstein chose Barcelona. Just why he should select a
Spanish city for a transaction involving Belgian politicians,
English financiers, and American currency was never
altogether clear. It may have been because he was working
on a grandiose scheme for hydro-electric generation in the
Pyrenees at the time, and thought he might as well impress
the hell out of the Spaniards while he was about it.

And impressive it certainly was. Loewenstein had
reserved the entire third floor of the Ritz Hotel and rented
seven additional villas in the city for his staff and guests.
These included wealthy industrialists from all over Europe,
several British MPs, and, of course, the world's press.

His own entourage arrived by air, rail, and road. There
were no fewer than forty secretaries, both male and female,
a publicity manager who had once been the youngest MP
in the House of Commons, and Loewenstein's personal

instructors in the arts of tennis, boxing, and dancing, plus a masseur. This perspiration of sportsmen had an airplane to themselves, as did Loewenstein. The third aircraft to bump on to the tarmac at Barcelona airport contained, to the delight of the assembled reporters, three English valets—all of them dressed in fur coats. The head valet, it was breathlessly reported, had his own personal servant, who was a dwarf. This may, however, have been an unkind reference to Fred Baxter, who was in all conscience a very small man.

There was one minor omission: Not one of the secretaries had remembered to bring a typewriter, and the official communiqué had finally to be written on a portable machine borrowed from a *Daily Express* reporter.

Everyone departed for the Ritz, where Loewenstein that night gave a banquet to remember. Caviar had been flown in from Moscow in his private plane, and the finest chicken from France. The cost was estimated at £20 per head, which was an expensive meal in 1926, and when the caviar ran out the aircraft was grandly dispatched to fetch more (though with the flying speeds of those days it is doubtful if it got back in time).

At last, with everyone wined and dined, Loewenstein told all. This was to be a private presentation—he was holding a press conference the next day—but the contents of it leaked out to the *Daily Telegraph*, which reported the story in its usual deadpan style. And just as well, too, for it proved to be the only detailed account of exactly what Loewenstein was up to.

———

THE FINANCIER SPOKE DEFENSIVELY, as though he guessed that his kite was a non-flier. Earlier, he had confided to the

correspondent of the Brussels paper *Le Soir* that if the
Belgian finance minister, M. Jaspar, failed to accept the
scheme, he would go to Brussels and "smash his face." He
had also threatened to send his fleet of ten aircraft over the
city to drop leaflets denouncing Jaspar as a traitor. Now,
however, Loewenstein's tone was mild:

> You will understand what I mean when I speak of a 'put
> and call.' This phrase means the right to sell at a certain
> price [a put], and to buy at a certain other price [a call],
> and it is upon this principle that my offer is based. In
> return for these dollars I ask no security, excepting the
> equivalent amount of Belgian francs, calculated at 225
> francs to the pound. I give them the right to sell me francs
> at 225 when they choose, *and I take the right to sell francs to
> them at 175 when I choose.*

> The francs which I thus obtain will be used in the first
> place for the purchase of shares in the Canadian
> companies held in France and Belgium. Later, the shares
> of other companies will be bought, and they will be
> provided with the capital necessary for their
> development.

> To give you an example: the French and Belgian Tubize
> companies want to increase their output, but have not the
> capital for the requisite plant. I have been able to put at
> their disposal the requisite sterling, and consequently to
> increase production in France and Belgium.

> This is an answer to those who say that I am seeking to
> damage the industry of my country by means of these
> successive purchases of shares. A steady stream of
> currencies possessing a gold value will be entering the

Belgian Treasury, of which the fifty million dollars now offered are the first instalment. And it is obvious that what I hope to do today for Belgium, I will shortly be able to do for France. The agency through which this operation will be carried out is a small company controlled by Belgian, French, and to a small extent British capital, on whose board of directors will sit persons whose eminence will be recognized in all countries. (Italics mine)

Just who these eminent personages were, Loewenstein never disclosed. Within hours, the point was to become academic, for news reached him that the Belgian government, with unseemly ingratitude, had rejected his altruistic offer out of hand. M. Jaspar had presumably read the small print and decided that a deal that gave Alfred Loewenstein a profit of nearly twenty-five percent—the difference between paying a pound to buy 225 francs and reselling the same francs at 175 to the pound—was one he could afford to refuse.

This was naturally not the way the financier saw it. He went on to tell his distinguished audience that night:

I have seen it hinted that my friends and myself are inspired by purely selfish motives in making this offer. Let us look at the facts. If today a Belgian company has need of capital and wants to issue bonds, first of all the Belgian government taxes them at twelve percent. Secondly, in as much as the Belgian franc is fluctuating, those bonds cannot be placed in Belgium and must be placed in a country which always answers our call, namely Great Britain. Our British friends, with whom I have worked so long and so much, exact a further twenty-two and a half percent in income tax, and therefore

Belgian industry must pay thirty-five percent a year simply because it cannot issue its bonds in its own country.

I have already mentioned, in addition, that the Belgian government will save about ten percent on its foreign loans, but I am not going to pretend that the offer is pure generosity. On the contrary, it is very advantageous for my group of French, Belgian, and English friends, because today, if we were to go to London to borrow French or Belgian bank notes, we should have to pay about eighteen percent to persons who are quite ready to lend them on the security of sterling and dollars, which later the Belgian and French governments will probably borrow next day from the same persons and pay ten or twelve percent gross for the privilege. The total commission on these transactions is therefore about thirty percent.

The bare fact remains, however many objections may be put forward, that my plan does offer to Belgium a stable franc, and to the Belgian government money at a cheaper rate than they ever dreamed of.

It was convoluted and highly plausible to those who neglected to read the fine print, but it cut no ice with M. Jaspar. Perhaps it was never intended to. Loewenstein had achieved his prime aim of appearing to the world at large to be a patriot of great wealth and selfless principle, a man to be followed and trusted. A man, moreover, with whom it would be safe to invest one's life savings. Not too many people were going to study that small print.

There was still the potential hazard of the scheduled press conference the next day, to which reporters had been summoned from great distances. The news of the Belgian government's rejection of the scheme had not yet been made public, and Loewenstein must have agonized over whether to carry on as though nothing had happened or to launch an attack on M. Jaspar. In the event, he did neither.

According to H.J. Greenwall, Paris correspondent of the *Daily Express*, Loewenstein walked on to the platform and began talking about Bolshevism. "Throughout the sultry afternoon he talked about Bolshevism. But not one single word about saving the franc. At the same time, the world press was receiving extraordinary communications from him, linking the names of visiting MPs with his financial scheme to develop the hydroelectric power of Spain."

Greenwall, who was writing after Loewenstein's death, was evidently not a reader of the *Daily Telegraph*, or he claimed that no one had ever discovered the details of Loewenstein's scheme. He himself believed that it had something to do with an exclusive agreement to print Belgian bank notes. However, he included one anecdote that revealed more about the financier's way of life than he would have wanted printed at the time.

"The following night [after the press conference]" wrote Greenwall,

> as I was passing his door, one of his valets stepped out of his room and, putting his fingers to his lips, said: 'Hush, we have just got him off.' I asked what he meant. He explained that Loewenstein had to be put to sleep like a child. Often he woke in the early hours of the morning and demanded of his valet, who slept in the same room, that a cold bath should be prepared. After the bath he would ring for a secretary, who had to rise and dress and take dictation.

What had we here? A financial wizard afraid of the dark? A millionaire who slept with his valet but not his wife? A cleanliness freak? A tyrant who worked his staff around the clock? Or simply a bad case of insomnia? Whatever the explanation, assuming Greenwall to be wholly accurate (which is a large assumption to make of any journalist), Loewenstein was emerging as a character of some complexity.

Five days later, it seemed that amnesia was also one of his personal failings. The Loewenstein circus had folded its tents and headed for London, where two suites had been reserved for him at the Ritz Hotel—one specially converted into offices. As usual, he arrived in style, complete with seven secretaries and a fleet of Daimler cars waiting for him at Croydon airport. The press called it "the great Loewenstein efficiency machine," which must have pleased him greatly.

What pleased him less was any talk of the great Belgian loan fiasco. A secretary was deputed to tell reporters that he had not gone to Barcelona for that purpose at all, but merely to look at his hydro-electric generating stations in the Pyrenees. It was Loewenstein's plan, the secretary said, to build five aerodromes close to the inaccessible power plants, so that engineers and workmen could be shuttled between them in a fleet of small aircraft. He had flown to Spain to demonstrate the feasibility of the scheme.

The Belgian loan? What Belgian loan? "He did not go to make himself a nine days wonder," the secretary added stiffly. "In fact Captain Loewenstein has been extremely annoyed at the publicity which his visit aroused. He does not like publicity in any shape or form."

The *Daily Chronicle* recorded this gem of absurdity in the middle of an unctuous account of the humming activity at the Ritz—"that quiet industry which is so impressive"—

and Loewenstein's dress: "a light grey suit with brown boots and a straw hat." It also described the disappointment of the villagers of Thorpe Satcheville at not seeing their squire on this trip, before adding, almost as an afterthought, that Loewenstein's aircraft had crashed on the way from Barcelona.

The final paragraph read:

> While on his way to London, Captain Loewenstein met with a mishap which has, however, in no way diminished his enthusiasm for air travel. He set out from Barcelona to Paris in one of his own airliners, but when near Le Bourget it was necessary to make a forced landing. The machine was badly damaged, but luckily both Captain Loewenstein and his English pilot were unhurt. The night was spent in Paris, and the journey to Croydon completed yesterday in one of the Imperial Airways planes.

I reflected that if things had turned out differently, or if Loewenstein had lost his taste for flying, this book would never have been written. I also mused that the priorities of news editors must have changed somewhat since 1926.

————

LOOKING BACK, it is possible to conclude that the whole currency fiasco was a smokescreen, designed to draw attention away from what Loewenstein was really up to in the autumn of 1926. He can hardly have supposed that he would be taken seriously by the French and Belgian governments. Though it scarcely seemed possible that he had time for any more activity in this period, what with this, the Dreyfus affair, the Villa Begonia robbery, et al., he was in fact engaged in heavy machinations elsewhere.

For details of what Loewenstein was doing in the early and mid-20s, I am indebted to Duncan McDowall, senior research associate at the Conference Board of Canada. McDowall had come across Loewenstein's name while researching a book on the history of Brazilian Traction and had written a long unpublished article on the financier's activities. On hearing that I was researching this book, he kindly agreed to let me see his material, on which the remainder of this chapter and some of the earlier references to Brazilian Traction are based.

Though F.S. Pearson had been dead for many years, Loewenstein had not forgotten the fairy godfather who gave him his first big break. He had, in a rather uncharacteristically sentimental gesture, bought the front door from the American engineer's country home in Great Barrington, Massachusetts, and had it installed in his own baronial mansion in Brussels. More importantly, he had not forgotten the potential of the companies that Pearson had founded, and for which Loewenstein had been instrumental in raising capital. With the concept of the holding company by this time in high fashion, he set about trying to amalgamate and control these widely spread public utilities.

Like most of Loewenstein's enterprises, it was an ambitious undertaking. With the assistance of a brilliant American named Dannie Heineman—who within a few short years would become his bitter enemy—he formed the Société Internationale d'Energie Hydro-Electrique, known to investors as SIDRO.

That was in 1923. SIDRO's main attraction on the stock markets was that it was closely associated with Heineman's company SOFINA, a vast power and traction conglomerate that already had worldwide interests. To these, through SIDRO, Loewenstein brought large interests in the Pearson companies of Barcelona Traction and Mexican Tramways, and in doing so established himself as a major force in European finance. But the jewel in the crown of the Pearson empire, Brazilian Traction, still eluded him. Still smarting from his failure to get a seat on the board, Loewenstein wanted that company and wanted it badly.

The Brazilian Traction directors watched nervously. Whenever their company's stock began to fluctuate on the market, they immediately suspected the activities of "Mr. Puffstein," as they had come, disparagingly, to call him. But Loewenstein bided his time, quietly buying what shares he could through SIDRO and cultivating his alliance with the powerful Dannie Heineman. The time would come, he was sure, when the right combination of market conditions and carefully planted rumors would deliver Brazilian Traction into his hands.

In 1924, he made his first overt move, inducing a Belgian named Derwa to take the company to court for failing to pay its mortgage bonds in anything but Belgian or French francs at the current rate of exchange. He himself, of course, was still enjoying the fruits of the 1921 "compromise" and was drawing his interest in sterling. But to the public eye, Loewenstein became the champion of the little man, defending him against the meanness of a large company. Brazilian Traction had little option but to fight the action, and to begin a court battle that was to last four years.

Toward the end of 1925, carefully placed rumors began to spread to the effect that Loewenstein was putting together a new undertaking that would join various Canadian-based utility companies into one enormous holding company. The shares of Brazilian Traction began to rise, more than doubling in value from a low of $52 in mid-1925 to a peak of $115 by August 1926 as Loewenstein boosted the stock and bought heavily.

This was not the good news it might seem to the Brazilian Traction board. Down in Rio, Sir Alexander Mackenzie grew more furious with every increase in the price. He was fighting for better concessions from the Brazilian government, claiming low earnings in order to get better payments and pay less tax. The rise in the price of the shares made it seem to Brazilian officials that the Traction company must be very profitable indeed.

And now a new bogey entered the scene, as the company learned from its spies in London that Sir Herbert Holt, the Montreal utilities tycoon, was willing to vest his own holdings in Brazilian Traction in Loewenstein's holding company. This, combined with the large block of shares that the Belgian was already rumored to possess, spelled real danger, for Holt was a man of power and influence in Canadian banking circles.

In some desperation, the directors sent an emissary to Paris to plead with Loewenstein to see reason. But he retired hurt when the Belgian boasted that he already possessed 125,000 Traction shares, and the heavy trading went on.

The projected new holding company, Hydro-Electric Securities, duly came into being in September 1926. Ominously, the board of directors contained the name of Andrew Holt, who was not only the son of Sir Herbert but also a director of Brazilian Traction. A triumphant Loewenstein let it be known that he was throwing the considerable financial weight of Hydro-Electric Securities behind his raid on Brazilian Traction and that his aim was the acquisition of at least thirty-five percent of the equity. He now had control of 167,500 shares and was prepared to spend up to $3.5 million to get more. The war was now to be fought in the open.

———

THE BRAZILIAN TRACTION directors decided that the best means of defense was attack. The Holt connection was the most worrying factor, and one of the directors, E.R. Peacock, wrote to Sir Herbert in a fairly blatant bid to scupper the budding alliance.

"As you know," ran Peacock's letter,

> our friend Loewenstein has been causing all of us a good deal of anxiety and trouble. He ran a high-class circus at Biarritz accompanied by a campaign in the press which took such forms that I began to doubt his sanity. . . . He made it quite clear, however, that he had committed himself so far that he must go on with his Canadian holding company, whether the others were prepared to do so or not. That is the difficulty with him, he always goes ahead with his things without taking advice until he has reached a position when he forces one's hand, and of course his promises to reform—while they are well meant—cannot be taken too seriously because the man's nature is such that he cannot avoid these spectacular things.

It was a letter from a worried man that ignored the fact that thus far in their long relationship, Loewenstein had managed to outsmart the Brazilian Traction board at every turn.

Peacock went on to point out that Loewenstein's interest in Brazilian Traction was entirely speculative, that he had dangerously overextended himself financially to acquire his shares, and that, if successful in his takeover bid, he would "wreck" the company within a year. "He is a market operator and splendid at that, but no man to control companies," Peacock concluded.

Exactly what effect this letter had is unclear. Brazilian Traction believed at the time that it had Holt's assurance that he would not give open backing to Loewenstein's scheme, but the association between the two men certainly continued. Holt was to become chairman of International Holdings and was the last man to speak to Loewenstein, apart from those on board the aircraft, on the day of his death.

The battle was now heating up, with Sir Alexander McKenzie warning publicly that any fusion of Brazilian Traction with the Mexican or Spanish utilities would lead to a violent outburst of Brazilian nationalism against the company. The Brazilians, he said, would conclude that they were being "bled" to prop up the ailing Spanish and Mexican companies. "Your scheme," he told Loewenstein bluntly, "is a negation of everything we have maintained for many years, and if realized would put an end to my usefulness here."

This might have made an impression on the shareholders. For Loewenstein, the prospect of early retirement for Sir Alexander, the man who had persistently snubbed his attempts to join the board, must have been sweet music. A more serious threat to his ambitions was the defection at this stage of Dannie Heineman.

Heineman wanted to see the autonomy of SIDRO preserved, and its absorption within Loewenstein's new empire of holding companies, with a consequent effect on the influence of SOFINA, was not to his liking. He was also afraid that the merger might form a precedent for further attacks on his company's financial interests. Heineman had clearly concluded that an alliance with Alfred Loewenstein was rather like trying to make friends with a shark.

The climax came on December 22, 1926, when Loewenstein called a mass meeting of SIDRO shareholders in Brussels to gain approval for his scheme. He was putting before them a complex package involving an increase in capitalization and a share exchange that would bring their company into the orbit of International Holdings. Heineman looked at the package closely and decided enough was enough. He would go to the meeting and speak out against Loewenstein in public.

For Heineman, this was an unusual decision. He was a retiring man who shunned all publicity, and as a result very little about him remains on record. But he must have been a formidable antagonist: When he joined SOFINA in 1905, the infant company had only two employees. By 1926, it was already a truly multinational concern, and in 1939 it employed 40,000 workers.

Before the SIDRO meeting took place, Heineman contacted Brazilian Traction and announced his intentions. Sir Alexander Mackenzie and his board were delighted. Heineman told them: "I definitely wish to put an end to this most unpleasant situation. We wish to do constructive work, and do it calmly. There are so many other things to attend to . . . and we have no time to waste in endless discussions of the fantastic schemes of a boxing financier."

Brazilian Traction promptly reversed its earlier plans to make an official appearance at the meeting, deciding to let Loewenstein and Heineman fight it out. Instead, they sent a young lawyer from their London office, Frank Schulman, to watch proceedings and report back.

Came the twenty-second, and almost a thousand Belgian investors crowded into a downtown Brussels theater to see the show. On the platform sat Loewenstein, flanked by many of the European directors of Hydro-Electric Securities and backed by a series of enormous charts depicting the assets of the world's leading electricity producers. Dannie Heineman sat quietly, alone, at the far end of the stage.

For Loewenstein, the evening began badly when the chairman ruled, in spite of the numbers present, that there was an insufficient quorum to vote on the share-exchange proposal. One suspects that someone, possibly Heineman, had been having a quiet word in his ear.

But having come this far, no one was going to prevent Loewenstein from having his say. "People have been astounded to see me inaugurate a new method by meetings of this kind," he declaimed. "And this method, so different from the policy of mystery usually adopted in financial matters, has even been criticized. . . . The operations which I have advised have always been based on the same general principle: the amalgamation of small concerns with powerful enterprises, and their control put into the hands of Trust companies."

It all sounded immensely reasonable. There was no mention of the fact that it was the promoter of these companies, namely himself, who tended to get rich. Frank Schulman described it later as "a good electioneering speech; all theory and phraseology but very little fact." At all events, it won applause.

Then it was Heineman's turn. In calm tones, which did nothing to diminish the viciousness of his attack, he described Loewenstein as a man of "crazy ideas" whose plan was a dream and whose ambitions were for personal power. For ten years, he said, Loewenstein had been wearing out the carpets in his house, trying to gain endorsement for his amalgamation plans. Why should Belgian investors allow an unproven Canadian holding company to usurp their rights, demanded Heineman. SIDRO was a Belgian company, and he intended it should stay that way. On a personal level, he accused Loewenstein of fighting with everyone, of being an exhibitionist who mistook his ideas for reality.

Heineman's speech stood the mood of the meeting on its head. When Loewenstein rose to speak again, he was hissed and booed, and when a vote was taken on his motion to increase the number of SIDRO directors, it was defeated by 218,992 to zero. Without raising a finger in their own defense, Brazilian Traction had won a notable victory. Messages of congratulation were sent from Toronto to Heineman, and Sir Alexander's spies learned that in the following week, Loewenstein had sold at least 20,000 Brazilian Traction shares on the New York and Montreal markets to relieve his dangerously overextended position at the banks.

The Brazilian Traction directors rejoiced. The threat to their company and their jobs from the Belgian Croesus, they told each other, had clearly passed, which just went to show how little they really knew Alfred Loewenstein.

11

To think of Alfred Loewenstein as chastened, let alone penitent, requires a hefty stretch of the imagination. But that was how he appeared in the early months of 1927, after his humiliation in Brussels. On January 14, he invited Heineman to his room in the Ritz Hotel in Paris, and there told him that he had honestly believed his Canadian scheme to be excellent, but that circumstances had shown he was wrong in his conception. He then burst into tears and admitted that he was in a bad state of health.

Heineman told friends later that it had been "a thrilling half hour"—which was an odd choice of words—and that it had left him feeling "deeply disturbed." Puzzled would probably be a better word. If Heineman's report of their meeting was true, it must have been like having one's face licked by a wounded Bengal tiger.

Brazilian Traction was quick to follow up its apparent advantage. The directors persuaded Loewenstein to make a public statement disavowing his fusion plan and announce that his interest in Brazilian Traction had been taken over by SOFINA and CHADE (another Heineman company).

Loewenstein, the newly tamed pussycat, complied. He put a notice in *The Times* that added: "Thanks to the good sense and tact of all the parties, concord, instead of strife, will prevail in the control and administration of these companies."

It was totally out of character, and Sir Alexander and his colleagues should have realized that the Belgian was never more dangerous than when down. One plan might have failed, but Loewenstein still held substantial numbers of their shares, and the vexing issue of the "gold" bonds was still before the Ontario Supreme Court. Loewenstein was supposed to have resigned from the SIDRO board, but by April 1927, he had still not done so, and suspicions grew that he had not yet finished with Brazilian Traction.

The fears were well justified. By early 1928, Loewenstein's financial fortunes had recovered. He had re-established International Holdings in Canada, the shares were booming, and he was buying up Brazilian Traction shares again. Just how many he had acquired was difficult to say, for most were bought from the pool of 300,000 "bearer" certificates that were floating about Europe. Best estimates put his new purchases at least 60,000 shares.

Nor was he weeping on Heineman's shoulder anymore. In fact, he was breathing fire and slaughter against the American and all his associates, considering himself, with some justification, to have been betrayed.

In Toronto, they waited to see what would happen next. An anxious cable went from one director, Miller Lash, to the London office. "We all dislike a fight," said Lash. "But if it is inevitable at some time in the future, I feel it would be much better to have it out now." Lash got his wish. On April 19, 1928, Loewenstein sailed for America on the *Île de France.*

He arrived in New York like a potentate. *The New York Times* said so, and there was no reason to doubt its word.

Not for Loewenstein an ordinary cabin on the liner, not even an ordinary suite. The Loewenstein entourage had no fewer than eight suites, one of which, of course, was the *grande suite de luxe*, consisting of three bedrooms, each with its own bathroom, a private parlor, and a private dining room. It was the same suite that had been used by Lord Astor on the liner's maiden voyage in the summer of 1927.

Loewenstein had never been to America before, though his investments in the United States were considerable. He brought with him his wife and five guests: the Count and Countess de Montalembert, the Count and Countess de Grunnes, and a Colonel Daufresne. In addition, there was a staff of fifteen, including Loewenstein's valet, his private detective, his pilot, his chauffeur, the masseur, four secretaries, and two stenographers. For what he claimed was merely a pleasure trip, it was quite a party. But then, it was not, of course, a pleasure trip.

Loewenstein's objective, which was disclosed to nobody at this stage, was to launch a two-pronged assault on Brazilian Traction. On the one hand, he would demand justice for the holders of the "gold" bonds; on the other, he would insist on a seat on the board by virtue of his large stock holdings.

The press loved the garish splendor of it all. They drooled over the cost of the passages—$20,000—and the amount of Loewenstein's radio bill on the trip across, which some estimates put as high as $3,500. To equate this spending with today's values, one must multiply by a factor of forty. It was a great deal of money in 1928.

Loewenstein had intended to leave the liner at Ellis Island to avoid reporters—or so he said. It was about as likely as P.T. Barnum taking a vow of silence. In the event, bad weather kept him on board until the ship docked. At the pier, he was welcomed by Prentiss Gray of the banking firm of J. Henry Shroder, and the party was whisked off to the old Ambassador Hotel, leaving the press to scavenge what they could.

This was not a great deal. Loewenstein must have felt wary of disclosing the real reason for his journey, for fear of the damage that a fresh humiliation would cause if he failed. The ostentation of his visit, and the impression he sought to give of a magnate bent upon mysterious but important deals, was also calculated to hoist the value of shares in International Holdings and perhaps do something to gain his secondary objective: a quotation on the New York Stock Exchange. Knowing nothing of all this, *The New York Times* had to fall back on describing him as a "man of mystery" and to saying that he was ranked "in some quarters" as the richest man in the world after Henry Ford and the Rockefellers. Whether or not this was accurate is a moot point. It was rumored that he was so rich, the *Times* reported, that during the First World War he had offered to buy back Belgium from the occupying Germans. (Loewenstein never denied this story. It fitted the image he was trying to create perfectly.)

Loewenstein moved around North America with remarkable speed for that era. In just over three weeks he managed to pay flying visits to Canada, Chicago, Philadelphia, and California, while the press panted in his wake. It is clear from the cuttings of the time that they never discovered what his true purpose was. At his one informal press conference in the United States, given at J. Henry Schroder's New York office on Pine Street, he was asked to what he attributed his great financial success. Loewenstein replied that it was due to his boyhood interest in chemistry and electricity.

At this point, Loewenstein departed for Toronto. The American press, blissfully unaware that battle was about to commence, lost contact and was reduced to reports about tests on the aircraft he hoped to use for the remainder of his visit. It happened, ironically enough, to be a Fokker F.VIIa/3m.

On his way to Toronto, Loewenstein stopped off in Montreal. This was hardly the most direct route, but the Belgian had his reasons. Crudely put, he wanted to make Brazilian Traction sweat, and Montreal was the headquarters of his great and good friend, Sir Herbert Holt. It would do no harm to give the impression, rightly or wrongly, that he was about to join with Holt in a bid to merge not only the Brazilian, Mexican, and Spanish utilities, but the Montreal Heat, Light, and Power Company as well.

In Montreal, Loewenstein met the press, aware that what he had to say would wing its way to Toronto before he arrived. After going through his usual performance of boosting the prospects for holding companies in general and Canadian holding companies in particular, he went on to launch a considered assault on Brazilian Traction.

He had come to Canada, he said, to gain justice for "the poor Belgian people of the streets" who had been so disgracefully treated by the company. It may have been news to the reporter from the *Mail and Empire*, whose account was published on May 1, that the street people of Brussels were investors on the Bourse, but he forbore to say so.

"I am going to fight like the devil for them," Loewenstein was quoted as saying. "We are asking for gold and we want it."

Next day, the Fokker having caught up with him, Loewenstein had Drew fly him to Toronto, along with as many of his entourage as could be squeezed on board. The Toronto press flocked to see the first business aircraft ever to visit the city and to get a few more juicy quotes. In the downtown boardroom of Brazilian Traction, they were putting up the metaphorical sandbags and preparing for an invasion. When Loewenstein walked in, he was met by no fewer than three directors (Miller Lash, Sir Thomas White and R.C. Brown), a lawyer (Walter Gow), an accountant (Gordon Scott), and a secretary.

No sooner had Loewenstein entered the room than he began a fierce diatribe against Dannie Heineman. Heineman and his SIDRO associates, he claimed, had made an attempt to kill him. Whether he meant this literally or figuratively is impossible to say. But in the light of what was to happen, the accusation is of more than passing interest. He went on to accuse Sir Alexander Mackenzie of using underhanded methods in thwarting his fusion plan a few months before and inveighed generally against the management of the Spanish, Mexican, and Brazilian companies.

"We all kept our tempers," Lash later cabled to Sir Alexander in Rio, "although it was not always easy. Loewenstein several times lost his and became very much excited and very unreasonable in attitudes and statements, as is customary."

Loewenstein left Toronto for New York, having achieved nothing. He had been told that since the question of the gold bonds was before the court, the company was not prepared to discuss it. But he had left behind him in the boardroom a fog of rumors and anxiety. How much stock did he really control? Was he really going to form "the largest company in the world," as he had told the press? Would he induce a bout of ruinous speculation in Brazilian Traction shares?

Nor had they seen the last of him on this trip, though four days later they almost said goodbye to him forever.

On May 5, Loewenstein made a flying visit to Philadelphia. As he left the cabin of the Fokker, he walked between the still-spinning propellers of the port and central engines, coming so close that one of the blades struck his Derby hat. Only a shout of "Duck!" from a spectator, which made him jump away at the last moment, saved his life.

The incident apparently did nothing to dent his enthusiasm for flying. A week later, he was reported to be trying to hire a faster version of the Fokker, three of which were about to start a passenger service on the west coast with Western Air Express. He was unsuccessful. The company had arranged for the aircraft to fly to California on a publicity campaign, and even Loewenstein's offer of a thousand dollars a day could not persuade them to change their minds.

It was, reported an impressed *New York Times*, the highest offer ever made for the hire of an aircraft in the United States.

On May 14, therefore, it was in his original hired Fokker, which had been having some mechanical problems, that Loewenstein returned to Toronto. He drove with a gaggle of secretaries, all heavily laden with files, to set up a base in the King Edward Hotel. There, while a small crowd of reporters watched in awed astonishment, he ran up a $500 telephone bill in the course of an hour, placing long-distance calls to finance houses in London, Paris, New York, Chicago, and Philadelphia.

Completing his last call, he turned and announced that he intended to attend the directors' meeting of Brazilian Traction that afternoon.

First, however, he went to a board meeting of the Mexican Light and Power Company, which also had its headquarters in the city. It was a brief visit.

Dannie Heineman, who was a director of the company, had hurried to Toronto on getting warning of Loewenstein's intention, and the two men faced each other across the table. Rather than listen to the man whom he alleged had tried to kill him, Loewenstein stormed out of the meeting and returned to his hotel.

An hour later, he was on his way again, this time to the Brazilian Traction meeting at 357 Bay Street. Seven directors awaited him, and to their intense surprise (having heard of his activities down the road and remembering his last visit), they found Loewenstein calm and reasonable. He quietly requested them to acknowledge the substantial amount of stock held by Belgians by granting him a seat on the board and to settle the "gold" bond dispute in favor of the Belgian bondholders.

Unmollified by this mild approach, which they probably saw as just another facet of Loewenstein's theatrical talent, the directors told him to go and play in traffic. The courts would settle the issue of the bonds, and if he wanted a seat on the board he would have to gather sufficient proxy votes to support his claim and present them at the next annual meeting. Loewenstein left.

The annual meeting was scheduled for July 16, and he had work to do in Belgium if he was to gather the votes he needed. In the meantime, the Brazilian Traction board was strengthening its determination to keep him out. "He is obsessed with his plans and importance," wrote Lash in a memorandum. "He is entirely unreliable and untruthful and cannot be depended on to keep any promise." The directors began their own urgent search for proxy votes, to outweigh the bearer warrants that Loewenstein would bring from Brussels.

But what were they to do if they were outvoted? In the event, of course, the problem was no problem at all. Alfred

Loewenstein spent the afternoon of July 16, 1928, bobbing gently on the surface of the English Channel, bothering no one.

The meeting duly took place, Loewenstein's name was never mentioned, and the directors produced more than two million proxy votes in their favor out of a possible 7.5 million. Could Loewenstein have beaten them? That is something we shall never know. Fate had intervened on July 4 to preempt the question. Fate, or something. Or somebody.

12

I BEGAN to review what I had discovered. It was not too encouraging. Loewenstein had fallen to his death from that airplane; that much was certain. There was a wealth of expert testimony to say he could not have done so by accident, and there was no reason for him to commit suicide. Nor could he have killed himself by this method if he had wanted to. The same forces preventing the door from opening by accident would stop him jumping out on purpose. Murder was the only other alternative, and there were those who thought it likely at the time. But that was hardly evidence. And if it was murder, how was it done? The same objections applied.

And not only how, but who? True, I had found in Henri Dreyfus one man who seemed to have good reason to hate Loewenstein, and in Dannie Heineman another who was alleged by Loewenstein himself to have tried to kill him. And then there were the directors of Brazilian Traction, who certainly breathed sighs of relief when he was safely out of their hair. But these things fell short of a country mile from being proof that someone had killed him. In any case, Dreyfus had achieved at least a nominal victory at the conclusion of their long-running conflict, more than a year before the Belgian's death. There seemed no profit for him in such a murder, and I knew of nothing to connect him with the fatal flight. Reluctantly, I had to put Dreyfus aside and look elsewhere. Where the others were concerned, I maintained a healthy scepticism.

Those on board the aircraft were the obvious candidates. Indeed, if it was murder, they must have been involved. Yet it bordered on the fantastic to think that six people, two of them young women, would act in collusion to murder their employer. What would they have to gain? Loewenstein may not have been the most loveable man to work for—I remembered the allegation that he had boxed the ears of those who displeased him—but if people went around murdering unpopular bosses, the world would soon be denuded of executives. And yet . . . and yet the confusions and contradictions in their statements, especially those of Donald Drew, still bothered my mind. Why had he landed on the beach when an aerodrome complete with officialdom was so near? Why had he not used his radio? Why had he lied so blatantly to the Brussels inquiry when he said the door had opened easily? As for the others, why should they claim to have noticed nothing when the opening of the outside door would have sent a blast of wind and noise through the cabin? Why should they be so insistent that Loewenstein was reading a book before his disappearance, when he was known never to do such a thing and when, in any case, no book had been found on board? Why did they act so strangely at their first interrogation?

And then there was the private autopsy, and the finding of alcohol in the stomach of a teetotal corpse. Plus, the curious reluctance of any police force to conduct an inquiry worthy of the name. Had influence been brought to bear; if so, by whom?

There were too many questions and too few answers. My gut feeling said this had to be murder. In order to prove it, the only things I had to find were motive, method, opportunity, and a credible suspect. I came to the conclusion that I was not doing very well.

————

THE PROBLEM WAS what it had always been: the chasing of ghosts. In my mind, I fantasized the tracking down of one of those who had been on the aircraft. I saw a confrontation with an old, old man, who would simply be awaiting my arrival to tell all. I would be gentle but persistent, and in the end he would unburden his soul and confess. Who would it be? Would it be Drew, or Little, or Baxter, or Hodgson? I had already abandoned hope of finding Ellen Clark or Paula Bidalon, though statistically they were the most likely survivors. As single young women at the time, they would almost certainly have changed their names by marriage over the years, and I had not so much as an address from which to start.

My daydreaming went further: I foresaw the complications if I did extract a confession. Should I report it to the police? Murder files, I knew, were never closed. But in this case no file had been opened, so that hardly applied. I felt myself absolved. But if I kept my discovery for the book, this book, would I then be accused of being an accessory after the fact? I had a sudden vision of myself in the dock at the Old Bailey, receiving sentence for complicity in the murder of a man who died before I was born. The thought was risible, but distinctly uncomfortable. I kept looking for these possible survivors, anyway.

The files of *The Times* revealed that Donald Drew was indeed dead. There was a brief formal report of a funeral service, which had been held for him at the church of St. Mark in London's North Audley Street on September 8, 1936. Among the mourners had been many fellow pilots from Imperial Airways, and a name I recognized instantly: Robert Little. The service at the church in the fashionable Mayfair district had been followed by a private cremation at Golders Green. There was nothing more; Drew had not been of sufficient importance to rate an obituary notice in *The Times*.

The fact of Drew's death was easy enough to accept. The date of it was not. I had seen pictures of him in the newspapers at the time of Loewenstein's disappearance, and he had been a strikingly handsome young man of thirty, perhaps thirty-two. Certainly no more.

Yet he had followed Loewenstein to the grave only eight years later. I wondered how he had died. An accident, perhaps? Flying was still a dangerous occupation in those days, even without the unpredictable hazard of doors that opened when doors should not. With one meager fact in my pocket, I began a round of long-neglected contacts in the aviation business. It took weeks, but I found them: men who had known, who had talked with, who had flown with Donald Drew.

———

THE FIRST WAS DENNIS BUSTARD, a sprightly septuagenarian whom I found living in retirement not far from the old Brooklands racetrack south of London. He had turned a considerable talent for glass engraving into a profitable hobby, but in 1934, he had been station manager for Imperial Airways at the Italian port of Brindisi. Bustard was only twenty-one at the time, but he had been with the company for four years and had been given his first station to run at the age of nineteen. "I regarded Drew as being in advanced middle age," he said. "I suppose he must have been in his early thirties."

Drew was a frequent visitor to Brindisi. After the Loewenstein affair, he had begun flying with Imperial Airways again as a regular line captain and operated three-engine Calcutta flying boats in the Mediterranean. He moved on to the four-engine Kent class when these were introduced shortly afterward.

The dashing pilot had made a great impression on young Dennis Bustard. He was the sort of flamboyant, devil-may-care adventurer who filled the airline cockpits of those early days; a veteran of the Royal Flying Corps (though he never wore his medal ribbons), and a gentleman to his fingertips. Well-spoken, and bearing the indelible imprint of a "good" school, Drew was the life and soul of the party in the mess. He had a great sense of humor, a contempt for authority, and a tremendous fund of stories. Oddly, though, he was never once heard to talk of the Loewenstein incident. All in all, Donald Drew was the archetypal flying hero of the roaring twenties, Biggles incarnate. Only one thing spoiled his clean-cut, knightly image: He was an inveterate womanizer.

Women were Drew's great weakness. Bustard was fairly sure he had been divorced ("he was the kind of man you would expect to get divorced"), and in an era when airline captains were required by company rules to have the moral standards of Benedictine monks, he committed the one unforgivable sin: He slept with the female passengers.

This was both easier and more difficult than it sounds. Easier, because the flying boats made frequent overnight stops. More difficult, because the number of female passengers was very small. Donald Drew, however, does not seem to have found this much of a handicap. His sexual activities appear to have been an open secret among his colleagues, but they kept it from the management. Had he been found out, the penalty would have been instant dismissal. But Donald Drew kept on merrily flying and fornicating until November 9, 1935.

At that time, the Italian war against Ethiopia was at its height. Mussolini's invasion of the helpless Horn of Africa had aroused public protests in Britain, and for this reason the British were less than popular in Brindisi. On that November morning, Donald Drew brought in his Kent flying boat to a perfect landing at about 10 a.m. He was late, though whether this was for mechanical reasons or a little too much dalliance during his overnight stop at the Greek port of Piraeus is not known. At all events, his machine had to be refueled and turned round quickly, and while it was being refueled—by a team of Italian mechanics—it caught fire. There was suspicion of sabotage, but it remained unproven. Drew was left stranded in Brindisi.

One of the Imperial Airways regulations laid down that pilots who lost their aircraft, through any cause, could not resume their duties until there had been a full investigation. Drew was sent back to London. He never flew again.

This was not because of his romantic proclivities. If the company ever knew of them, it decided to turn a blind eye. But Donald Drew had another secret: For years he had been suffering from stomach cancer, and lately the pain had been so bad that he drank while flying to keep it in check. He kept a bottle of brandy tied to the control column. That, too, would have been a terminal offense on any airline that got to know about it, but Imperial Airways almost certainly did not. I learned it myself from an eyewitness who, even after all these years, would only disclose the information off the record. But once back in London, a routine medical examination discovered his cancer, and Drew was given immediate retirement. He died a few months later.

Confirmation that Drew knew he was gravely ill awaited me a few miles away, in the London suburb of South Croydon. E.T. Hatchett, affectionately known as "Chopper," had been stationed in Cairo in the early 1930s as chief of communications in the Middle East for Imperial Airways. He knew Drew and his fellow pilots well, and since there was a shortage of aircrew at the time, he often flew with them as second pilot and radio operator.

There were five pilots flying the route, which led from Brindisi via Piraeus, Rhodes, Cairo, and Alexandria, down to Entebbe on Lake Victoria.

In addition to Drew, there were Captain Wilson, Captain Lumsden, Captain Cummings, and Captain Cross —the last, for some long-forgotten reason, known as "Slack-Arse Charlie." Drew himself was stationed in Alexandria, where he had a luxurious apartment and lived, by all accounts, the life of a pasha. Exactly how he managed to do so on his salary of £500 a year—even though this was augmented by flying pay—is something of a mystery. He was certainly not saving for his old age: He knew there was no need.

Chopper Hatchett flew about four trips with Donald Drew and remembers him as "a most charming person."

"You could not have wished for a better pilot," he said. "He was always very calm and calculating, but there was something that made you wonder about him." Hatchett and Drew talked a good deal on those flights, and the radio operator came to know that Drew was aware of his fatal illness. Noticing that the pilot was in pain, he asked him about it point-blank. "He told me himself that he had this trouble," he said, "but he didn't want to give up the job."

But how, I asked, had he managed to pass his mandatory medical examinations? Chopper, an immensely tall man, now bent with age, shrugged his shoulders. "They were not very strict in those days," he said. "When I was stationed at Croydon I knew one pilot who could only see out of one eye. It was the sort of thing that used to go on." But he was sure that Drew would never have continued to fly if he felt himself incapable of doing it safely. "He was not that sort of man."

Chopper confirmed that Drew was "quite a story-teller," but, like Dennis Bustard, he had never once heard him mention the Loewenstein affair.

"Probably it was something he would want to put in the background," he said. "Nobody wants to be tied up with a thing like that."

Perhaps not.

And yet if Drew was totally innocent, why should he not talk about it? He had been, after all, a central character in one of the greatest flying mysteries of the age. Given his loquacious character, confirmed by two independent sources, it seems extraordinary that he should take a vow of silence on this one subject; especially among his fellow airmen. If he knew that Loewenstein had been murdered, of course, his reluctance to talk becomes much more explicable.

And then there was the question of his illness. Did he know of it in July 1928?

If he did, and was offered enough money to enable him to live life to the full for his remaining years, might this have tempted him? Donald Drew certainly had little to lose, and it was a fact that he made the most of his remaining years.

One other possibility nagged at the back of my mind. Drew was a handsome man with a philandering reputation, and as Loewenstein's personal pilot he would have had closer contact with the financier and his family than most employees.

Madeleine Loewenstein was a beautiful woman in a passionless marriage, whose husband was frequently away. She was also to become a very wealthy widow. Could it have been ... I wondered. But no, such speculation was the stuff of romantic fiction and I put it behind me. All the same ...

13

DONALD DREW WAS NOT the only key witness who never talked about the death of Alfred Loewenstein. Nor was he the only one to find a premature grave. Fred Baxter, the valet, kept quiet too, in the few short years remaining to him. Then he died a death as violent, and almost as mysterious, as that of his master. Fred Baxter had come a long way from his origins as a street urchin in Melton Mowbray. He had been born on Regent Street, in a row of terraced houses that no longer exists, and after leaving school had gone to work at The Pinfold as a boot boy in 1921. His main duties were cleaning the family shoes and carrying coal from the outside story, which must have been heavy work for a lad with his pint-sized frame.

Baxter was small, but he seems to have been bright. In such a horse-oriented society, it is perhaps surprising that he did not become a jockey. But young Fred showed no interest in riding and clearly had other ideas of the best way to improve his station in life. From the bottom rung of Loewenstein's large domestic staff, Baxter slowly worked his way through the feudal ranks until he caught the financier's attention and was promoted to footman. After that, he never looked back. It became Baxter's job every morning to take the newspapers up to Loewenstein's bedroom, where he would sit beside the bed and read out the latest stock-market prices—these being the only part of the paper in which Loewenstein was interested.

Before very long, the Belgian came to regard him as indispensable. Baxter rose to the exalted rank of valet, and began to travel everywhere with the great man. It was a giant step for a working-class Melton lad. Suddenly he was flying in airplanes, visiting the capitals of Europe, and crossing the Atlantic in luxury liners. It would have been surprising if it had not gone to his head, and he was generally disliked by his peers. Teddy Morris, who worked for Loewenstein as an under-gardener and still lives nearby, remembers him as "a bumptious little bugger," inclined to violence when he had been drinking. Morris once asked Baxter outright about the financier's death, but the valet refused to discuss it. With the demise of Loewenstein, Baxter was taken on as valet by Bobby, his son. Bobby Loewenstein had been eighteen at the time of his father's death, a slim boy with his mother's looks and much of Loewenstein's panache and an infectious charm that seems to have been all his own. He was young, rich, and wild: the archetypal playboy. And with no need to work for his living, there is no evidence that he ever bothered to do so.

Bobby, it was said in Thorpe Satcheville, "liked the girls and liked his 'pop' [champagne]," and there were stories of wild parties at The Pinfold after Loewenstein's death, with young women being tossed from bedroom windows in a state of undress. He also liked fast driving. On the road between Melton and Thorpe Satcheville, in the little village of Great Dalby, there is a tight left-hand bend as the road twists downhill. The hedge that separates it from a narrow cottage-fringed field is a little tattered, as though recovering from an old injury. As indeed it is. This was the point where Bobby Loewenstein regularly ran his sports car off the road, driving back from Melton after too much "pop."

But though he terrorized the villagers with his driving and generally behaved like a juvenile delinquent, Bobby seems to have aroused no resentment in Thorpe Satcheville. They were used to young men with too much money and too little to do. They knew their place.

Bobby's charm won him the status in the Melton social set that his father had never been able to achieve. Or it may have been the fact that he, like them, was living on inherited money rather than having earned it. Mrs. Ulrica Murray-Smith, a formidable lady who still rides to hounds and lives with a Rhodesian Ridgeback dog the size of a small donkey, remembers dining with him around 1930. He never, she said, mentioned his father or the way in which he died. Bobby was totally involved in the gaiety of his life.

But in the early 1930s, life at The Pinfold seems to have become too tame for Bobby Loewenstein. He moved to Paris, where he took an elegant studio apartment at 6 Rue Antoine Bourdelle, which is an old cul-de-sac in the district of Montparnasse. And he took Fred Baxter with him.

———

BAXTER DID NOT LIVE in the apartment. He had a room nearby in the Hôtel de Commerce on the Avenue du Maine from which he walked daily to his valet duties in the Rue Antoine Bourdelle. By 1932, at the age of twenty-eight, Baxter had worked for the Loewenstein family for eleven years. He had known Bobby, six years his junior, since he was a small boy. The two men seem to have been more like friends than master and servant, often seen drinking together or visiting race meetings. On April 22, 1932, the relationship ended. Tragically and permanently. It was a Sunday. Baxter, as was his habit, wandered across from the Hôtel du Commerce to the small restaurant on the other side of the road where he took most of his meals. Each Sunday after lunch, he sat for some time reading the newspapers, and this day was no different from the rest. Except for one thing: According to the owner of the restaurant, who knew Baxter well, he received a telephone call that afternoon. The restaurateur later described the call as "mysterious," but this may have been due to a natural desire to dramatize. At all events, the call does not seem to have affected the valet unduly. He was cheerful and in high spirits when he folded his newspapers and went back to the hotel. There he paid his weekly account with a check from his employer, and then walked around the corner to Bobby Loewenstein's apartment.

What passed between the two men during the next few hours will probably never be known. By Loewenstein's account, given to the police, he left the apartment on foot at about 4 p.m., returning two hours later. When he came back, he found the front door locked. A note pinned to it said: "Don't come in. Go and stay with the Countess."

Bobby Loewenstein claimed that he went through a neighbor's apartment and forced his way into his own home through a balcony window. There he found Baxter lying on the floor of the living room, a gunshot wound in his right temple. A revolver lay nearby. The valet was still breathing and was rushed to hospital, but he died three hours later without regaining consciousness. If Fred Baxter knew what had really happened to Alfred Loewenstein, he would never tell anyone now.

On the face of it, Baxter's death was a simple suicide. But nothing involving the Loewenstein family was ever that simple. For a start, there was the matter of Bobby's behavior. The young millionaire appears to have panicked. He left the apartment immediately, going to the home of a friend's parents on the Avenue d'Iéna, from which he telephoned Baxter's parents to tell them of their son's death. He then spoke to his mother, who was staying at the family villa in Biarritz, and promptly got in his car and drove to Brussels. From there, two days later, he traveled to London. But before he left Paris, Bobby Loewenstein did one curious thing: He persuaded the police to keep the news of Baxter's death a secret. It is reasonable to suppose that money changed hands. Certainly the Parisian police did as they were asked, and it was not until almost a week later that the press got to hear of the affair. When they did, it was through a British reporter who had learned of it from Baxter's father. French newspapers promptly bombarded the police with questions, but they were, according to the reports of the day, extremely reticent.

Slowly, from this source and that, the story was pieced together. It transpired that the revolver that had killed Baxter belonged to Bobby Loewenstein and was normally kept in the glove compartment of his car. A razor and a knife had been found on the living-room table, and the official theory was that Baxter had been intending to kill himself with one of these. On seeing Loewenstein leave on foot, however, he had gone down to the garage and got the revolver instead. As to why he should have killed himself, the theory advanced by the police was that Baxter had spent money borrowed from Bobby Loewenstein on gambling and high living and had been worried because he could not pay it back. It was a tenable theory, but for two factors. In the first place, several friends testified that Baxter was well paid, always seemed to have plenty of money, and appeared cheerful and unworried up to the time of his death. Second, the amount of money said to have been involved—five hundred francs—was a pittance. It was the equivalent of £20 at the then-current rate of exchange, or less than $100. Nothing in Bobby Loewenstein's easy-going character suggests that he would have made a fuss about such a small sum, especially when his relationship with Baxter had been so long and apparently so close. Yet for fear of what would happen when his peccadillo was revealed, the normally ebullient valet was supposed to have drunk a bottle of liquor (found in his stomach during the autopsy) and then killed himself. Before he did so, he had carefully ironed and laid out his master's linen and written a farewell letter. If the text published in the *Melton Times* of June 6, 1932, is accurate—and there is no reason to suppose it is not—it was a fairly unusual kind of suicide note. This is what Baxter wrote:

Goodbye, sir.

I recommend my friend Alexandre to replace me. Take him—he's a good man. Pay him well, at least three times what you paid me. Your laundry is the first on the right going down the Avenue de Maine. In future don't drive so fast, for that's what has ruined my nerves. Give the money that you owe the Countess for the picture to the concierge. I've spent your Swiss and Belgian money. I'm a coward and haven't got the pluck to face the consequences.

Good-bye, sir.
—Fred.

P.S. Don't drive so fast.

The Countess referred to in Baxter's letter appears to have been Countess Anna Carolina Minici, who until April 14 of that year had occupied the apartment next door to Bobby Loewenstein with her husband, Captain William Henry Patterson. Patterson was an artist, and the couple had known Baxter well. He used to do work for them on the side, cleaning shoes and pressing suits. They called him "le petit Fred." On hearing of his death, they were astonished, especially when they learned of the small amount of money involved. Baxter, they said, had many friends and could easily have borrowed such a sum if necessary. "He was a good lad," Patterson said. "He never gave us the impression that he was tired of life." He could think of only one reason for Baxter's suicide: "that he was familiar with the intimate details of the Loewenstein tragedy, and might have become tired to knowing too much."

The French press, which thought the whole affair extremely fishy and was loud in its criticisms of Bobby Loewenstein for gagging the police, seized on the point. *Le Matin* asserted bluntly that Baxter had known the secret of Alfred Loewenstein's death and had left behind a note explaining the mystery. But if he did, it never came to light. The furor died down quite quickly, and Fred Baxter was buried quietly in the Cimetière de Thiais, Paris. His secret, if he had one, was buried with him.

It was an odd affair; the valet shot with Bobby Loewenstein's gun in Bobby Loewenstein's apartment, with the only evidence a note that could equally have been a simple letter of resignation. Add to that the playboy's rapid departure from France and his remarkable action in trying to keep the death under wraps, and suspicions begin to mount. Was it possible that Baxter, under the influence of alcohol, had finally blurted out his part in the death of Bobby's father and had been killed as an act of revenge?

Nothing I knew of Bobby suggested that he was capable of
such a thing, but who knows what any of us might do on
impulse under such circumstances? I dearly wished that I
could talk to Bobby Loewenstein, but I already knew that
that was impossible. Bobby, too, was dead.

It had happened in England, on March 29, 1941, at an
aerodrome near Maidstone, in Kent. Until 1938, when
Madeleine Loewenstein died (of natural causes, as far as I
know) and was placed beside her husband under the plain
black marble slab at Evere, Bobby had continued his
carefree existence. He became a noted polo player and a
well-known figure in the high society of both London and
Paris. He also learned to pilot his own aircraft.

After the death of his mother, however, he was
compelled to devote himself at long last to managing the
family's financial business. For reasons we shall come to,
this was a fraction of the size it had been in this father's day,
but he was still substantially wealthy.

At the outbreak of war, in September 1939, Bobby found
himself in the United States. He could have stayed where
he was in safety, but he caught the first Clipper flight across
the Atlantic and enlisted in the Belgian forces. When King
Leopold capitulated to the Germans, Bobby escaped to
England and joined the Air Transport Auxiliary, whose
duties involved the delivery of warplanes from the factories
to RAF airfields. And it was on one such flight that the
engines failed shortly after take-off and he crashed and was
killed. He was thirty years old.

Bobby never married. He was the last of the
Loewensteins. And even in his own death he could not
escape the hot breath of scandal and mystery. It was said in
Thorpe Satcheville, and still remembered when I went
there, that Bobby had been having an affair with the wife of
a friend in the Air Transport Auxiliary and that the friend

had sabotaged his aircraft. The friend was named, though it would be unfair to identify him, but for interest's sake I checked through the local paper to find the list of mourners at Bobby's funeral. The friend's name was there, and so was that of his wife.

Bobby still owned The Pinfold at the time of his death, though Mina Burnaby was living there and the stables had been converted to accommodate German prisoners of war who worked on surrounding farms. He was brought home to lie in state in the little Roman Catholic church of St. John's, Melton Mowbray—the same church where his father had prayed before his own fatal flight thirteen years before. The coffin was draped with the Belgian flag and the Union Jack, and lay throughout the night with two lighted candles at head and foot. There were two funeral services and a requiem mass before Bobby was finally left in peace in St. Andrew's churchyard, Twyford, just a mile from his home. Whether he still remains there or not is something of an open question. I could find no gravestone, and local inhabitants thought the body had been exhumed and taken to Brussels for interment in the family vault. But the cemetery records at Evere showed no sign of it.

Among the long list of mourners, I recognized another name that was to play an important part in my search. Major Albert Pam had come to pay his respects.

14

Major Albert Pam, Officer of the Order of the British Empire, Fellow of the Linnaean Society, known as "Pamski" to his friends, lived to the age of eighty and died peacefully at his home in the English village of Broxbourne, Hertfordshire, on September 2, 1955. I mention this only because death by natural causes among the leading characters in the Loewenstein saga is something of a novelty.

It had been an adventurous life. Pam was part Jewish, the eldest son of a London merchant, and was educated at the City of London School and at universities in Germany and Switzerland. He began his business career working without pay for a sugar merchant in Mincing Lane. His father had been known as an ill-tempered man, a character trait that Albert inherited in full measure. The young Pam was efficient and highly intelligent, which won him respect. But a gruff and prickly manner made him difficult to work with. He was admired by many and liked by very few.

One of those few was Alfred Loewenstein, who first crossed his path in 1922. Perhaps because of their Jewish background, or possibly because they shared a basic insecurity despite their wealth, the two men seem to have been drawn to one another. According to those who knew them at the time, there was an atmosphere of complete trust between them. In Loewenstein's case, this may have been a mistake.

Pam was in his late forties, a figure of rectitude and respectability in the financial establishment of the city, by the time he became associated with the Belgian financier. His war record had been impeccable: three mentions in dispatches, the star of an Officer of the Order of the British Empire, the cross of a Chevalier of the Legion of Honour, the star of an Officer of the Belgian Order of the Crown, and the Belgian Croix de Guerre. All these had accrued during his service in France, spent mostly on the headquarters staff of the Third Army, which had culminated in his appointment as chief of staff to the general in command of the British section of the International Armistice Commission at Spa, where Pam's knowledge of languages was put to good use.

Pam was also a man of science and culture, acknowledged as the foremost authority on the flora and fauna of South America, and a member of the Council of the Zoological Society of London from 1907 onwards. The garden of his Broxbourne home, which had been planted in the reign of George III, contained many rare South American plants and a private menagerie and aviary. He even had a species named after him: pamienthe peruviana —the Flower of Pam. In fact, it was said of him that he was more interested in his hobby than in making money. In later years, this may have been true. It was not always so.

Pam's business career had really taken off in 1903 when, together with a friend, he founded the Marmite Food Extract Company. Expatriate Englishmen have yearned for the stuff ever since, though it is doubtful if any of them have heard of Albert Pam. Ironically, for all the vastly greater enterprises he was later involved with, his most enduring legacy to the world is a pot of yeast extract.

Three years before this, in 1900, Pam had paid his first visit to South America with his uncle, Otto Fuerth, who had business interests on the Amazon. It may have been Fuerth, an able linguist of Australian extraction, who introduced him to the Ethelburga Syndicate.

The Ethelburga Syndicate was not, to put it mildly, the kind of enterprise that fitted the pristine image of Pam in his later years. Apart from Pam, Fuerth, and other members of the Pam family, its members were Francis Voules, a London solicitor; Arthur Stanley, a member of parliament and son of the Earl of Derby; Henry Mauborget of Paris; and T.M.C. Steuart. Voules and Stanley were later knighted, though probably not for their involvement with the Ethelburga Syndicate, the activities of which were regarded with distinct distaste by the British Foreign Office.

Established with a registered capital of only £20,000, the syndicate set about getting monopoly concessions from various South American dictators. The first of these was General Cipriano Castro of Venezuela, a man described by Pam himself in his later years as "completely uneducated, despotic, and cruel." Pam had a poor opinion of the general who, he said, "had managed to retain his position by killing or incarcerating anyone who opposed him politically."

———

"HE HAD NEVER BEEN OUTSIDE VENEZUELA," Pam went on in his memoirs, "but seemed to possess a crude instinct for business. He acquired by sheer robbery a substantial interest in many enterprises, farming lands and coffee plantations. He was addicted to many vices and was altogether an unpleasant individual."

None of this prevented Albert Pam from doing business with Castro, to whom he gave thirty percent of his company's shares and agreed to pay him rent at four times the going rate, in return for a monopoly agreement to mine salt in Venezuela.

He followed this up by obtaining a monopoly to make matches in the general's fiefdom.

British diplomats on the spot, who had witnessed Castro's sequestration of other profitable foreign enterprises, were not greatly pleased by Pam's initiative. They suspected that the Ethelburga Syndicate would ask to be bailed out by the British government when they suffered a similar fate, and Sir Outram Bax-Ironside said as much in a cable to the Foreign Office from Caracas.

Sure enough, in 1908, the treacherous general canceled both monopolies. Albert Pam had discovered the truism that when you lie down with dogs you get up with fleas, but he was not averse to a little underhanded revenge. His pleas to the British government having fallen on predictably deaf ears, he went to New York, where he managed to spread a few unhelpful words about Venezuela to American politicians and financiers. General Castro did not mind scuppering the Ethelburga Syndicate, but he could not afford to offend Wall Street. In early 1911, Pam got his monopolies back.

A similar deal was struck in Bolivia, where in 1907 the Ethelburga Syndicate was granted a monopoly on matches to run until 1929, for payment to the government of half their net profits. Shrewdly, Pam sold out this enterprise in 1927 to Ivan Kreuger, the Swedish match king, who found to his distress what Pam must have strongly suspected: The monopoly was not to be renewed.

But not all Pam's South American enterprises turned out so well. In 1910, having ousted a competitor from a contract worth £4 million to build a railway in Chile, he lost a million on the deal because, he said, the builders allowed a diversion of the line over a longer route. He also lost out on a deal to link London to Venezuela by cable because of his row with General Castro.

Elsewhere in the world, he attracted official displeasure by becoming involved in a £500,000 loan to a Chinese provincial government of which the British disapproved and drew the attention of the Anti-Slavery Society. The latter was more than a little interested in the labor conditions on some sugar plantations in Mozambique, of which Pam was a director.

Albert Pam's character in those pre-war years was summed up in a Foreign Office telegram of May 1908. Sir Vincent Corbett described him as "a keen businessman, used to fishing in troubled waters, who does not hesitate to push his own interests by any means that may come to hand," but who "acted quite frankly in his dealings." Translated into less diplomatic English, Albert Pam was a ruthless and unashamed financial buccaneer. Small wonder that he got on so well with Alfred Loewenstein.

The change in his image came in 1919, when Pam became firmly linked to the merchant banking firm of J. Henry Schroder and Company. He had already had dealings with Schroder's ever since they had been involved in the Chilean railway affair in 1905, and the firm seems to have employed his special talents when they needed a trouble-shooter. In Pam's own words: "Whenever Henry Schroder and Co. had a difficult problem to solve I was sent for, and was able to help on two or three by finding a solution where none was evident. I became a member of the 'family' and was appointed to several boards where my services were useful."

In 1919, Schroder's had a difficult problem indeed. The firm was of German origin, having been founded in 1804 by Johann Heinrich Schroder, who became a naturalized British subject in 1864. Under Johann, who became a Prussian baron in 1868 and lived to the ripe old age of ninety-nine, the business prospered mightily. It continued to do well under his son, John Henry, and the J. Henry Schroder Banking Corporation of New York was established. But the link with Germany had never been lost. Prior to 1914, Schroder's had been heavily involved with business in that country, to its subsequent embarrassment. Now those profits were gone, and in the immediate post-war climate, the prospects were bleak. They badly needed a man of proven enterprise, to put it politely. And so they turned to Albert Pam.

By this time the senior partners in the London bank were Baron Bruno Schroder, grandson of the founder, and Frank Tiarks—who was a director of the Bank of England from 1912 to 1945. It was Tiarks who made the approach to Albert Pam.

In 1919, Tiarks had been appointed Civil Commissioner to the Commander of the Occupation Forces in Cologne. Pam was still working for the International Armistice Commission at Spa and came to Cologne at the banker's invitation. The two met at the Ewige Lampe, a restaurant that had been taken over by the occupation forces exclusively for officers, and Tiarks lost no time in making his offer. Pam was to become a junior partner, with a percentage of the profits but no state in the ownership. It was an arrangement that suited him very well. As soon as he was able to return to London, Albert Pam moved into the offices of Henry Schroder, and there he stayed, growing more and more important as other partners became ill or drifted away. He never did own any part of the bank, but to those in the know in the city, the name of J. Henry Schroder was synonymous with Albert Pam.

It appears to have been Tiarks who first brought Pam and Alfred Loewenstein into contact. Unlike Bruno Schroder, who was an arch conservative, Frank Tiarks was brilliant, volatile, and aggressive. He was also something of a showman, and it was precisely those qualities in Loewenstein that he noted and admired. Though their first business encounter was abortive—an attempt by Loewenstein to organize a £5 million debenture issue for Tanganyika Concessions Ltd. to secure the future of the Benguela Railway—the Belgian became Tiarks's protégé. Which meant an ongoing relationship with Albert Pam.

I was frustrated in my efforts to find out more details of the dealings between Loewenstein and the Schroders by the fact that most of the merchant bank's records were destroyed by fire during the Second World War. On the face of it, it appeared that they acted as his advisers, for which they collected fees, and headed the list of underwriters when he made an issue of shares in his companies. Which was frequently. Pam's association with Loewenstein, however, seems to have gone beyond this role. His business activities outside his position with Schroder's were many and various, and he became part of the three-man "advisory committee" that controlled International Holdings and Investment Ltd.—Loewenstein's key enterprise.

The other member of the triumvirate, apart from Loewenstein himself, was a man named Frederick Szarvasy.

———

IF PAM WAS A SLIGHTLY shadowy figure, he was a beacon in the night compared with Frederick Alexander Szarvasy. Born in Hungary, a naturalized citizen of Czechoslovakia, he too had spent some years in South America before coming to London in 1901 at the age of twenty-six. I kept thinking that there must be some sinister significance to the South American connection—Loewenstein, Pam, and Szarvasy all had interests there. But I never could pin it down.

Like Loewenstein, Szarvasy was the son of a banker. And as with the Belgian, almost nothing is known of his early years. But by 1919, he had become chairman and managing director of the British Foreign and Colonial Corporation, in which he owned 22,780 five-shilling shares. BFCC, which had been registered nine years previously, was an issuing house that specialized in the flotation of new companies. At the time when Szarvasy took control, its major shareholders included the Earl of Derby (whose son had been involved with Pam in the Ethelburga Syndicate), Count Edmond de Fels, and Baron Rothschild. Loewenstein, who had a great weakness for titles, was drawn into association with Szarvasy like a moth to a candle. They also had the common bond of being foreigners in a society that tolerated but did not exactly welcome them. Both, too, were Roman Catholics.

Pam, Loewenstein, Szarvasy. They made a powerful trio. Each in his own way was ruthless and talented, and each had interests that spread far beyond their joint control of International Holdings and Investment—though this in itself was a hydra-headed monster.

In the case of Szarvasy, these interests spread to the Dunlop Rubber Company, which he was instrumental in rescuing during the early 1920s, and to coal mines, banking, insurance, and newspapers. He also played a leading role in the formation of British Imperial Airways.

———

To all outward appearances, Szarvasy was a successful and respected member of the British establishment—he had changed his nationality for a second time in 1919—and was deeply interested in music and in art. In association with Sir Thomas Beecham and Lady Cunard, he founded the Covent Garden Opera Syndicate and became its chairman. He was a generous patron of young musicians and a more than passable violinist himself. Could such a man have been involved in any way with the demise of Alfred Loewenstein? It seemed hardly credible. And yet, I found the odd straw blowing in the wind of my suspicion.

There had been, for instance, his involvement in the Panama Corporation, which prospected widely for gold in that country in the late 1920s before going into voluntary liquidation in 1932. Szarvasy was the corporation's financial adviser and, after its collapse, was threatened with legal action for conspiracy and fraud. It is difficult to tell from the surviving records exactly what was being alleged against him. The Panama Corporation, like International Holdings and Investments, operated as a holding company. And like the latter, it had transferred its operations to Canada.

Was there some connection? My initial research could only tell me that after the charge against Szarvasy and the British Foreign and Colonial Corporation had been made by Hugh Marriott, president of the Panama Company, the Hungarian had launched a countersuit for libel. This may have been ill advised. In the outcome, Szarvasy had to withdraw the libel action and pay all Marriott's costs. He also had to settle the action for conspiracy and fraud out of court, paying damages of £25,000 plus costs of £6,000 and returning 196,000 out of 225,000 shares he had held in the enterprise.

There was another story, more difficult to substantiate, in which it was alleged that Szarvasy had used sharp practice to oust a British financier, Sir James Dunn, from a valuable foreign deal. All in all, it began to look as though Mr. Frederick Alexander Szarvasy, who died in 1948 at the age of seventy-three, was not quite the pillar of propriety he had at first seemed.

I extended my research beyond the death of Loewenstein into the period when Pam and Szarvasy had been left in virtual sole control of the affairs of International Holdings. There were indications in scattered reports on the business pages that they had been active in acquiring more shares in the enterprise, but no proof of the amounts involved. I found to my disappointment that the company itself, after going through various changes of name, had finally been wound up in December 1964 and that all records of shareholdings had been destroyed. It was going to be difficult, if not impossible, to prove the extent to which these gentlemen had benefited from Loewenstein's demise.

I did discover, however, that Szarvasy's financial house, the British Foreign and Colonial Corporation, had not survived for long. In May 1930, it was being sued by Loewenstein's widow for the return of securities worth some £300,000, which had evidently been security for a loan. In return, the company was claiming £212,019 from Loewenstein's estate.

Whether this action was responsible for dragging BFCC down, or whether it was a casualty of the general economic slump of the time, is unclear. At all events, before the affair could be settled in court, the company had slipped gently beneath the waves, going into voluntary liquidation on March 9, 1932.

Szarvasy himself survived the crash, though his personal shareholding, which by then had been expanded to 90,675 shares, was worth only £2,266 17/6d after all debts had been paid. Since he held directorships in eleven major companies as well as his interest in International Holdings, the blow was probably not too severe. And he did draw a salary of £200 a month from BFCC, in accordance with his service agreement, until December of that year.

One thing he left behind, to be sold with the rest of the firm's assets, was a book titled *100 Best Investments*. Presumably, Frederick Szarvasy no longer had need of such advice. It was sold for four shillings and sixpence.

15

I HAD a feeling that the key to Alfred Loewenstein's death must lie *somewhere* in the convoluted history of his business affairs during those last two turbulent years. But the notion was one thing—checking it out was quite another. It soon became clear that Loewenstein was a financial juggler, with at least fifty-two deals in the air at any given moment. Trying to keep track of them all was like trying to pick up mercury with a toothpick. The man was everywhere, dashing off in airplanes and fast cars at a moment's notice to swoop down on this company or that. Small wonder that boards of directors from Poland to Brazil were forever organizing their defenses to stave off his impudent takeover bids. Equally small wonder that around the brokers on the London Stock Exchange who dealt in his shares, a crowd of gamblers was in constant attendance.

For whether Loewenstein won or lost, there was always money to be made by hanging around his coattails. He was the Pied Piper of Lombard Street. The trouble was that too many people who followed the tune had forgotten the end of the story.

An *Evening Standard* editorial writer wrote on the day after his death: "It was not merely that everything (or almost everything) he touched turned to gold—it turned to drama as well. Here at last was a financier such as a novelist might have conceived when in a carefree mood."

The same paper's financial columnist had a more penetrating analysis. "I do not know," he wrote,

> that there has been a greater financial propagandist in our time. He used everything and everybody, from aeroplanes to princes, to bring himself and his schemes into favourable notice.
>
> I am bound to say that I never felt attracted by his personality. He was a large, awkward, rather flashily-dressed man, whose appearance was scarcely one of his assets, though his face showed the strength of a powerful and dominating character. As a financier, he created nothing. From start to finish, he was a speculator whose interests were bounded by the market and ways of manipulating it. . . . His vanity was colossal, and it went with a rather cynical nature. He made millions and spent millions, and was therefore never really worth millions.

Being owned by Lord Beaverbrook, who was never averse to using his paper to promote his personal views, the *Evening Standard* could be relied on to provide an unflattering view of Loewenstein. Beaverbrook, after all, had been a fervent supporter of Grant Morden, and therefore Dreyfus, at the time of the dope scandal. The enemies of his friends were his enemies also.

There was certainly an element of truth in what the columnist had to say: Money did flow in and out of the Loewenstein coffers in vast quantities, and it is hard to estimate how much the man was worth in terms of hard cash at any given time.

But the writer missed the point. It was all a matter of confidence. However much or little money he had in the bank, Loewenstein and those around him would always be rich as long as the public believed in his power to generate wealth. The Belgian's flamboyance, his huge spending, his fleet of cars and aircraft, were necessary props to establish his image, as one Belgian newspaper put it, as *le grand brasseur d'argent*—the great brewer of money. Nor was this wholly dishonest. The companies into which the public's money flowed were, by and large, sound concerns. They were not being conned into investing in useless enterprises. The trick lay in mesmerizing the investor into believing that he was jumping on to an escalator that would continue to climb for ever more, thus paying far more for his shares than they were really worth.

It seems to have taken Loewenstein some little time to find the catalyst that would turn this talent into the true touch of a Midas. Before 1926, he had been investing and speculating in all sorts of different ventures. There had been railways in Belgium, manganese mines in Silesia, steel furnaces in Spain, rubber plantations in the Congo, and coal mines in the Saar basin and the Ruhr. Plus, of course, the artificial silk factories and the public utility companies that were to be the focus of his last two fateful years. The new factor that made the difference, that changed him from a merely rich man to a truly bloated capitalist, was the concept of the holding company.

Some observers of the time credited Loewenstein with inventing this phenomenon. This is doubtful, but the existence of companies whose only purpose in life is to own the shares of others was far less common in the 1920s than it is today. And Loewenstein developed it into a form of fine art, building company upon company in a great inverted pyramid of investors' money, which he balanced on his own fingertips with apparent ease. At the heart of it all was International Holdings.

The International Holdings and Investment Company Ltd., to give it its full title, had come a long way from its humble beginning as a mere financial tool to help Henri Dreyfus and British Celanese survive. In those days, in 1922, it had a share capital of only £50,000, divided into shares of one shilling each, and though Loewenstein was on the board of directors he was not prepared to risk much money on it. The company register for 1923 shows that at that time he owned only 1,210 shares—an investment of only just over £60. Later that year, when the royalty agreement began to pay off, he hurriedly bought some more. By November, he and his wife jointly owned 67,055 shares, with a nominal worth of £3,352.

It was still very small beer, but after the row with Dreyfus reached boiling point in 1926 and the company name was altered to International Holdings, everything changed. Now the authorized share capital was £500,000, divided into ten million one-shilling shares, but at first, comparatively few were issued. Of the 1,557,486 sold for one shilling each, Loewenstein snapped up 18,169, and most of the rest went to his fellow directors. These included Gustave Popelier, fresh from his firing from the British Celanese board, his Royal Highness the Duc de Vendôme, and Andrew Holt.

Loewenstein, whose name was very much in the public eye at that point, then made a bold move. He persuaded the board to issue more than four million of the remaining shares—this time not at the officially quoted price, but at a premium of no less than 1,500 percent. Each one shilling share was to cost the buyer fifteen shillings, which in theory would raise £3 million—or more than £120 million in today's money.

And it worked, though the share register shows that Loewenstein may have had to exert some personal influence to sell the shares at this inflated price. Among those who bought them were his father- and mother-in-law, Pierre and Anna Misonne, who each had about two thousand; Mina Burnaby, wife of Algy, who bought 6,800; a Captain William Higson of Melton Mowbray (twenty thousand); a Mrs. Gladys Fenwick of Melton Mowbray (eight hundred), and Andrew Holt (twenty-four thousand). He even sold one hundred forty to his secretary, Arthur Hodgson.

They may have had their arms twisted, but they had little cause to regret their decision in the months that followed. Loewenstein had set an example by taking up almost three million of the premium shares himself, although because he paid only five shillings each for them "on account," the total benefit to the company funds was somewhat less than it might have been. Nevertheless, it still represented a personal investment of £750,000, which was no small sum in 1926. The Belgian was demonstrating that he had money and was prepared to put it where his mouth was.

———

ALTOGETHER, International Holdings had now accumulated more than a million pounds in cash, and with the help of a further £430,000 borrowed from its bankers, it began its corporate raiding among the artificial silk companies. The only dent to Loewenstein's self-esteem at this stage was the withdrawal from the company of Baron Bruno Schroder and Frank Tiarks, both of whom decided to sell their shareholdings and distance themselves when Loewenstein made the premium issue. Their motives are difficult to assess, although it seems probable that they thought the Belgian might be overreaching himself or that the enterprise was becoming less respectable than Schroder would wish to be associated with. On either count, Albert Pam does not seem to have been discouraged.

The next move, in November 1927, was to transfer the whole operation to Canada, where the tax laws were far more favorable to holding companies. International Holdings already had a subsidiary there in the form of the Hydro-Electric Securities Corporation, which had invested heavily in American public utility companies and was causing such palpitations in the heart of Brazilian Traction. Now Loewenstein decided to wind up the British company, to register the enterprise in Quebec under the same name, and to offer shareholders one new share of common stock in the new company for every twenty of the old one shilling shares, plus one $10 bond carrying interest at six percent for every forty of the old shares held.

On this basis, the reconstituted International Holdings had a capital of 500,000 shares (although not all had been issued), each valued at around $65 (£13). The stock market seemed to agree. When trading began in London on January 3, 1928, ordinary shares in International Holdings were quoted at $68.

It was the start of a quite remarkable few months. Up to the middle of January, the shares followed the usual pattern of Loewenstein investments during the hunting season: increasing in value early in the week as his rich acquaintances called their brokers following his weekend tips, then falling slightly on Fridays. The overall trend was unspectacular, but upward. And then, on January 14, International Holdings jumped from $69 to $74. Next day it had climbed to $79, and it kept on rising. By January 31, the company's shares stood at $95 each—a profit of almost fifty percent in less than a month for the lucky shareholders.

Loewenstein's star soared, and his personal fortune in International Holdings now stood at $19 million. For a few days in early February, the shares stood still, and then they recommenced their rapid climb. On February 29 (it was a leap year), anyone who wanted to buy a share in Loewenstein's company had to pay $161 for the privilege. The shares seemed to have got a fresh boost from a report in the *Financial Times* that Henri Dreyfus was now warring with Courtaulds, claiming that they, too, had stolen his patents.

In a single month, the financier's wealth had increased by a further $13 million, and still the rise went on. Another 100,000 shares were released from the unissued stock and were snapped up at $150 each, putting an extra $15 million in the coffers of International Holdings. The move might have been expected to put a brake on the market, but it did nothing of the kind. An exultant Loewenstein announced that his holding company now had investments worth nearly $73 million, not taking into account the value of the controlling interests that it was acquiring in increasing numbers. It was his aim, he said, to rank among the biggest of the artificial silk companies and to compete with the Courtaulds-Snia Viscosa cartel.

There was much eating of words among those in the city who had been scornful of the upstart Belgian. The *Financial Times* reminded its readers smugly that it had tipped the Loewenstein shares for a rise in early January and forecast that they would soon top the $200 mark. International Holdings then announced that it would not only be paying an initial dividend of $1.25 per common share but would also be redeeming in full the $10 preference shares it had given away only four months previously.

Along with the parent company, its various offspring were also riding on the tide of success. Tubize, Brazilian Traction, Mexican Tramways, Hydro-Electric Securities, Glanztoff, and all the rest were watching their shares climb steadily in value.

It was roses all the way. Loewenstein was even back in control of SIDRO, which he had finally left after the row with Heineman, vowing that he would soon return. He was a man who enjoyed revenge, but even the sweetness of this could hardly compare with his satisfaction at the progress of International Holdings. The shares duly passed the $200 mark on March 20, jumping from $194 to $211 in a single day and finishing the month on $218. At present-day values, this made every individual share worth $8,720 and increased Loewenstein's personal fortune from this source alone to a staggering $1,744 million. He could well afford to book suites for his entourage on the *Île de France* before sailing off to New York on what he hoped would be fresh conquests at the expense of Brazilian Traction and Dannie Heineman.

In early April, it began to look as though the boom had reached its peak, as some of the more nervous stockholders began to sell out and take their profits. International Holdings dropped back at one point on the London Stock Exchange to $203, but it was only a temporary hiccup. On the thirtieth of the month, which was a Friday, the shares confounded the superstitious by rebounding to $243 and then resumed their steady climb. It had become a ridiculously easy way to make money.

Alfred Loewenstein thought so too. Before leaving for the United States, he laid plans to launch two more holding companies, one in France and one in Canada, each designed to attract large sums of cash and strengthen his grip on the artificial silk industry. By dint of crafty manipulation, he ensured that these latest ventures would remain under the control of International Holdings, thus boosting his personal empire at very little cost. Holding companies, he had become convinced, were a Good Idea. He intended to make the most of them.

There were no premonitions of disaster as he set off across the Atlantic, nor did the value of the shares suffer in the absence of their chief promoter. On the contrary, as news of his awed reception in New York filtered back to London, they bounded still higher in value. On April 28, International Holdings stood at $273; on May 1, they were $278; and two days later, they had breached the $300 barrier to stand at $318 per share. And the boom was still not over. On May 7, 1928, each share of International Holdings cost the bold investor $352, equivalent to $14,000 in the devalued currency of 1985. By the same yardstick, Loewenstein's 200,000 shares were now worth almost $3 billion.

As it turned out, that was the end of the joy ride. And the incident that turned the tide had nothing to do with the soundness of the company or the wisdom of its investments, or even with any underlying fear that it could not go on capping its own success. It was a simple news story recounting the fact that Alfred Loewenstein had almost walked into the propeller of his aircraft in Philadelphia. Investors suddenly realized that the charismatic figure they were following so blindly was, like themselves, merely mortal.

Two inches closer to a circle of whirling steel, and the brains of Alfred Loewenstein would have been scattered on a distant tarmac. And with them would have gone a great deal of their money.

The moment of panic was short-lived, but it was enough to knock $25 from the price of the shares, and from this point, they drifted slowly downward. Even so, when the May account closed, International Holdings still stood $62 higher than it had at the start of the month, and during his absence, Loewenstein's wealth had increased by $9.6 million in the money of 1928. He must have been well satisfied.

The mushrooming strength of International Holdings was being watched with anxiety by the members of the artificial silk cartel. Though they still held the dominant share of the market, there were ominous straws in the wind. Trade figures were showing that the profit margins on their viscose silk were less than those of Loewenstein's acetate variety, and the Tubize company was doing very well indeed. In Europe, International Holdings now controlled the Polish firm of Tomaszow and had substantial interests in the German companies of Glanztoff and Bemberg, while the formation of Loewenstein's new French holding company, the Société Financière de Soie Artificielle, had been a phenomenal success. Now rumors reached them that he was about to make a bid for the artificial silk industry in The Netherlands, dominated by the Enka and Breda factories. This was striking close to home. Enka were virtually members of the international cartel. The enemy was at the gates.

Many of the shares in Dutch Enka were held by British investors, which made them especially vulnerable to attack. In desperation, the board bought up as many as they could before Loewenstein had a chance to purchase a controlling stake. Then they formed their own holding company, for the purpose, they said bluntly, "of protecting the Dutch artificial silk industry from domination by foreign interests." By which they meant International Holdings.

The move appears to have been successful. Loewenstein turned his attention from Dutch Enka to Dutch Breda, buying heavily on the market. But again he was outwitted. The Breda directors defended themselves by creating fifty thousand new shares in the company and distributing them among members of the board. The move diluted the capital, but it achieved its object: they now commanded sufficient votes to ensure that Loewenstein could never gain control. "They seem to be very fond of paper," he remarked caustically.

These were setbacks to Loewenstein's grand design, but the confidence of the speculators does not seem to have been unduly affected.

The price of shares in International Holdings on the London market picked up again on his return from America, and though they failed to regain the giddy heights of May 7, they kept comfortably above $300.

Hydro-Electric Securities, too, was doing well, with more than $40 million invested in public utilities and railways in the United States. The shares had been placed on the London market only in March 1928, and already they stood at more than $80 each. Since Loewenstein, along with Schroder's and Szarvasy, had acquired an option months before to buy more than half a million at $25 each, this was another cause for satisfaction.

And then, on the morning of Tuesday, June 12, 1928, the bubble burst. The shares of International Holdings, which had been declining gently for some days for no apparent reason, suddenly fell by $35 on the London market to finish the day at $263. On the continental exchanges, they fell even further to $240. And the slide continued.

On June 20, London brokers were marking them at $235, before another wave of selling in Montreal and Brussels sent them plunging to $198. Hydro-Electric

Securities, reacting in sympathy, saw their share value almost halved to $47. And a quick check through the Stock Exchange prices in the *Financial Times* showed me that every company with which Loewenstein was associated had suffered similar losses. Something had happened.

But what?

Whatever it was, it had cost some people a great deal of money. In the course of a few days, Loewenstein's personal fortune, at least on paper, had dwindled by $30.8 million. His was undoubtedly the greatest loss, but others less able to afford it must have had their fingers burned severely. For some reason the Pied Piper's tune had become discordant, and that vital factor of confidence had deserted him.

I scanned the financial commentators in search of the answer, but they seem to have been just as mystified as I was. No great disaster had befallen the Belgian; there was no slump in the market for artificial silk; his American investments were doing well; and although there had been setbacks in his Dutch takeover attempts, these were a very small part of the total picture. "All kinds of stories are in circulation to account for the severity of the slump," reported the *Financial Times*. "As in the wild upward movement, a genuine sense of value became confused. As with the easy way in which money was made through the purchase of these two companies' shares, on the abrupt descent speculation has resolved itself into more or less of a gamble. Among the principal firms of stock exchange dealers and speculators in these shares there stand, for the greater part of the day, eager and excited groups watching the gyrations in prices, and occasionally taking a hand in the speculation that is afoot."

In other words, the *Financial Times* either did not know what was behind the slump or was not prepared to say. The one clue that did emerge was that the wave of selling had apparently begun in Brussels. Whatever had happened to turn the all-conquering Loewenstein into a financial liability so soon before his death had taken place in his native city. I packed my bags and caught the boat-train to Brussels.

16

It was autumn 1984, and rotting leaves made the path slippery underfoot as I trudged through the cemetery of Evere in search of the grave of Alfred Loewenstein. A fairly pointless pilgrimage to see a tomb, to stand above the broken body, long rotted into dust, of the man who had become an obsession to me. Did I expect some voice from beyond the grave to tell me where I should look next, to give some ghostly seal of approval to my quest? I cannot say. I only know it seemed important at the time to see the place where it had all ended and to re-create in my mind the scene of that lonely burial.

What I did not expect was to find the grave covered in flowers. Heaps of wreaths and floral tributes, all decaying, were piled over the plain black marble slab and the enclosed plots on either side. It was a shock. Was Loewenstein still remembered after all? But I turned over one of the cards attached to a wreath, still just legible, and read a tribute to "Chère Maman." A check with the burial records in the cemetery office showed that a member of the Misonne family had been buried in the vault just three weeks before, and I wondered whether she, unlike Alfred, would get to have her name inscribed on the tombstone. Somehow that omission seemed the ultimate indignity.

Brussels had been through a lot in the fifty-six years since the death of Alfred Loewenstein: a world war, occupation by the Germans, and liberation by the Allies. I wandered down the Rue de la Science, not far from the royal palace in the old part of the city, with little expectation of finding his old home at number 35 still intact. But it was there, facing a grassy square studded with ornamental flowerbeds and mature trees that must have been there in the days of Loewenstein.

It was, to say the least, impressive: less a house than a bijou palace of classic proportions, with elegant carvings and a stone balcony on its five-window frontage. But it was no longer a private home, which was hardly surprising. It would need the wealth of a Loewenstein to own and maintain 35 Rue de la Science, and I found it occupied by the Dutch embassy. Inside, behind a newly installed security desk, I could see a stately Empire-style staircase leading to the upper floor. Loewenstein, I thought, had trod those stairs. And his dogs, which were reported to have wandered the street outside after his death, looking for their master, would have run in the huge paved enclosure at the rear. Madeleine had been here, and so had Bobby. So had Baxter and Hodgson, and possibly Drew and Little. But the friendly Dutch officials I spoke to knew nothing of the history of the place. They had bought it from the Canadians some years previously and now preserved it as a national monument. Alfred Loewenstein, I thought, would have been pleased to know that.

My sightseeing was getting me no closer to the crux of the problem, however, and I headed for the Bibliothèque

Nationale to see if the Belgian press of the day held any clues.

———

I DISCOVERED, as I expected, that the demise of Loewenstein had dominated the papers in Brussels to an even greater extent than it had those in London and New York. But there was nothing essentially new. Not, that is, until I began to search backward to the date of the slide in the share prices. And then I found it.

Neptune is a financial newspaper that no longer exists. It was published in Antwerp from the turn of the century until shortly before the Second World War, apart from 1914 to 1919, when it transferred its operation to London during the German occupation. It appears to have been an authoritative and outspoken journal and was doubtless widely read among speculators on the stock market. The issue of June 8, 1928, crucified Alfred Loewenstein in print.

With growing fascination, and the hope that my powers of translation were adequate, I picked my way through the French journalese, wondering at the bravery of the anonymous author or the laxity of the Belgian libel laws. The theme was Loewenstein's creation of his new French holding company, La Société de la Soie Artificielle (FISA), which had been launched in Paris six weeks before. Seems the financier, was accused of defrauding his investors. According to *Neptune*, the history of the affair went something like this:

On April 17, less than twenty-four hours after Loewenstein had announced his intention to form the company, the necessary documents had been filed in Paris. Two weeks later, on April 30, it had been declared that FISA would have a capital of forty million francs (roughly

£400,000 at the prevailing rate of exchange). This would be divided between three hundred thousand "B" shares of one hundred francs each and one hundred thousand "A" shares of the same value. International Holdings announced that it would be taking up all the "B" shares, with an investment of thirty million francs, giving Loewenstein a substantial voting majority. The A and B shareholders, under the rules of the company, were to have equal benefits according to the amount invested.

But within two days, on May 2, a further announcement was made. The capital of FISA was to be increased by 190 million francs, and the shares would be offered to the public at 117.5 francs each. *Neptune* thought this more than odd. If you want to raise 230 million francs, said the article, why not create a company with a capital of 230 million francs in the first place. Why take two bites at the cherry?

It soon provided the answer. Although the new shareholders were to subscribe a vastly greater proportion of the capital than International Holdings, the voting rules for the new issue had been subtly changed.

Their 190 million francs would entitle them to only nineteen thousand votes in the company's affairs, and even when these were added to the ten thousand vote of the original A shareholders, Loewenstein would retain absolute control. It might seem that they would still be entitled to a fair share of the profits under the company Articles, but it was not necessarily so. Loewenstein, *Neptune* pointed out, would be in a position to oppose the declaration of any dividend at all and to retain the profits to do with as he wished.

The capital had been created in two stages so that the later proposal, containing this denial of shareholders' rights, would not be subject to legal scrutiny by the commissioner when he vetted the company's Articles.

"A veritable dictatorship," *Neptune* said, "is arrogating the major benefits to itself. We don't know if this arrangement is truly legal. What we can say is that it is very much in the style of M. Loewenstein. Altogether, we don't see the benefit to the public of participating in an affair where, under the Articles, it is treated unfairly."

Neptune had delved further into the offending Articles and discovered that Loewenstein had also required that his investors renounce their rights under a law of July 27, 1867, which gave certain rights to minority shareholders. The article continued:

> To make things easy for him, Loewenstein apparently sees nothing wrong in making people give up the protection of the law. His lawyer must bear a heavy responsibility for not warning him of the stupidity and danger of such a precaution. It's stupid, because the clause can have no effect. The Articles can reinforce guarantees given under the law, but they cannot diminish them. It's an illegal precaution, null and void.

> All the indications are that FISA, like the Société Financière Belgo-Canadienne, which was created at the same time, is for the sole object of furnishing the great brewer of money, Loewenstein, with the wherewithal to continue the multifarious operations in which he is engaged. And the only thing we can be sure of is that the theoretical beneficiaries are certain of heartbreak.

Whether or not these accusations were true, and they seemed to be well documented, they must have come as a severe blow to those who invested in FISA, few of whom can have read the Articles. The new share issue had been oversubscribed many times by the closing date of May 21, and the shares were subsequently changing hands at more than double the launch price. On May 19, *The New York Times* reported that they had been oversubscribed twenty-five times from 11,000 buyers and were being quoted at $300 each on the open market. After the *Neptune* article, their value was halved to $150.

The allegations had exposed Loewenstein to the Belgian investors who read *Neptune* as a man whose star it might no longer be safe to follow. It was one thing to hitch your wagon to a man who made money for you by outsmarting everyone else, even though you might suspect his honesty. It was quite another to stick with him when he had been exposed in the public prints. The Bourse had taken fright.

Nor had *Neptune* finished with Loewenstein yet. In the same issue, under the heading THE GREAT GAME OF M. LOEWENSTEIN, the paper conducted an exhaustive examination of the financier's affairs that bespoke of a good deal of inside knowledge. At the time, I wondered where they got their information. It was not until some weeks later that I found out.

Over the past two years, the anonymous writer calculated, Loewenstein had accumulated capital equivalent to about a billion Belgian francs. With money in hand, he had thrown himself headlong into a wide spectrum of investments. The story listed the companies involved, and they made an impressive array:

- Adamello
- Atchison
- Allied Chemical
- Atchison Topeka Railroad
- Bemberg
- Brazilian Traction

- Breda
- Buffalo Niagara
- Commonwealth Edison
- Consolidated Gas of New York
- Energie Electrique du Meditérr234néen
- Glanztoff
- Hydro-Electric Securities
- I.G. Farben
- Middlewest Standard Gas Corporation
- Missouri Pacific Railroad
- Pennsylvania Railroad
- Sicilienne Electricité
- Tomaszow
- Tubize

Neptune doubted if even a billion francs could be made to stretch so far. Certain of the operations, it added, were deceptive. There had been problems with Tubize, centering on Loewenstein's failure to launch the stock on the New York and London markets. This plan had apparently been dropped, but he was still buying shares to keep the price up. He had also failed to open up the international viscose silk cartel with a combination of the Glanztoff and Bemberg artificial silk companies, and Brazilian Traction had refused to cooperate with him.

Now that he had invested all his spare cash, the paper continued, Loewenstein was in need of money to pursue his aim of dominating the world market in artificial silk and was seeking it from the public. He was aiming to raise 200 million francs from FISA, 100 million francs from the new holding company in Canada, 300 million francs via a new finance company to be set up with a group of Belgian financiers, plus a $25 million bond issue in New York. Neptune did not say so, but I already knew from other sources that the last deal had gone sour some weeks before.

Neptune did disclose, however, that contrary to the optimistic reports being put about by Loewenstein, the public had not taken up all the controversial A shares of FISA. A large block had had to be absorbed by certain London banks, which had underwritten the issue and would presumably not be pleased by the latest revelation.

"Loewenstein," trumpeted *Neptune*,

> has dreamed up a new way of getting money: without guaranteeing interest and by never repaying the capital. Better still, he has found a means to bend the law to his wishes by securing three votes to two. In these circumstances, we cannot advise the public to buy FISA shares. Loewenstein has not, in business affairs, had such a reputation that one should follow him blindly into this new enterprise.

The Belgian stock market dithered nervously at these revelations, and two days later *Neptune* returned to the attack with a scornful dismissal of Loewenstein's visit to America. He had left, said the editorial, with a fanfare. He had returned without an orchestra. He had gone proclaiming that he wanted to invest money in North America because of the good Canadian taxation laws and to encourage other Belgians to do likewise. In fact, he had gone to make a show, to call attention to himself because he wanted to borrow money. And the trip had been a failure.

"His fortune, one of the largest in the world—let's put it modestly—can really be translated as gigantic appeals for money," said *Neptune*. And it added a prophetic footnote: *"Take note that these billions depend on the life or on the health of one man alone."*

The market took note. The shares plunged.

————

THE ASSAULT in the Belgian press came as little surprise to Alfred Loewenstein. He had been expecting something of the kind since he arrived back in London from the United States in the third week of May. Someone, he discovered, had been doing a fine piece of character-assassination on him, circulating a twenty-five-page duplicated typescript that examined and attacked every aspect of his career. Copies had been distributed widely—for the most part to bankers and financial houses where the allegations could be calculated to do him most harm. It was inevitable that they would reach the press sooner or later, although the strict British libel laws would probably protect him from publication in London.

Loewenstein's reaction was angry and immediate. He sent for John Bell, the private detective who had investigated the jewel robbery at the Villa Begonia in 1926, and hired him to find the author of the offending document. The fee, if he was successful, was to be £20,000. "He was more upset than I have ever seen him," Bell said later. "His piercing black eyes were sparkling with rage, and his usually immaculate hair was badly rumpled. 'Bell,' he said, 'I've sent for you because I liked the way you handled that jewel job. I wouldn't entrust this job to anyone else. Find me the author of that.' He thrust the document across the desk."

Bell must have been mildly surprised at his new commission. He had, after all, failed to find the culprit in the Biarritz robbery, nor had he recovered Madeleine Loewenstein's jewels. However, his investigation on behalf of the insurance company had led to Loewenstein's claim being paid in full. Perhaps that was the cause of the financier's gratitude. Among a host of other allegations, the document suggested that he had staged the theft himself to collect the insurance.

———

THE DETECTIVE LOOKED at the offending typewritten sheets. Six years later, he wrote in a *Daily Express* article:

> A moment's quick reading was enough to take my breath away. It was the most vicious and detailed attack on a public man I have ever seen. The anonymous author's intention was obvious: He wanted to see the downfall of Loewenstein. To achieve his purpose he had set down a carefully documented and forthright attack on every aspect of Loewenstein's career. Event after event was examined and attacked.
>
> If a fraction of the allegations were true, Loewenstein was finished. He would be better dead. If it was a pack of lies, then Loewenstein's only course was to discover the author and sue him for libel.

Bell began his search with small hopes of success. The document, he decided, had probably been produced by a typewriting and duplicating office, but there were scores of these in Central London alone. His only clue was a slight misalignment in the typeface, which might enable him to identify the machine it was written on. With dogged persistence he wrote to every typing bureau in the telephone directory, asking for specimens of their work. It was a very long shot. As Bell knew only too well, even the smallest firm was likely to have more than one typewriter, and if the guilty party happened to reply to him on a different machine he was lost. As the replies began to come in he studied each one with a magnifying glass.

Luck was with him. From a tiny office in the West End of London came a letter with exactly the type of fault he had found in the Loewenstein document. Bell promptly hired a girl to pose as a trainee typist looking for work, and had his second stroke of good fortune when the suspected office took her on the staff as a "learner-improver." She quickly found the suspect machine, but at this point Bell's investigation stalled. For several weeks, whenever she was left alone in the office, the girl went through the firm's books. There was no trace of the Loewenstein transaction.

———

LOEWENSTEIN WAS A LION IN A CAGE, roaring in frustration. True or false, the document had done its work, and the aura of confidence that had surrounded him for so long was beginning to dissipate like morning mist. London bankers had never loved him. Now, when he came looking for new loans to pursue fresh schemes, he was politely turned away. Even his closest associates, while not abandoning him, were beginning to look askance. And J. Henry Schroder sent a watchdog from America to report on his every move.

The watchdog's name was Norbert Bogden. Late in my investigation, in the autumn of 1984, I discovered that Bogden was still alive and living in New York. I telephoned, only to be told that he was in hospital and seriously ill, unable to see anyone. It was bad timing. Here was a man, perhaps the only man left, who had known the business side of Loewenstein at the highest level. With the wartime loss of the Schroder records, and the deaths of Pam and

Szarvasy, he was probably my only means of discovering what had been going on. I am not religious by nature, but I prayed for the recovery of Norbert Bogden.

In the event, it was May 1985 before I could meet him. And then it was a close-run thing. I arrived at his elegant duplex on Park Avenue on the afternoon of May 16 to be told by his wife that he had collapsed while lunching at a nearby restaurant that day, and she was not sure if he was fit enough to talk.

This time I got lucky. A thin voice from upstairs insisted that he wanted to see me, and with clucking reluctance, I was ushered into the study where he lay full-length on the couch.

Norbert Bogden proved to be a stocky, ruddy-faced man, extremely polite and highly articulate. He had been twenty-six in the year that Loewenstein died, and already had a reputation in the New York office of J. Henry Schroder for being the man the bank turned to when something difficult, complicated, or unpredictable turned up. Alfred Loewenstein was all three of these things.

At that time the president of the New York branch of the firm was a man named Prentiss Gray. When Loewenstein was due to visit the city, Gray sent for Bogden and asked him to act as the Belgian's guide and companion. Bogden remembered the conversation well. "From all I hear," Gray had said, "he's a very peculiar and difficult man." Bogden accepted the assignment and saw Loewenstein every day as the Belgian wheeled and dealed his way around Wall Street. Remarkably, in view of the differences in their ages, backgrounds, and temperaments, the two men became friends.

"He was incredibly shy and insecure," Bogden told me. "Unless you knew him well enough to discover that, you would have taken him for the brashest, most arrogant, and most conceited man in the world. And he wasn't like that at all. He was very insecure and fragile; a man with a heart. Not a big heart, or a warm heart, but a heart just the same."

It was a new slant on the character of Alfred Loewenstein, but somehow believable. Madeleine, too, had fallen under the lens of Norbert Bogden's microscope:

> She was pretty much of a cold fish as far as any emotions or sex or anything like that was concerned. She liked the atmosphere of excitement around her. She always said that she didn't, but that was not true. She lapped it up. She wasn't around much, because she didn't mix in his affairs at all. She had some influence on him in a general way, and always a moderating and calming influence. She was an extraordinary woman. Very good-looking and very well balanced. A remarkable woman, really. Her sister, to whom she was very close, was the exact opposite. They were just like night and day.

Bogden confirmed what I had suspected: that the Loewensteins had lived separate lives, with Alfred too involved in business to have much time for his family. "But that did not mean," he said, "that his wife was on bad terms with him. They respected each other enormously. He adored his wife. He was extremely proud of her because she was so beautiful. There was not much tenderness or passion involved, I am sure. But it was not a bad marriage."

On Loewenstein's return to Europe, he had left Bogden with an invitation to visit him in Brussels. It was to be taken up sooner than either man expected. The young American was not told the reason, but in June 1928, he was dispatched to London by Prentiss Gray with orders to proceed to Brussels and keep a very close eye on Alfred Loewenstein and his business activities. It was an unconventional move for such a staid firm of merchant bankers, and a clear indication that doubts were beginning to creep in about the wisdom of their association with the Belgian financier.

Bogden was sure that Gray must have cleared it with Baron Bruno Schroder "because it was all very much against the grain." His instructions, too, were unusual for a relatively junior employee: He was to return to London at intervals and report in the boardroom, in person, to the six men who controlled the bank of J. Henry Schroder. But in the event Bogden was spared the embarrassment of spying on his new friend. Death intervened.

He arrived in London from New York on the third of July, settled into a hotel, and the following day went to Schroder's office in the city. He was feeling virtuous, not merely because he was forsaking the American national holiday, but because it was too hot for anyone to work. "I shall never forget that July the fourth as long as I live," he said. "It was the hottest day I have ever experienced in London."

But that day left more than the heat to remember it by. As Bogden was going into his office he was surprised to see Loewenstein, who he believed to be in Brussels, emerging from the Partners' Room. The Belgian took him by the arm. "Look," he said, "I think I will be going to Brussels this afternoon. Why don't you come with me? I have invited you before, and this way we could go together on my plane."

It was all a little too sudden for Norbert Bogden. He had hardly got the salt air of the Atlantic crossing out of his lungs, and he was being plunged into instant close contact with the man on whom he had been sent to spy. He searched for a reasonable excuse.

"Look, Captain," he said. "It's goddamned hot. I have to run home now to pick up some clothing and toilet articles. Wouldn't it be just as good if I came tomorrow? Maybe it's going to be cooler. I will take an early plane and join you in Brussels tomorrow, rather than rush to the hotel now and then down to the airport."

Loewenstein looked at him for a moment. "Sure," he said calmly. "That's all right. You go ahead, and I will see you tomorrow."

On the couch in his New York apartment, so far away in time and space, Norbert Bogden remembered the moment. "We shook hands," he said, "and off he went. Nothing in the whole world could have been less like a man contemplating suicide, or any kind of accident whatever, than Loewenstein when I saw him on July fourth. If it hadn't been for my feeling so hot and irritable because of the heat, I would have joined him. Then again, if he had any thoughts of suicide, he would hardly have invited a good friend to come with him."

If Bogden had accepted that invitation, would Loewenstein still have died, I wondered? Would the sudden presence of a stranger on the aircraft have disrupted the conspiracy, if conspiracy there was? No one will ever know. Wryly, I reflected that but for Bogden's spur-of-the-moment decision on that day in 1928, I would now be talking to a living eyewitness of what had happened to Alfred Loewenstein. But then again, it might not have happened at all.

Norbert Bogden had been as good as his word and caught the early flight to Brussels next morning, totally unaware that Loewenstein had disappeared. He had neither seen a newspaper nor listened to the radio before he left and only heard the news when his aircraft landed. He went straight to the Rue de la Science, where Madeleine Loewenstein had already returned from Calais. "She was absolutely, totally broken," he said. "She couldn't understand what had happened."

Arthur Hodgson was there as well.

"You sure are a smart fellow not to have come with us on the plane," the secretary said. "He mentioned to me that he was going to ask you to come with him, but you were supposed to have told him that you didn't like the heat and didn't want to rush back to the hotel."

Bogden, as he spoke to me, saw this as having been fresh confirmation that Loewenstein's intention to have him on board had been well formed and that suicide was therefore an unlikely theory for his death. His own belief was still, as it had been through the years, that the Belgian had died by accident. For my part, I could not help wondering whether Arthur Hodgson's tone that day had been one of relief rather than congratulation.

I mentioned my suspicions of murder to the old man on the couch. "Hodgson?" he said, genuinely surprised.

My God. I thought he was a lousy secretary. He was rather naïve and not up to standard as a professional secretary. He was a nice boy, but very primitive and not a bit smart. When I spoke to him on that day in Brussels he was completely baffled. He was absolutely lost in a cloud. He was very admiring of Loewenstein, and in some ways, Loewenstein did not treat him too badly. He was very demanding, but he treated him as humanly as he treated anybody.

I always thought that he could have picked a better man as secretary, a more fitting man. Hodgson wasn't exactly a playboy, but he was a little bit that type. Superficial. He was not the type of secretary you would expect an empire builder like Loewenstein to hire. He was very English. I don't think he came from a very highly bred background. He was always very well dressed and loved to put on a show, but in an innocent way. Like a kid. He was very young. I would no more think of him having any criminal motivations . . . [F]or a man to plan or execute a murder for gain calls for some kind of mental agility and sharpness. I certainly didn't see that in Hodgson. All I can tell you is that he was one of the people who believed most strongly in the theory that Loewenstein had pushed the wrong door.

Bogden was equally convinced of the innocence of Albert Pam, whom he had known well.

An absolutely wonderful guy once you knew him, but widely misunderstood because he always seemed to be in a bad humor. But he was the softest, most considerate man inside, really, when you knew him. I visited him very often at his wonderful place just north of London. He was tremendously interested in plants and animals. That is what he really lived for. Pam was a tower of integrity in my view, one hundred percent pure.

I reflected on some of the things that I knew, and wondered if retirement and the passing years had not given Norbert Bogden a slightly roseate view of human nature. But he did confirm for me one vital fact: The spawning empire of International Holdings had been controlled by three men: Loewenstein, Pam, and Szarvasy. The board of directors, headed by Sir Herbert Holt, had been a mere cipher.

———

THOUGH HIS MISSION had been rendered pointless by the death of his quarry, Norbert Bogden stayed on in Brussels for about three weeks and represented Schroder's at the funeral, recalling clearly that the sorrowing widow had not been present. "It was very small," he said. "That didn't surprise me, because he had very few friends, only business acquaintances. He had many enemies, whom you would not expect to see at his funeral, but I do remember saying to myself at the time that some of his business associates might have showed up."

17

If Alfred Loewenstein was alarmed by the sudden reversal of his fortunes, it certainly did not show. It was not in the nature of the man to retire and lick his wounds. Like a gambler convinced that the next turn of a card will complete a straight flush, he raised the stakes and tried to pull off the biggest deal of his career.

The target of his ambition was no less than the Banque de Bruxelles, one of the two largest banks in Belgium at that time. If he managed to achieve control, the implications for his other business activities would be considerable. No more would he have to go cap in hand to the creatures of Lombard Street or Wall Street to borrow money for his takeover ventures. He would have his own bank.

But to get the bank, he first of all needed money. It was a Catch-22 situation. And with public confidence draining away, doors were closing in his face. Loewenstein's personal fortune was still very considerable. Even at the depressed share values of June 1928, he was worth, on conservative estimates, at least £10 million. However, with the cash tied up in the shares of International Holdings, it was of little value in his attempt to get control of the Banque de Bruxelles. While the shares were rising in value, he would have had no problem in using them as collateral to raise a major loan, but now the banks were nervous.

Loewenstein went looking for a loan of $8 million in the City of London. He was turned away empty-handed.

Even the firm of J. Henry Schroder was not prepared to back him on this one. They felt the scheme was too far-fetched. "We didn't exactly advise him not to do it," said Norbert Bogden, "but we took it rather coldly and asked many questions."

Loewenstein confessed to them that the deal was causing him more trouble than he had expected. The $25 million bond issue that he had hoped to float in New York would probably have solved his problems, but that was stalled indefinitely because of the state of the market and the reluctance on the part of Schroder's to launch the issue. Help came from only one quarter: Frederick Szarvasy, head of the British and Foreign Colonial Corporation and the third member of the triumvirate in charge of International Holdings, loaned him about $2 million. As collateral, Szarvasy took 11,500 of Loewenstein's shares in the company, worth at that time £500,000—which was slightly more than the amount of the loan at the current rate of exchange.

Loewenstein had one other ally: Charles Farbré, head of the Société Générale in Brussels. The Société Générale was Belgium's other leading bank, and an intense competitor of the Banque de Bruxelles. Fabré and Loewenstein had agreed that once the latter's takeover bid had succeeded, the two banks would merge and create one dominant financial institution. For Loewenstein, apart from the prestige and access to finance involved, the deal had another attraction. The Société Générale was the financial power behind SOFINA, the empire of Dannie Heineman. The implications of the scheme as far as Heineman was concerned were therefore dire. They far exceeded the potential threat posed by Loewenstein's fusion proposals of the previous year, and given the Belgian's known feelings about him and his penchant for revenge, Heineman could be certain that he would suffer.

The Banque de Bruxelles itself controlled another group of public utility companies. Putting these together with SOFINA, and bringing in SIDRO, Barcelona Traction, and the other assorted electrical undertakings with which he was involved, including many in the United States, might indeed make Loewenstein ruler of the "largest company in the world," of which he had boasted so often. And Heineman, it seems safe to say, would be finished. Loewenstein was not about to forget the insult he had suffered at the SIDRO meeting, nor the fact that Heineman had seen him cry. In retrospect, perhaps Heineman had been right to feel "deeply disturbed" about that episode in Paris.

The directors of the Bank de Bruxelles were proving obdurate in their opposition to Loewenstein's bid for control. Had he found a way to outwit them? It was in connection with this bid that he was making the flight to Brussels that was to be his last, and his optimism during his dinner with Algy Burnaby at Baggrave Hall three days previously seems to indicate that he thought he had the problem solved. He spoke, too, with the city correspondent of the *Evening Standard* shortly before his death, claiming that he was beginning "some of the greatest schemes I have ever planned." But whether this meant that he was winning the battle in Brussels or whether he had abandoned the project and was off on some other tack is impossible to say. Loewenstein, according to Monica Sheriffe, was no poker player. But when the stakes were high enough, he would have made a good one.

One problem did resolve itself for the Belgian financier during his final days. He found, or believed he had found, the author of the scurrilous exposé that had cost him so dearly. During that last press interview with the *Evening Standard*, Loewenstein had been asked if there was any possibility of a truce between himself and Henri Dreyfus. He had replied: "Never. I am busy now, but when I come back from Brussels, I shall have more time. Then I will settle with Dr. Dreyfus once and forever."

The quotation had puzzled me when I first came across it in the British Museum archives. All connection between Dreyfus and Loewenstein seemed to have been ended when the shares in British Celanese had been sold and the royalty agreement terminated many months before. That the Belgian should have felt some lingering enmity toward Dreyfus for his boardroom defeat was understandable, but he had certainly not suffered financially. In fact, it could be said that Dreyfus had, unintentionally, been the making of International Holdings. Why, then, should Loewenstein be planning some unspecified revenge at this late date? And what did he have in mind?

The latter question was soon answered. Like the good journalist he undoubtedly was, the anonymous city correspondent of the *Standard* had been equally curious. In an article published after Loewenstein's death, he wrote that through "a close friend" of the good doctor, he had learned that Henri Dreyfus was about to be sued for criminal libel. The "friend" claimed that Dreyfus knew of the impending action, had a complete answer to the charge, and in fact was looking forward to his day in court.

He had in the past, it was said, received a number of threatening letters from Loewenstein.

"If the case had been brought," said the article,

> I learnt that it would probably have been one of the most sensational ever known. Leading financiers whose names are known all over the world might have been called as witnesses by both sides, and the evidence would have been followed with interest not only by the general public but on the stock exchanges of every capital.

Dreyfus himself, when questioned, did not wish to discuss the matter. "My principle," he said, "is *De mortuis nil nisi bonum*"—of the dead speak nothing but good—"and I would rather not say anything further." His unnamed friend, however, seemed remarkably well informed and had no hesitation in saying that Dr. Dreyfus's resources were such that he could have faced the long legal action without fear.

I doubted this. English libel actions are notorious for their remarkable expense and total unpredictability, and Dreyfus's funds at this point must have been as heavily tied up in British Celanese as Loewenstein's were in International Holdings. He had just spent a vast amount of money to gain control of the company. I also doubted the identity of the source, for almost the whole article read as though it had been dictated by Henri Dreyfus.

"At the same time that he brought the law case," the city correspondent went on,

> Captain Loewenstein intended to start a bear attack on the shares of British Celanese, in an attempt to reduce the value of Dr. Dreyfus's holdings, and thus hamper him in his legal fight. Here again, however, Captain

Loewenstein had been misled, for I understand that Dr.
Dreyfus has command of cash resources of a sufficient
magnitude for any temporary fall in his shares not to
have affected him in meeting the expense of the lawsuit.
It is possible that Captain Loewenstein learned that his
opponent's position was much stronger than he
anticipated before he left London for Brussels.

The last sentence was interesting. A seed was being
planted in the public mind that Loewenstein might have
had reason to commit suicide rather than risk another
humiliating defeat at the hands of Dreyfus. The last three
paragraphs of the piece confirmed it:

Although the enmity between Captain Loewenstein and
Dr. Dreyfus was of long standing, it had increased in
intensity recently. Loewenstein's greatest ambition was
the creation of a world artificial silk combine. This was
made difficult, if not impossible of accomplishment, by
Dr. Dreyfus's opposition.

A short time ago, in an effort to save the situation,
Captain Loewenstein decided to try and sink his enmity
for Dr. Dreyfus. Through intermediaries, he approached
him and asked if his company would link up with the
Loewenstein scheme. Dr. Dreyfus refused. He believed
that British Celanese had a greater future as an
independent concern, and he stated definitely that he
would not consider Captain Loewenstein as a business
associate ever again.

Captain Loewenstein then started his attack on British
Celanese shares, and succeeded in forcing them down in
market value in an attempt to make Dr. Dreyfus

capitulate. Dr. Dreyfus's resources were, however, much stronger than he realised, and when Captain Loewenstein again approached Dr. Dreyfus, he was rebuffed more definitely than before.

It was subtle, but it was there. Someone in the British Celanese camp was anxious to paint a picture of Loewenstein as an all-around failure; the sort of man who might well have killed himself. The only person I could think of with a conceivable reason for doing so was Henri Dreyfus himself. With the libel action hanging in the background as a possible motive for murder, it would be in his interest to foster a belief in suicide. And there was something about the way in which the article was phrased that indicated, to my own journalistic senses, that the interview had been with a prime source who had asked not to be identified.

Dreyfus's "friend," if such a person existed, had been extremely vague about the nature of the libel allegations, and understandably so. With Loewenstein vanished and presumably dead—a point on which he seemed to speak with certain knowledge—it was a case of the least said, soonest mended. There would be no libel action now, and no suggestion that the head of British Celanese might have been responsible for circulating a document that had been the indirect cause of financial loss to many besides Loewenstein. Such an allegation, even if unproven, might have been extremely damaging. Now it need never be known.

All this must have come as a severe disappointment to one man in particular. John William Bell, the private detective, had finally provided Loewenstein with the ammunition he needed.

It had happened by accident.

The girl whom he had placed in the suspect typing bureau had one day been asked to take dictation from the woman who ran the firm. Having forgotten her shorthand notebook, she picked up a sheet of paper from her employer's desk, only to be told sternly to put it down again

"You mustn't waste paper like that," she was told. "If you want scrap paper you will always find plenty in this drawer." The principal was an economical woman.

The girl duly went to the drawer, where she found a stock of scrap paper. It consisted of sheets that had been spoiled by typists' errors and torn into convenient sizes. She picked out a few and took down the letter.

Back at her desk she turned over one of the sheets. And on the other side was a spoiled version of one page of the Loewenstein document. Within a few days, she was able to trace the whole transaction, including the name of the author. She took it to Bell and was paid a hundred guineas —not overgenerous in view of the fee the detective was expecting, but business is business.

Bell took the evidence to Loewenstein. "He seemed pleased," he wrote later. "I think he was relieved to know the truth. It let him see where he stood."

Pleased he may have been, but not sufficiently to reach for his checkbook on the instant. This was unfortunate for Bell. Pleading pressure of business, Loewenstein promised to settle his £20,000 fee as soon as he returned from Brussels. It was never paid.

Writing this story when he did, in 1934, Bell understandably decided not to reveal the name of the man he had found to be the author of the Loewenstein document. Henri Dreyfus was still very much alive and had a litigious reputation. But given that Alfred Loewenstein had launched no other suits for criminal libel in the last days before his death, or at any other time, it would be remarkable coincidence if Bell's discovery was not the trigger that fired the action against Dreyfus.

"*De mortuis nil nisi bonum*," said Dreyfus. A commendable sentiment, but it begged the question. What had he said about Loewenstein *before* he died? And how anxious was he to avoid the consequences?

———

ON JULY 16, 1928, while the bloated body of Alfred Loewenstein was still floating, undiscovered, in the English Channel, the ninth Ordinary General Meeting of British Celanese was held at the Cannon Street Hotel, London. It was addressed at great length by the new chairman and managing director, Dr. Henri Dreyfus.

Dreyfus's speech was remarkable—not for what it said, but for what it left unmentioned. Here was a situation in which a man who had been a leading figure in the company's fortunes, who had in fact rescued it from bankruptcy only six years previously, had disappeared in tragic circumstances and was presumed dead.

Common usage, not to say common decency, might have dictated some expression of sorrow, however insincere, some phrase of gratitude for past services, or some word of condolence for the bereaved. But from Dr. Henri Dreyfus there was nothing. In all his long and turgid speech on that steamy afternoon, the name of Loewenstein never crossed his lips. It was as though the Belgian to whom he had once gone cap in hand for money had never existed.

Instead, Dreyfus devoted himself to a convoluted explanation of why he had spent a great deal of the company's money in buying out the royalty agreement with International Holdings.

Though none of his charges was specific, and his arguments were hard to comprehend, his hatred shone through. Four days later, on July 20, the *Stock Exchange Gazette* published a verbatim record of his speech. It epitomized Henri Dreyfus.

Loewenstein's company, which had been his financial savior a few short years before, was castigated by Dreyfus for impeding the progress of British Celanese "in every direction." The shareholders were told of "direct and indirect activities against your company"—though none of these was specified. Agreements were alleged to have been broken, promised forgotten, or ignored. What agreement? What promises? Dreyfus never said.

Tubize was dragged in, savaged vaguely, and discarded. "I have expressed my views about the Tubize company," he said, "in a statement issued some months ago, when it was a question of introducing the shares of this company here. However, we do not attach any further importance to these activities, or to those of the Tubize company against your company. This is proved by the fact that we have not even mentioned them in this report, as we do not wish to waste any more time on these relations. I only want to mention it so that you have, once and for all, the true history of it."

The true history of what? In all this diatribe—and it went on for thousands of words—Dreyfus had not come up with one specific charge against Loewenstein, his company, or Tubize. It was easy to see why the tribunal of inquiry into the dope scandal had become so frustrated in their efforts to understand what the man was saying.

In fact, the nub of the matter was Dreyfus's belief that Loewenstein had stolen his precious patents for the manufacture of acetate silk. "It is flattering to your company," Dreyfus continued in one of his more lucid passages, that all the biggest artificial silk interests are keen to imitate your products. What you must realize, however, is that your company, being pioneers in this industry and possessing the master patents, can make their own choice of the time or period when, if ever, they will start legal proceedings in order to enforce the observance of their rights. The other companies will have to await the moment when it is convenient for us to take such action. The damage is only done and due when you have a production. The damages to be awarded are more or less directly proportional to the amounts produced and sold. It would be a waste of money to start a legal fight today over the amount of production going on. Once we find it is that proper time, damages may be enormous. Then, and only then, will we consider the possibility of devoting a relatively small amount of the profits to this task.

The shareholders who listened to all this in patience, but without marked enthusiasm, were at least encouraged by Dreyfus's forecast of substantial dividends now that the incubus of International Holdings had been removed from their necks. It was a promise they were to hear from him many times over the ensuing years. But for British Celanese, success always lay just over a tantalizing horizon, a mirage painted by Henri Dreyfus on the fertile canvas of his imagination. The company made profits, to be sure, but they were eaten up in a series of lengthy and curious legal actions in defense of his treasured patents, all of which, without exception, were lost.

Henri Dreyfus died, a week short of his sixty-third birthday, on December 31, 1944. It was then that his company paid its first ever dividend on the ordinary shares and was shortly afterward swallowed up by Courtaulds. His brother Camille outlived him, dying in his apartment in the Hotel Pierre in New York on September 27, 1956. He was seventy-eight, and under his much quieter leadership, the American Celanese company had made huge profits for many years.

18

AT LAST I had found someone—or more accurately, two people—with a motive for killing Loewenstein. But were their motives plausible? In the case of Heineman, whose character was still obscure to me—and likely to remain so —the possibility of losing all he had worked for at the hands of a man he held in contempt might well have been unbearable. And there was the added factor that Loewenstein, rightly or wrongly, had been convinced that Heineman and his associates had threatened his life.

But what of Dreyfus? Would a man, even so volatile a character as Henri Dreyfus, kill in order to avoid being taken to court? The Belgian's death had freed him from the threat of a libel action, which, if he had lost, might have resulted in crippling damages. It was not just harm to Loewenstein's reputation that a court would take into account; there was the actual financial loss, easily proved, which had run into millions of dollars.

Loewenstein v. Dreyfus could well have been the most expensive libel action in history, and would have been fought to the bitter end. Neither man was a quitter by nature. The importance that Loewenstein himself attached to it was indicated by his willingness to pay twenty thousand pounds to a private detective. This was a huge sum in 1928—almost $100,000 at the prevailing rate of exchange back then. If Loewenstein could prove that Dreyfus was the author of the document, which seemed highly likely, then the truth or otherwise of what had been written would scarcely be relevant. Under the strict English libel laws, it would not be sufficient for Dreyfus to claim that the gist of what he wrote was true. He would have to prove the truth of every single word, a virtually impossible task.

Once taken to court, therefore, provided Bell's evidence stood up, the Swiss chemist would face near certain ruin. He would be in the center of a scandal even more damaging than his dope escapade, and this time there would be no Loewenstein to haul him from the mire.

But in spite of all this, I felt far from certain that I had found the answer. Fear of ruin, and deep hatred for the man whom he believed was stealing the fruits of his genius, might well have turned the thoughts of Henri Dreyfus towards murder. But one inescapable fact gnawed at my mind: Loewenstein had only been told of the identity of his accuser, and had decided to launch the libel action, a very short time before he died. I was not sure of the exact date John William Bell had completed his inquiries, but circumstantial evidence indicated that it was not more than a week and possibly only a day or two before Loewenstein made his last flight. It seemed to me too short a time for a complex conspiracy to be set in motion. By whatever method the deed had been done, and that I had yet to discover, it would have required imagination and careful planning. And the persuasion of at least some of those on board to take part in the plot, without which the whole thing was impossible, could hardly have been accomplished overnight.

I decided to keep Henri Dreyfus at the back of my mind, but to continue the search elsewhere. What I needed to find was someone who had gained direct and considerable financial benefit from Loewenstein's death. His will was the first and obvious place to look, and I found it without difficulty. It had been opened and read in Brussels on Friday, July 20, 1928, less than twenty-four hours after the financier's body had been found floating in the Channel.

Madeleine Loewenstein, who had not felt able to attend her husband's funeral two days later, managed to attend *this* ceremony without difficulty. It was, as lawyers are fond of saying on such occasions, to her advantage.

Loewenstein had drawn up the will a year previously, and, considering the complexity of his estate, it was a simple document. His fortune was estimated at this time to be worth about $24 million (more than $1 billion in 2000 currency)—though this represented only the value of his shares in International Holdings and was certainly a conservative figure. At the moment when he boarded the aircraft, of course, the shares had been worth some $53 million. Loewenstein on the hoof was far more valuable than Loewenstein on the mortuary slab.

But it was still a tidy sum, and it was to be divided equally between Madeleine and his son, Robert. Since Robert was only eighteen, and legally a minor at this time, under the terms of the will his mother was appointed his legal guardian with power to look after his share of the money until he came of age. Madeleine Loewenstein was also appointed sole executrix. In essence, she had gotten the lot. The will contained only one admonition: Alfred Loewenstein asked that if she needed advice on how to handle the money, she should go to one of his close business associates.

All this was really no more than Madeleine Loewenstein's legal entitlement. Her marriage contract stipulated that she should receive one half of her husband's estate, and there was a similar provision in Belgian law. As joint owner of the palatial house in Brussels, The Pinfold at Thorpe Satcheville, and the Villa Begonia in Biarritz, she had already inherited these automatically. And with the exception of the airplane, which she had already instructed Donald Drew to sell, she announced that she intended to keep everything. Life for Madeleine Loewenstein would go on much as before, with periodic seasonal migrations among her various homes. The only difference would be the absence of Alfred, but then she had never seen very much of him, anyway.

Young Bobby, questioned by reporters after the contents of the will were made public, seemed to be chiefly moved by the fact that he would now be able to run the Loewenstein stable of racehorses under his own colors. He was looking forward, he said, to the hunting season. As for taking up a business career himself, he thought he might in course of time, but for the moment he confessed that he was too interested in sport.

There was no evidence of great and lasting sorrow in the Loewenstein family, and it was tempting to construct a plot in the imagination that would involve the willing seduction of Donald Drew by the beautiful and frustrated Madeleine. The trouble was that I had encountered not one whiff of scandal surrounding the lady, nor any evidence that she was unhappy with Loewenstein, save for the fact that he left her on her own a great deal. And if that were grounds for murder, the streets would be carpeted with the bodies of overworked husbands. She had certainly inherited a great deal of money. That much was undeniable. But all my information seemed to show that Loewenstein had treated her generously in his lifetime, and she had everything she could possibly have wanted already.

There were only a few small things that made Madeleine a possible suspect. She had been extraordinarily anxious to find the body—a task in which Drew helped, though it was hardly his job to do so. And it had been at her request that the pilot had come to Brussels and told his dubious story of opening the door of the aircraft with ease, which had effectively quelled any more thorough inquiry. She would also have known all those who were on the aircraft that day and would have been able to made contact with them without arousing suspicion. But my gut feeling still said she was innocent, though I could have been wrong. Like most men, I have a built-in tendency not to think ill of beautiful women. I decided to carry on looking for someone else, someone who might have made money from Loewenstein's death in ways that were less obvious. But, as I quickly discovered, it was easier to find those who had lost.

The stock exchanges of Europe were closed at the moment Alfred Loewenstein fell out of the sky. If television had been invented in 1928, there might well have been a few defenestrations on the night of July 4, but as it was, most of the brokers, the jobbers and the speculators, learned of his disappearance as they opened their newspapers on the morning journey to the office. And then, in Berlin and Brussels, Paris and London, there was instant panic.

On the London Stock Exchange, as investors surged around the stalls in a frantic effort to sell before the bottom dropped out of the market completely, jobbers at first refused to deal at all in the shares of International Holdings and Hydro-Electric Securities. Overnight the price of these

shares had stood at $215 and $51, far below the peaks they
had reached before the bad news from Brussels three
weeks earlier, but still highly respectable. Now that
Loewenstein was almost certainly dead, they seemed like
worthless pieces of paper to the frightened speculators.

It was all in the mind, but then it always had been.
There was as little economic justification for the
catastrophic fall in July as there had been for the meteoric
rise in May. Somewhere in between lay the true value of the
companies, and now that the mountain had closed behind
the pied piper, the market was going to have to decide that
for itself.

When trading finally began, International Holdings
were being quoted at $100 a share, and *The Times* of
London reported that large blocks were traded at that price.
Hydro-Electric Securities were being sold for less than half
their previous value, at $20. Something had to be done to
steady the market, and Albert Pam and Frederick Szarvasy
rushed out a statement.

> In view of the regrettable death of Captain Alfred
> Loewenstein, president of the International Holdings and
> Investment Company and the Hydro-Electric Securities
> Corporation, we the undersigned, as members of the
> advisory committee acting for the two companies, state
> that the financial position of both companies is sound
> and that the very large shareholdings of the late Captain
> Loewenstein in the two companies are, in the main, to
> the best of our knowledge, unencumbered.

The words "in the main," of course, could have covered
a variety of sins. They certainly obscured the fact that
Szarvasy himself had lent $2 million to Loewenstein on the
security of his shares. The statement continued:

It is as yet too early to say what arrangements are to be made to fill the place of Captain Loewenstein as president of the two companies, but due consideration is being given to the matter by the Board in Canada, and an early announcement will be made.

There is nothing in the situation as we understand it today which, in our opinion, need give rise to any anxiety. Our advice to the companies will be to continue and further develop the well-conceived policy agreed on by us with Captain Loewenstein.

The contemplated sale by the International Holdings and Investment Company of the unissued shares in the company will be proceeded with forthwith.

The last sentence of the statement was curious. On the face of it, it seemed intended to impress the stock exchange with the fact that business would carry on as usual in spite of Loewenstein's death. Yet it implied that still more shares were going to be unloaded on a market that was already in steep decline, further diluting the capital of the company and probably depressing the price even further. There were around 62,000 shares involved, on which International Holdings had been expecting to raise, prior to the Belgian's disappearance, roughly $13 million. Now they would be lucky to get half that sum. To proceed with the sale before investors had had a chance to recover from the shock was an odd decision to be made by financiers as smart as Albert Pam and Frederick Szarvasy.

Subsequent events showed that the rump of the advisory committee knew exactly what they were doing. And in fairness it must be said that their statement that day did steady the nerve of the market to some extent. At close of business on July 5, International Holdings had recovered to $145 and Hydro-Electric to $39.59.

The losses were still enormous. In London alone, it was estimated that $43 million was lost the day after Loewenstein died. Even Courtaulds suffered, on the ground that Loewenstein was believed to have been buying into the giant textile firm.

It was ironic that one of the few companies to buck the trend was none other than British Celanese. In a surge that must have had Loewenstein turning furiously in his watery grave, Dreyfus's preference shares rose by one shilling and sixpence to forty-four shillings and sixpence, and the Swiss announced that he was about to launch an issue of new ten-shilling ordinary shares at two pounds ten shilling: a premium of five hundred percent. If Dreyfus had known that Loewenstein was about to die, he could have dreamed up no more suitable triumphant blast to trumpet over the corpse.

The pattern of panic was repeated in Berlin, Brussels, and Paris, where there were heavy slumps in the shares of any companies in which Loewenstein had an interest. From the German capital it was reported that his death had "struck the business and industrial world like lightning from a clear sky," although it was believed that he had already sold most of his German holdings when heavily pressed over the previous few weeks.

As well as International Holdings and Hydro-Electric Securities, FISA, Barcelona Traction, Mexico Tramways, SIDRO, and Brazilian Traction all suffered sharp declines on the European exchanges. In Brussels, investors in Belgian Tubize saw the value of their company drop by thirty percent as the rumors of suicide and murder spread around the Bourse. A statement by the Brussels representative of International Holdings (a man named

Fischer who was cordially disliked by Norbert Bogden), to the effect that Loewenstein's affairs were in order and there was no question of his companies being liquidated, did little to stem the tide of selling.

The ripples from the great splash in the Channel even spread as far as Mexico, where the inhabitants of Chihuahua waited anxiously to see what was going to happen to their forests. In the weeks before his death, Loewenstein had been completing negotiations to take over vast lumber concessions in the state and had been promising to invest several million dollars in a new sawmill and other projects. Chihuahua, which had been suffering badly from an economic recession in Mexico, had looked on him as a fairy godfather come to rescue them. Now he was gone, and with him their hopes of prosperity.

Only New York remained calm. It could afford to, since Loewenstein's companies had been refused a quotation on Wall Street during his transatlantic sortie two months before. American Tubize, having seen what happened in Brussels and afraid of disaster by association, promptly issued a statement denying any connection with the Belgian company of the same name. My information said otherwise, but their reaction was understandable. True or false, the statement probably saved the shareholders a great deal of money.

The New York Times reported that although Loewenstein had invested considerable sums in American securities, both for his companies and himself, the investments were not large enough to affect prices. Nor would his American bank loans, which varied from $1 million to $4 million on any given day, cause any embarrassment.

Officials in the New York office of Schroder's were quoted as saying that from their knowledge of Loewenstein and his financial plans, they could not believe that he had ended his life deliberately.

In all the lamentation over speculators' burned fingers, it was at first difficult to imagine that anyone could actually have made a profit on the stock market from Loewenstein's death. Only the London correspondent of *The Toronto Daily Mail and Empire* had the perspicacity to point out that "anyone who knew Loewenstein was going to die, or apparently going to die, would have made millions by selling shares short."

I suddenly realized that this was quite true. Given foreknowledge of the Belgian's death, and the fact that the basic soundness of his companies was bound to be lost sight of in the blind panic of the speculators, a large investor could have sold his shares at $215 and bought them back for less than half the price the following day. It was possible, but had it taken place? There was really no way of knowing. But newspaper reports in the days that followed showed that interesting things were happening.

For a start, quotations in the *Financial Times* of July 12, a week after Loewenstein's disappearance, disclosed that the price of shares in International Holdings had suddenly slumped to $13. The day before they had been $130, and I could see nothing to account for the catastrophic decline until I discovered that the board had made a ten-for-one share issue, increasing the capital from five hundred thousand to five million shares. This move had been decided upon in mid-May, at which time the shares were selling for $325 each. Loewenstein must have realized that this was putting them beyond the reach of the small investors, from whom he had always drawn much of his support. By diluting the capital tenfold, he would make renewed speculation in his shares attractive to a wide audience once again. His own holding would be multiplied to 2.2 million shares, and every time the price rose by a dollar—which at that time looked like it was a regular event—he would have been more than $2 million richer. Had he lived, of course.

Pam and Szarvasy had evidently decided to stick with the plan, perhaps for the same reasons, even though the price of the shares had slumped. The move may have had some other significance, but for the moment, it eluded me. The importance of what happened next, however, was unmistakable.

They were great makers of statements, Pam and Szarvasy. A few weeks before, following the Brussels debacle, they had tried to reassure the nervous market with an impressive list of the investments held by International Holdings. Now, in *The Times* of London of July 16, 1928, they trotted out much the same panegyric. It took a keen eye and a good memory to detect that the figures had altered fairly radically in the space of a month.

"The company," they said, "has acquired and now holds options on certain securities which, if the options were exercised and the securities realized at current market prices, would represent a further profit of over $4 million."

On the face of it, this was impressive. The trouble was that less than a month before those securities and options had been forecast to yield a further profit of $12.9 million. It is doubtful that even Loewenstein's death, from which the markets had, in any case, partially recovered, would have accounted for such a loss on the books.

The net result, said Pam and Szarvasy, was that after deducting all liabilities, the value of International Holdings assets now represented $12 per share, break-up value. They were not taking into account the undoubted potential value of the company's control of various undertakings, nor goodwill. The pair then proceeded to go into great detail about the investments held by the company in artificial silk (worth $41,664,000), public utilities ($13,826,000), and American railroads ($2,850,000).

The significance of all this emerged next day, when it was announced that a syndicate headed by Albert Pam and Frederick Szarvasy had been formed to buy all the previously unissued shares in International Holdings. They were to pay $12 each for 380,000 shares and to take an option at $15 each on the remaining 244,400. In other words, the surviving members of the "advisory committee" had advised the board to sell to them, rather than to the general public, shares on which they themselves had fixed the value. Assuming that they took up the option, those 624,400 shares would cost them $8,256,000—an average of $13.22 per share. Had they bought them on the day before Loewenstein died, the same shares in the same company with the same investments would have cost them around £13.5 million. A saving of more than $5 million was not to be sneezed at, most especially in light of yet another statement from Pam and Szarvasy that appeared in the *Stock Exchange Gazette* only ten days later, on July 27, 1928.

I almost missed it. At first sight this seemed to be a mere repetition of what I had already read in *The Times*. The *Stock Exchange Gazette* was a weekly publication, and I assumed as I scanned the yellowing columns that the statement must have been issued too late for its deadline the previous week.

There was the announcement of the syndicate's share purchase (the market price had risen to $14 by this date, so they were already doing nicely), and there was the forecast of an additional $4 million profit, just as before. The actual profits for International Holdings from interest, underwriting profits, and the sale of securities were said to be running at $328,500 for the full year. Given the amount of capital involved, this seemed a good return, though not remarkable. But the line of small print that followed was remarkable indeed. I read it once and then read it again, hardly able to believe my eyes.

"In addition to the profits stated," said the Pam/Szarvasy statement, *"the company has realized profit arising out of the transactions of a special nature amounting to $13,226,137."*

Transactions of a special nature? What did that mean? Somehow or other International Holdings had brought off a deal that had not only increased its profits for the year but had *quadrupled* them. What sort of transaction was that, to be dismissed in two lines of small print without a word of explanation of this extraordinary coup? It was surely a feat of which any businessman ought to be proud (especially since it had to boost the value of their shares). Yet, Pam and Szarvasy had not thought it worthy of any more attention than a passing reference at the bottom of their report. I wondered why.

I also wondered why there had been no mention of this sensational success in the statement of July 16 that had made the syndicate's share offer of $12 per share look so fair and reasonable. Could it be that these two honorable men had wanted to make International Holdings appear less valuable than it was at that moment?

Perish the thought.

There was one other possibility: that this windfall had actually accrued to the company *after* the statement of July 16. I looked further down the figures and noted that a mere $422,346 was being distributed in dividends, while $6,701,300 was being put in the company's capital account, and $8,566,693 was described as "undivided profit remaining in the surplus account." Either the directors were being extraordinarily stingy with their shareholders or my latter theory was right: The profit had been made very recently, and too late for the board to decide what to do with it.

As far as I knew there had been only one relevant event between July 16 and July 27, 1928: The body of Alfred Loewenstein had been found floating in the English Channel on July 19. Now how could that possibly be linked with a profit of more than $13 million?

19

BLINDED by columns of figures and the small print of financial reports, I was in danger of losing sight of the central enigma of the Loewenstein affair: his exit from that airplane through a door that would not open.

But until I solved that conundrum, all my speculations on the who and why of Loewenstein's departure from the world were useless. It was a classical locked-door mystery, a crime that could never have happened, but did.

Contemporary sources were proving to be of very little use in this part of my quest.

In the absence of any official investigation worthy of the name, I was left with uninformed opinion that said, on the one hand, that the door could open so easily that Loewenstein had stepped out in a fit of absent-mindedness, and on the other that he had been so determined to die that he used superhuman strength to force it open.

The first explanation I knew beyond all reasonable doubt to be wrong. The second was implausible for two reasons: First, Loewenstein had no good reason to end his life. Nothing in his behavior suggested he was contemplating such a thing.

Second, as for the notion that he had powered his way through the door, I had learned that though Loewenstein was generally strong, during his last days, he had suffered from such bad rheumatism that he had had to be lifted from his horse.

––––––

BUT IF LOEWENSTEIN could not have opened the door, who did? On the evidence of the tests, it took two men acting in concert to force the door open far enough to thrust a body through. That in itself posed no particular problem, for there had certainly been sufficient people on board the Fokker that day. Leaving aside the two women, there were Hodgson, Baxter, Little, and Drew. One of the crew would be needed to control the aircraft, which did not have an automatic pilot, but that still left three to do the dirty work. Yet I could not believe it had been done in this way. The toilet compartment on the Fokker measured roughly five feet by four, with scant standing headroom. It was inconceivable that four men should crowd into it, one of them unwilling or unconscious, and that two should force open the door and hold it against the slipstream while the third struggled to throw the fourth out into space. Even if such a scenario were possible, which I doubted, it would almost certainly have left traces on the aircraft or the participants, and none had been found.

I would have to go back to basics, and in this case the bottom line was the aircraft itself. There had to be something about that airplane, some factor in the design or construction, that would make the impossible credible. But I was damned if I knew what it might be.

The Fokker Tri-motor, with its heavy cantilevered wing and box-like fuselage, was an unlovely machine by modern standards. But in the mid-1920s, when aviation was struggling out of its barnstorming cocoon and seeking commercial respectability, it was an outstanding success. With a wingspan of seventy feet and a length of forty-seven feet, six inches, it could carry eight passengers at a cruising speed of ninety-three miles an hour for 480 miles. Top speed was 115 miles per hour, and the service ceiling ten thousand feet—though it took forty minutes to reach that altitude.

The machine had been born almost by accident. In July 1925, Henry Ford and his son Edsel announced an annual competition, to be known as the Ford Reliability Tour, for commercial aircraft. Entrants were to fly a course of 1,900 miles over six days, in an effort to demonstrate to the public that the airplane was a reliable means of transportation. Anthony Fokker, best known for his design of German fighter aircraft during the First World War, was in the United States at the time and decided to enter one of his own machines. The only snag was that his current model, the F.VIIa, had only one engine and lacked the necessary reliability.

Fokker cabled his main factory in Amsterdam and instructed it to design an aircraft capable of winning. There was not much time. The tour was due to start on September 28, and the machine had to be designed, built, test-flown, and transported across the Atlantic, all in less than three months.

The Fokker engineers solved the problem by fitting two more engines, one on either side of the fuselage, to their existing design. It was ugly, but it worked. On September 7, Fokker himself demonstrated the Tri-motor at Schiphol, flying it "hands off" down the main runway. It was promptly dismantled, crated up, and shipped to America.

In the event, no one won that first Reliability Tour. None of the sixteen entrants managed to finish the course. But the Fokker Tri-motor had done as well as any and better than most and had managed to garner more publicity than all the others combined. The era of the three-engined aircraft, which was to reign over the world airline scene for the next ten years, had been launched. Though the Ford Tri-motor, a similar but somewhat more sophisticated design, came to dominate the American market, it was the Fokker that was flown by airlines from Europe to Japan.

By 1932, no fewer than ninety-six were in operation, accounting for fifty-six percent of all tri-motors in service with European airlines—the remainder being built by twelve different manufacturers. They were bought by the U.S. Navy and Army, flew with the Byrd expedition to the North Pole, and but for an unfortunate accident would probably have beaten Lindbergh's *Spirit of St. Louis* to become the first aircraft to fly from New York to Paris nonstop.

The Fokker F.VIIa/3m was *the* airplane to have, which was why Alfred Loewenstein wanted one. They were also in very short supply for the first two years of production because the Fokker factory was heavily committed to building military aircraft. He had to wait his turn. Of the first six built, five were sold in the United States and one to the British Air Ministry. Finally, in December 1926, Loewenstein's name came to the top of the list.

The machine he had ordered was no ordinary airplane. *The New York Times* described it as "the most luxuriously equipped 'air yacht' in the world." It would have, said the *Times*, "a salon with rich carpets and hangings, comfortable armchairs which can be removed and beds substituted for night flying, plus a completely equipped lavatory with washbasins and mirrors. A small foyer will lead to the apartments, which will be heated in winter and cooled by a diffused air system in summer."

But Loewenstein was destined never to take delivery of this marvel of the skies. The record shows that the machine that was allocated to him on Fokker's production line—H-NADS—was in fact delivered to the Rt. Hon. Frederick Guest and registered as G-EBPV. Guest, who was a prominent figure in British government circles, had bought a single-engined Fokker from the Dutch airline KLM some two months previously, but apparently decided that he needed the extra power and range of the tri-motor.

He must have persuaded Loewenstein to give up his place on the delivery schedule, but the financier was not going to relinquish his new toy without a quid pro quo. Shortly thereafter, the name of Frederick Guest was to be found on the board of directors of International Holdings and Investments Ltd.—a valuable and influential catch, which Loewenstein probably thought well worth the temporary sacrifice of the aircraft he so badly wanted. It was also a moment when the Belgian's finances were at a temporarily low ebb following the failure of his Brazilian Traction merger scheme, so he may not have been all that sorry to pass up the order.

It was June 1928 before his turn came around again. The twenty-first Fokker F.VIIa/3m to roll off the production line, again specially fitted for Loewenstein's requirements (though less like a flying brothel than the machine described in *The New York Times* eighteen months before) was delivered to Donald Drew on Loewenstein's behalf shortly after the latter's party returned from the United States.

Drew flew it to England, re-registered it as G-EBYI, and thus set in motion the final chapter of Alfred Loewenstein's life.

I needed to see that airplane, or at least one of the same model. G-EBYI, I knew, no longer existed. After the death of Loewenstein, it had been sold by Drew on Madeleine's instructions to a Lieutenant-Commander Glen Kidston. Kidston flew it to Africa and, in July 1929, made a forced landing in the Sudan that caused serious damage to the aircraft. In March 1930, all that remained of the machine at the center of the world's most intractable aviation mystery was sold back to Fokker for use as spare parts.

I began hunting among the aeronautical museums, hoping that someone, somewhere, would have an intact model of the Fokker F.VIIa/3m. The Smithsonian Air and Space Museum in Washington, D.C., seemed the best bet, and as luck would have it I was due to make a short business trip to the United States. I had visited the museum before and knew there was no example in the main exhibit, but I hoped that one might exist among the overflow collection of historic aircraft kept at Silver Hill, Maryland.

It was a wasted journey. The Smithsonian officials were friendly and helpful, poring through great piles of old blueprints to see if there was any relevant material, but without success. As far as they knew there were only three extant examples of the Fokker: one in Australia, one in Dearborn, Michigan, and one in Holland.

Of the Dearborn aircraft, however, very little remained. And the Australian exhibit, which was the famous Southern Cross in which Sir Charles Kingsford-Smith had cross the Atlantic and the Pacific and broken the Australia-to-U.K. record, was said to have been heavily modified. In particular, the critical port-side door had been sealed up. Since I could not possibly afford to go to Australia to see it, this news was almost a relief. There remained the Dutch example, housed in the museum at Schiphol Airport, Amsterdam. I resolved to go there as soon as I could.

I had begun to formulate a theory. On various light aircraft in which I had flown, there had been a device fitted to the cockpit-door hinges, which would allow the door to be jettisoned before an emergency landing or possibly removed before take-off if the machine was to be used for parachuting or aerial photography. As I remembered it, there was a simple lever that withdrew the hinge pins at the forward edge of the door, after which a light push would allow it to be carried away in the slipstream.

I wondered whether Loewenstein's aircraft had been equipped with a similar gadget. It seemed likely. After all, it was a passenger aircraft, and there would have to be some provision for emergency escape. Ordinary doors, which can jam on impact, are not normally considered adequate for emergency use, though whether air safety regulations had gotten this far in 1928 I had not yet discovered.

There were two pieces of evidence to support my theory. One was the examination of the plane when it had arrived back in Croydon, when it was discovered that the wooden framing on the inside of the door latch had splintered. Such damage could hardly have been caused by a heavy impact from the inside—in which case it would have been expected on the outside edge of the frame—but I reasoned that it might well have been caused by the tongue of the lock twisting violently in its mortise as the door was torn open by the wind. The latch had been a simple spring-loaded handle, backed up by two interior bolts. Whoever released the front hinges on the door would presumably have withdrawn the latter first but might well have forgotten the latch or been unable to reach it at the same time as the emergency lever.

The second piece of evidence concerned the French fisherman who had reported seeing a "parachute" descending at about the time that Loewenstein's aircraft flew over his boat. The report had been associated with the discredited rumors that Loewenstein had staged a deliberate disappearance and had been generally dismissed as fantasy. But what if that fisherman really had seen something? Not a falling body, which he would have been unlikely to mistake for a parachute, but a light plywood door windmilling down from the sky? Such a door would have fallen slowly, tumbling and spinning. From a couple of miles away it might very well have looked like a parachute, especially to someone who had probably never seen such a thing in his life.

There was, I realized only too well, one very serious objection to my newfound theory: When the aircraft was discovered by the French soldiers on Mardyk beach, there was no mention of a missing door. It was possible that they approached from the starboard side and did not notice, but the gaping hole could hardly have escaped attention at St. Inglevert and would certainly have caused some comment when the aircraft was returned to Croydon. Nowhere had I found any such suggestion. Indeed, the whole core of the problem was that the door was very much there and very much intact, with the exception of that splintered frame. Feeling slightly depressed, I went back to see Dennis Bustard. Having flown in the aircraft of that period, he was the one man I could think of who might possibly have an answer.

Bustard remembered the Fokker Tri-motor very well. Too well for the sake of my theory. He began by pouring cold water on my idea of an emergency release for the door. No, he was quite certain that there had been no such device. To the best of his recollection, the emergency exit had been via a rip panel in the fabric of the fuselage above the toilet. I subsequently discovered that this was quite correct. So much, I thought, for bright ideas. But Dennis Bustard had not finished. "You know," he said, "it could have been done that way."

"How?" I asked, hardly daring to hear the answer.

"As I recall it," he explained, "there were two small hinges on that door at the forward edge. Quite simple things they were. And there were sliding windows that you could open. I seem to remember that they went right back to the end of the cabin. So it would be quite easy to get rid of that door—all you would need to do would be to open the window, put your arm out, and unfasten the hinges."

I felt my heart beating a little faster. "Okay," I said, "but how do you account for the fact that there was quite definitely a door on that aircraft when it landed?"

Bustard thought for a moment. "How long did you say it was before they were found on that beach?"

I told him.

He grinned. "No problem," he said. "No problem at all. All they had to do was to make a spare door. Or maybe get one from the stores at Croydon. But that was a very simple door. The mechanics who flew in those days were trained to do that sort of thing, just in case the plane was damaged while they were away from base. Any competent flight engineer could make a thing like that in a day."

"But how would they carry a complete door on a small airplane without Loewenstein noticing?" I found myself playing devil's advocate. I wanted Bustard's theory to offer a possible solution, but surely there had to be a snag somewhere.

"There was plenty of room in the back of the Fokker," he explained. "Aft of the cabin it was just empty space all the way to the tail. My guess would be that you could reach it via some sort of access panel in the rear wall of the toilet compartment. They could have taken off the real door and stowed it in there, and put the spare door on for the actual flight. No one would have noticed. Then, after the spare had been jettisoned, they could put the real one back on for the investigators to see."

It all began to fit together. The scheme was outlandish, but it was not impossible. Indeed, it was just about the only solution that fitted all the known facts. There had been a mechanic on that flight. And the damage to the doorframe could have been caused because it was impossible to operate the latch while leaning out of the cabin window to disengage the hinges. Most important of all, Bustard's theory provided a logical explanation for Donald Drew's strange decision to land on a deserted beach rather than fly on for a mere five minutes to the nearest airfield. Had he been seen to land at St. Inglevert with a gaping hole where the door should have been, there would have been no mystery. Loewenstein's fate would have been only too obvious. But he chose instead to put the aircraft down at a spot where there would be no curious eyes.

It would have been the work of a moment to pull out the true door the moment the aircraft came to a halt, and slip it back on its hinges before officialdom came puffing over the sand dunes. I felt in my bones that I had found the solution that had been hidden for almost sixty years. Everything depended now on finding an actual Fokker F.VIIa/3m and checking to see if it was really possible. I packed my camera and measuring tape and set off for Amsterdam.

———

THE NATIONAAL LUCHTVAART MUSEUM, better known as the Aviodome, is housed in a futuristic building on the edge of Schiphol airport. To reach it from the main terminal requires the navigational skills of Marco Polo, which are needed to thread one's way through a maze of parking lots and hotels, plus a certain fleetness of foot to avoid being run down by Dutch motorists as you cross the access freeway. Of course, you could always take a cab, but I was on a strict budget—which was why I had traveled to Schiphol by boat, and train, and bus. A ridiculous way to visit an airport, unless you consider the equally ridiculous levels of European airfares.

Somewhat out of breath from my dash across the freeway, I finally squelched my way over a marshy field and found the entrance to the dome. The place was empty, and I reflected that the local inhabitants either had little interest in old airplanes or lacked the Dutch courage to make the trip. It was also smaller than I expected, and I could see at a glance that the massive box-like shape of the Fokker F.VIIa/3m that I had come to see was not there. If it had been, it would have dominated the hall. There were, it is true, one or two models of the type on display, but models were of no use for my purpose.

I needed to poke and pry and measure, to climb inside and get the ambience, the feel of the machine in which Loewenstein had died. And it was palpably not here; my information had been wrong.

My heart sank.

It was not just the waste of time and money, though that was serious enough. It was the sheer frustration of being close to a tenable solution of the mystery and having no way in the world to check it out. I looked around for an attendant, failed to find one, and went in search of the curator.

Considering that our two nations spent so much time fighting each other in centuries past, the Dutch are unfailingly courteous towards the English. They also speak our language, probably better than we do, and so my anguished plea for information on the Fokker was received with grave concern. The curator was very sorry: The museum did indeed have a Fokker F.VIIa, but at the present time it was being stripped down for restoration. Sometime next year, he said proudly, or perhaps the year after, it would be returned to flying condition. There were even plans to demonstrate the machine in the air before it was returned to the exhibition. Perhaps I would like to come back and see it then?

I smiled through my tears. That would be splendid, I said, though I doubted if my publisher would be very happy at the delay. Still, there was no sense in getting upset about it. The curator spread his hands helplessly. Would I care to talk to the museum's research department? They might have some information or perhaps some blueprints that might help.

I allowed myself to be steered into a small, paper-cluttered room, where I was introduced to the research officer, Peter van de Noort. For the umpteenth time, I found myself telling the Loewenstein story.

Van de Noort, a blond young man with a thirst for knowledge and a passion for old airplanes, heard me out with apparent fascination. He rummaged through files and produced enough information about the Fokker F.VIIa to fill a small book on the subject. There they were: the serial number, delivery dates, and flying histories of every single machine built by the Fokker factory and its licensees. There was an exploded drawing of the design in immense detail, but of Production No. 5063, the machine purchased by Alfred Loewenstein, there was only the barest mention

—and no suggestion that it had been at the center of one of aviation's most puzzling mysteries. Van de Noort's information was useful, but only in peripheral way. The Dutchman sensed my disappointment. What was it, he asked, that I really wanted?

I explained.

"But we have one here," said Peter van de Noort.

I was puzzled. "But I thought it was away for restoration?" I said.

"It's being restored, yes. But we're doing the work here. Come, I'll show you." He led the way back into the museum.

And there it was. It had been there all the time, but I had been too blind to see it. I had been looking for a complete aircraft, not its component parts, and I had failed to recognize the framework of metal tubing against one wall for what it was: the fuselage of an F.VIIa, stripped of its fabric.

Van de Noort pointed upward, and I saw the massive wings suspended in the ceiling of the dome. Various other bits and pieces were scattered around, quite recognizable now that I knew what I was looking at. But there was no door.

"Wait a minute," van de Noort said blithely, "I think I've seen it somewhere." He vanished into a back room and came back carrying a piece of plywood with a small glass panel set into the upper half. "Is this what you were looking for?"

Trustingly, the researcher went off for his lunch and left me on my own. I looked at the door, which I had seen in so many fuzzy newspaper photographs, with something like reverence. As a piece of aviation technology, it was laughable: simply two sheets of flat plywood over a light wooden frame, with an alloy strip riveted to the outer edge.

The lock, with a Bakelite handle instead of the metal one I knew was fitted to Loewenstein's aircraft, looked like a standard fitting that could be bought from any hardware store. That was probably what it was.

Could a duplicate door have been made, realistic enough to look like the real thing? I am no carpenter, but I decided that with a few simple tools I could make one myself.

It was the hinges that interested me most. They were merely U-shaped pieces of metal, pierced at top and bottom and held in place by two ordinary 3/16-inch-diameter bolts, one and a half inches long. There were no retaining pins, and no holes drilled to take them—just an ordinary nut on the bottom. Those nuts, I thought, could easily have been loosened, or even left off altogether, without anyone boarding the aircraft being the wiser. Gravity would have held the bolts in place for the short time necessary.

I photographed the door from every angle, then carried it over to the fuselage, wedging it into position. Thankful that there was no one around to see me clambering on an exhibit—which was certainly forbidden—I climbed into the framework and stretched my arm out of the space where the sliding windows had once been.

And I could reach the hinges. The lower one was a bit of a stretch, but the feat was perfectly possible. That door *could* have been released in mid-air, in exactly the way that Dennis Bustard had theorized. And with the door gone, there would have been no impediment to Loewenstein's abrupt exit.

There was one more question to answer: Could a spare door have been stowed on board in a position where Loewenstein would not have seen it, and from where it could be retrieved in a matter of seconds when the aircraft landed on the beach? Bustard had postulated that it could have been stowed in the empty space at the rear of the fuselage, with access through a maintenance panel in the back wall of the toilet compartment.

But from van de Noort's engineering drawings, and from what I could see of the actual fuselage, this solution was impossible. The "empty" space was not really empty at all—it was filled with a mass of bracing wires, which would have ruled out any chance of fitting such a bulky object inside, at least without considerable contortions. It would have been like trying to put a grand piano in a bathroom. Nor did there seem to be any means of access to the tail section, though I guessed there might well have been some form of rip panel in the fabric to permit mechanics to work on the control wires to the tail.

For a spare door to have been carried on Loewenstein's aircraft that day, however, no contortions would have been necessary. For I found out something about the F.VIIa that no written account had thought to mention: Behind the toilet was a luggage compartment. And that compartment was reached by a door on the starboard side of the aircraft —the opposite side to the passenger door and, therefore, invisible in all the photographs I had seen of Loewenstein's plane.

I waited impatiently for Mr. van de Noort to return from his lunch. Did he have the door to the luggage space, by any chance? Obligingly, he disappeared into the back room again and fetched it. It was almost identical to the passenger door, differing only in the absence of a window and the beveling to one top corner. The lock was a patent key arrangement, operated only from the outside.

I located the area of the fuselage space frame where the luggage compartment would have been and measured it carefully. The starboard door was of full height, so there would have been no problem of access, but was the volume of the space sufficient? With a wondering museum official looking on, I carried the passenger door across and slotted it into the empty hole. Then I grinned with delight. It fit perfectly.

Suddenly, *everything* had begun to fit.

20

Y OU NEED luck when researching a book. Experience and dogged persistence are a help, but without luck, it can all count for nothing. I had been lucky in Amsterdam; now, as I returned to London feeling absurdly pleased with myself, I got a message that seemed to prove that I was on a winning streak. *Robert Little, Loewenstein's mechanic, was alive.*

At least, Chopper Hatchett thought he was alive. Chopper re-entered my life with a telephone call, the wires vibrating with excitement. It seemed that he had been caught up in the Loewenstein legend almost as completely as I was and had been doing some digging on his own account. As a spare-time activity, he helped to look after the interests of his fellow pensioners from British Airways— the lineal successor to Imperial Airways—and hence had access to the computer at Heathrow Airport containing all their names. It had occurred to him, as it should have occurred to me, that if Robert Little was still alive, he might well be on that computer. So he had gone to search the files.

"Would you like to know Bob Little's address?" asked Chopper, casually. I nearly dropped the telephone. He gave it to me, right down to the last letter of the postal code. Robert Little, it appeared, had retired to the small seaside town of Littlehampton on the south coast of England.

I knew Littlehampton well; it was less than ten miles away from where I had grown up, and I had often gone to play there as a child, riding my bicycle along the flat and windy coastal road. I remembered the amusement park where I squandered my pocket money on the Ghost Train and the Whip and the stomach-wrenching roller coaster, and where for sixpence you could still see What the Butler Saw. I remembered being disappointed, even then, in the butler's ocular achievements: flickering pictures of ladies in 1920s underwear, cavorting coyly in glorious sepia, were not much of a turn-on for a ten-year-old. All gone now, I supposed. But what I remembered most vividly about Littlehampton was the wreck. It lay on a white sand beach on the far side of the River Arun estuary, the rotting hulk of a sailing ship, perhaps a hundred feet in length, abandoned and forgotten by all but the wheeling gulls and small boys like me.

To climb on to the bleached deck of that ship, to hold the worn spokes of the wheel and explore the dark recesses of the crab-infested hold, was the stuff of dreams. I had once sailed to faraway places on that ship, flying the skull-and-crossbones from its masthead and buccaneering through the fantasies of boyhood. And now I was going back to Littlehampton, chasing an adult fantasy. I was on my way to see a man who I thought might be a murderer. The prospect stopped me dead in my tracks. How could I manage such an encounter? Robert Little would be an old man, secure in his secret for more than half a century. How would he react to a perfect stranger knocking on his door and accusing him of murder? How would I feel if he suffered a heart attack? What would I do if he denied everything, as he probably would? The anxieties I had suffered at the outset of my quest, and long since forgotten, came crowding back now that I faced the actual prospect of meeting one of the men on that airplane. What if he sued me for libel? For a brief moment, I was tempted to forget the whole thing. But curiosity is a powerful master. I decided to write Robert Little a letter, setting up an interview on some innocent pretext. Once inside the door, I would simply have to play it by ear. I tore up several drafts before I finally decided that my letter struck the right balance of honest innocence concealing downright deceit:

Dear Mr. Little,

I am currently writing a book on the early days of British commercial aviation, and have been interviewing many of those who served with Imperial Airways in the 1920s and '30s. It has been gratifying to find so many still with us, and rewarding to discover their memories so sharp. I understand that you yourself served as a flight engineer and would be most grateful if you would agree to talk about your experiences. I am sure they would add much to my book. I shall be coming down to Littlehampton on Saturday afternoon and hope it will be convenient for me to see you then. If this is not so, perhaps you would be kind enough to telephone me at the above number.

I look forward to seeing you.

Yours sincerely,
William Norris

I read and reread the letter, signed it, and addressed the envelope with no more than a slight sinking feeling. I was not particularly proud of my deception, but it ought to serve the purpose, and at least I had told no lies. Just a great deal less than the whole truth.

There were four days to go before I was due to make the trip to Littlehampton. In the event I did not have to wait so long, for on the Thursday I got a telephone call from a very puzzled Mr. Robert Little. He was flattered by my interest, he said, but did I really want to interview a former British Airways ticket clerk who had recently retired after serving the airline since 1960? He would be delighted to see me, but having never been a flight engineer and having no recollection of aviation in the 1920s, he doubted if he could be of much help.

I knew not whether to laugh or cry. All that anticipation, all that worry and scheming, and at the end of the day I had got the wrong man. I should have realized that the name was not all that uncommon, and there might well be other Robert Littles on the British Airways computer. But I had become so driven, my focus so narrow and my enthusiasm so high, that the thought had never occurred to me.

I thanked the wrong Mr. Little for his courtesy, apologized for troubling him, and went back to the drawing board.

———

CHOPPER HATCHETT SEEMED to be more distressed at this minor debacle than I was. Like some lean and ancient bulldog, he had gotten his teeth into the problem and would not let go. He vowed to return to his precious computer at the first opportunity and batter its electronic brains into submission until it came up with the right answer. I thanked him and wished him luck, but I did not rate his chances highly. Something told me that Robert Little was long departed.

Four days later, the telephone rang again. It was Chopper.

He had failed to find any trace of the elusive engineer, but he had come across a Mrs. Julie Little in the files. She lived at Wallington, just south of London in the Surrey commuter belt. Was I interested?

Why not?

I was not about to make a fool of myself with another phony letter, but it was worth a telephone call on the off chance. To my surprise, the frail voice that answered had a distinct American accent.

"Mrs. Julie Little?" I inquired.

"This is she."

I introduced myself.

"Forgive me for troubling you, but I'm trying to trace a Mr. Robert Little who flew with a man named Alfred Loewenstein back in 1928. I wondered if by any chance he might be a relative of yours?" I anticipated blank incomprehension or a curt denial. In anticipation I began mumbling some inanity about coincidence of names. She cut me short.

"Why yes," she said, "that was my husband, Bob. But I'm afraid he died a long time ago. What did you want to know?"

What indeed? Actually, madam, I have a strong suspicion that your late husband was part of a successful plot to kill Mr. Loewenstein, and I want to know if he ever confessed to you.

But there are some things you do not say to widowed ladies of advanced years. I temporized.

"I'm writing a book about Loewenstein," I said truthfully, "and I want to find out all I can. I'm sure your husband must have talked about him ..."

"You mean about how he died, and that sort of thing?" Mrs. Julie Little was smart as a whip. She knew exactly what I was driving at.

"Well, yes," I said. I was not even going to get to first base. There was steel in that gentle voice, and if Robert Little had made any confessions to his wife, she was not going to see me, let alone tell me about it.

But I was wrong. Mrs. Little was hesitant, but she agreed to an interview. At the appointed time next day, I knocked on the door of her small suburban house and was ushered into a living room crammed with memorabilia of her dead husband. On a shelf in one corner stood a near-life-size bust of a young girl, carved in some black stone. It was finely done, and the model had clearly been very beautiful. She saw me looking at it.

"That's me," said Mrs. Julie Little.

I looked again at the bust, and I looked at the frail old lady who stood beside me and tried to keep the disbelief from my eyes. Then she smiled and I could see that it was true. The bone structure was still there, and the way she held her head. And I knew that whatever cruel tales the mirror might tell, in her own mind it lied. The basalt truth was sitting on that shelf.

We sat down, and I laid my pocket tape recorder on the table in full view and switched it on. Of all my interviews, this was one I needed to have on the record. Mrs. Little looked at it nervously, the red light blinking as I made some soothing (and truthful) explanation about my poor memory. But she raised no objection and began to tell her story. She had been Julie Johnson in July 1928, born in St. Louis, Missouri, the daughter of Lewis Charles Johnson, a corporation lawyer. When she was still a child, the family moved to New York, and her father became very rich. The source of his wealth was oil; it provided Rolls-Royce cars in the garage and genuine Rembrandts on the walls of the family apartment. But to the vivacious Julie, a child of the "flapper" era, it was dullsville. She wanted to go on the stage and began to take dancing lessons from the wife of a friend. "I always adored dancing," she said.

———

LEWIS JOHNSON, rich and respectable, was horrified when he found out about his daughter's ambition. He promptly packed her off to Paris, out of harm's way, where it was arranged that she should stay with a French family. There she went to the Sorbonne, where she studied fencing and sculpture, which was the origin of the bust and the cause of a few more grey hairs on her father's head.

Julie Johnson was having a good time. On July 5, 1928, she was on holiday with friends in the South of France when she picked up a newspaper and read the account of Loewenstein's death.

"I was sure they were guilty. Guilty as hell," she told me.

I was sipping a cup of tea at that moment. I almost choked. *"Who* did you think were as 'guilty as hell'?" I asked, hardly daring to hear the answer.

"The crew," she replied. "My husband. Well, he wasn't my husband then, of course. Why should they land on the beach? I thought it was all most peculiar."

That seemed to be the understatement of the year. I tried to picture the scene: the lovely, vivacious young heiress, scanning a newspaper on a Mediterranean beach, and reaching an instant verdict of murder on a man she had never met but would later marry. It was bizarre. In spite of the bonds that must have formed during many years of marriage—and the evidence of that was all around me—the memory that stuck in Julie Little's mind, the first thing she chose to tell a stranger, was her initial conviction that Robert Little and Donald Drew were killers.

By the time they did meet, Julie's suspicions must have subsided. Or else the charm of Robert Little was sufficient to override them. It happened the following summer, ironically enough at Croydon Airport, from which Loewenstein had taken off on his fatal flight.

Robert Little was twenty-eight years old when he met Julie Johnson. He had been born and brought up in Cumberland, a rural county in the northwest corner of England, and been educated at the minor public school of Sedburgh. Which meant that his parents must have been reasonably well-to-do, a public school in England being precisely the reverse of its American counterpart and demanding the payment of tuition.

Little's interest in flying began early. At Sedburgh, he was a member of the school's Air Training Corps, but luckily for him the 1914-18 war ended before he could join the RAF. Robert, who was a gutsy lad, probably did not see it that way. Deprived of the opportunity to fly in action, he did the next best thing. Together with his brother, Graham, he bought an aircraft, an Avro 504 biplane. They started up a barnstorming operation, Border Aviation, giving joyrides to innocent civilians up and down the north of England. It was nearly, but not quite, as dangerous as being in action.

Robert was the mechanic/navigator of the team, and though he got his own pilot's license in the mid-'20s, navigation was to be his major forte. He received his navigator's certificate from Johnny Johnson, commander of the ill-fated R-101 airship, and enlivened his flying hours with wing walking, parachute jumping, and various other stunts common to the barnstorming circuses of the time.

Then, in 1923, the Little brothers decided to try for the big time. They flew south in their trusty Avro and set up Surrey Flying Services in Croydon, the center of British civil aviation. It was a small, tightly knit community. Inevitably, Robert Little met Donald Drew, who was flying for Imperial Airways.

The two men had much in common; both were handsome, adventurous, lady-killing types of the leather-helmet-and-silk-scarf brigade, and they seem to have formed an instant friendship. When Drew was seconded to become Loewenstein's chief pilot in the spring of 1928—his predecessor, Captain R.H. McIntosh, having been killed in a flying accident—it was only natural that he should wangle the job of second pilot and mechanic for his friend Robert Little.

When that job came to an abrupt end on July 4, the two appear to have separated. Little did not go back to barnstorming, but somehow found the capital to set up his own aviation consultancy business at 148 Strand, in the heart of fashionable London.

Business seems to have been good. In those pioneering days, with new air routes being opened up all the time and virtually no navigational aids on the ground, Little's skills as a navigator were in demand. The following year he was approached by the Duchess of Bedford, a redoubtable lady who had just become the oldest woman to fly solo at the age of sixty-four, to navigate her attempt to break the record for a flight from London to Cape Town and back again. The aircraft chosen by the Duchess was the Fokker F.VIIa, with which Little was all too familiar. Save for having one engine instead of three, it was identical to that used by Loewenstein.

It was while planning the route for this trip that Robert Little met Julie Johnson, the girl who believed he was a killer. She was staying with her sister and brother-in-law at Croydon's Aerodrome Hotel, on the fringe of the airfield, where they had taken a suite. Julie was still a rich young heiress then. In a few months' time, after the Wall Street crash, all her father's money would be gone, the Rembrandts stripped from the walls, and the Rolls-Royces sold to pay the creditors. But in the summer of 1929, Julie was still enjoying herself.

The party had hired a car, a Morris Cowley. It was a lemon. Sometimes it worked, and sometimes it didn't, and on this particular day, when they were headed for the golf course, it refused to start at all. Julie's escort and her brother-in-law sweated over it to no avail.

Enter Robert Little, smoking a large cigar. "This is right up my street," he said. He leaned inside the hood and had it going in a moment.

"The other men went off in a huff," Julie recalled at a distance of fifty-six years. "He offered to show us the way to the golf course. My sister said we knew it, but I kicked her and said, 'Let him show us the way.' He had just bought a brand new Riley, and we had trouble keeping up with him. He winked at me when we got there, and that was that. We got engaged just before he left for Cape Town, and we got married soon after he got back."

Little was lucky to survive that trip. With the duchess on board and a Captain Barnard as first pilot, the Fokker made three forced landings in the African bush. Nevertheless, they flew an average of a thousand miles a day on the outward journey and maintained that pace for eight days on the way back, which was a considerable achievement. Finally, shortly after leaving Sofia, an oil line fractured and forced them down once more.

The record attempt was a failure, but Robert Little returned home a hero nonetheless. He was filthy and unshaven, and Julie put him straight into the bathtub. When the welcoming committee arrived, they found him there, fast asleep.

The couple was married in Paris in 1930. Robert Little told his future father-in-law when they became engaged that he could hardly afford to keep Julie in the manner to which she was accustomed and had been assured that there would always be plenty of money. Lewis Johnson had spoken too soon.

Nonetheless, there was no sign of poverty in the new Little household. After a splendid wedding, attended by virtually all the pilots from Imperial Airways, including Donald Drew, the couple settled down in a Paris house that featured a pillared living room with an ornamental pool in the middle. It was not bad for a barnstorming flight mechanic.

———

IN THE YEARS THAT FOLLOWED, Robert Little carried on with his freelance consultancy business, made an unsuccessful attempt to fly the Atlantic in a Dornier, and finally joined the staff of the Air Ministry. There he spent most of his time teaching navigation to airline pilots, and he continued the same job with Coastal Command and later in the United States during the Second World War. When that ended, he went back into the Air Ministry, working on research and development.

Robert Little died in August 1970, a few months after his seventieth birthday. He had long suffered from heart trouble, but it was cancer that finally killed him, and Julie nursed him for the final year. During our interview, she looked back on that time almost with affection.

"He had been away such a lot," she told me, wistfully. "It was only in that year that we really got to know each other. He never complained of the pain. He was absolutely wonderful."

Tattered cuttings, yellowing letters, and testimonials dragged from an old cardboard box backed up Julie's story. Robert Little had led a daring and distinguished life, apparently beloved by all. He had been a brilliant navigator, a patient teacher, and a witty raconteur. Was it possible that such a man had yielded to one moment of temptation in his youth and been part of the Loewenstein plot?

Was it possible that he had been, as Julie Johnson first thought, "as guilty as hell" and that she had been too blinded by love to care? Improbable, perhaps. But not impossible.

———

ONE THING I badly needed to know: Had Robert Little, unlike everyone else on that aircraft, talked about the Loewenstein incident in later years? Julie did not seem to me the sort of woman who would be content with silence on the subject, however deeply in love. Yes, she said, Bob had told her what had happened. I pinned back my ears. It was not first-hand information, but it was as close as I was likely to get.

Her husband, said Julie Little, had liked Alfred Loewenstein. Before the final flight he had talked with him about the weather. He had also known about the flimsy door fastening on the Fokker, having had it pointed out by a friend, Charles Dickson, some two days earlier.

At the time Loewenstein disappeared, she went on, her husband had been at the controls.

A few minutes before, he had glanced over his shoulder, looking through the glass partition into the cabin behind, and had seen Loewenstein remove his jacket, collar, and tie. Then the financier had stood at the window, as if gasping for air. "Bob was convinced that he must have been poisoned," she said.

After Hodgson had passed the note, saying that Loewenstein had disappeared, Little had handed control of the plane back to Donald Drew. It had been Drew's decision to land on the beach, taken, Little had told his wife, in a moment of panic. They had made no attempt to turn around and search. "It was their amazement at the time," she said. "They just wanted to get down and see what had happened—to examine the door. It was so amazing, because they knew they couldn't push the door open."

Julie Little's story ended there. Her husband, she claimed, had never told her what had happened on the beach, had never mentioned the Brussels inquiry or the "experiment" on the journey home when he and Drew were supposed to have opened the door without difficulty. Nor had he given any real explanation of why they had not flown to St. Inglevert, except the suggestion that Drew had panicked. Nothing I knew of Donald Drew, or of Robert Little for that matter, suggested that they were the panicking kind. Frankly, I did not believe a word of it, but there are limits to how far one can go in cross-examining fragile old ladies. I tried every interviewing trick I knew, trying to dislodge some admission that her Bobby had told all.

It was no use. If Julie Little knew more than she was telling, and I was sure that she did, she was going to keep her secret.

But there was one other thing. "Did you know," she asked me, "that Loewenstein was making notes before he disappeared?"

No, I did not know that. Furthermore, the information from those on board the aircraft, principally Hodgson, had been that he was reading a book before getting up and going to the toilet. Hodgson had made a point of saying that Loewenstein had marked his place.

"Oh yes," said Julie brightly. "Bob found them scattered on the floor of the aircraft after they landed. That was what convinced him that Loewenstein had not killed himself like they were saying. Bob had picked these notes up, and he knew he hadn't. It wasn't a suicide note or anything like that."

I held my breath. "I suppose he handed them to the French police when they questioned him?" I said.

"Oh, no. He stuffed them in his pocket. He never gave them to anyone." She rummaged in the cardboard box. "I've got them here. Would you like to see them?"

21

IT WAS AN EXTRAORDINARY FEELING. I held in my hand the last things that Alfred Loewenstein had ever written, the last things he touched before dying. And apart from Robert and Julie Little, no one had seen them or touched them in more than half a century. Even if they proved to be worthless from the point of view of content, they were still an experience to savor. Did I imagine it, or was there something, some psychic force adhering to those sheets of paper, telling me to go on with my quest? A foolish thought. I do not believe in that sort of thing.

I had no doubt that the notes were genuine. Specimens of Loewenstein's handwriting were not common, but I had obtained several samples on company documents from the public records office at Kew. There was no mistaking that florid, aggressive hand, in spite of the distortion that must have been caused by the vibration of the Fokker's engines. Since he was known to prefer dictation, and had two stenographers on board, I guessed that in spite of the attempts at sound-proofing, Loewenstein had found the noise in the cabin too loud to make himself heard and had scribbled the notes for later transcription.

Hodgson had made the same point when he claimed to have written down the message to the pilot announcing that Loewenstein was missing—though in the light of my research, I doubted if *that* note had ever existed.

The Loewenstein notes were in pencil, written on sheets of pale green, fine-lined graph paper measuring 7-1/2 by 5-1/8 inches. Serrations along the upper edge indicated that they had probably been torn from a spiral-backed notebook. In all there were thirty-five pages, so Loewenstein must have spent most of the flight before his disappearance in writing them. Some pages were full, some contained only a few words, and even the former were so widely spaced that few had more than thirty words scrawled across them.

The writing was hard to decipher, but that was not the major problem. The main difficulty was that the pages were not numbered. If they had been scattered on the floor of the Fokker—and I asked myself why that should have been if Loewenstein had made his supposed calm progress to the toilet—they must have become shuffled like a pack of cards when Little picked them up. A quick glance showed me that hardly one sheet was consecutive with another.

This might not have mattered so much if Loewenstein had been writing a complete draft of his letters or even if he had prefaced each one with the name of the addressee, but he had not done so. What I held was a sort of aide-mémoire from which he intended to dictate. To make some sense of what he had written was going to require time and patience and a certain degree of ingenuity. I needed to take those notes away.

I did not foresee any problem; Mrs. Little had been becoming more friendly and relaxed as our interview progressed. But I presumed too much. During the ten minutes or so that I had been studying the notes, she had begun to nurture a deep suspicion that what I intended to write about her late husband might not be altogether to his credit. She was also remembering what she had said earlier. And when I asked if I might borrow the notes, at least long enough to make copies, she refused. All my pleas were to of no avail: Mrs. Julie Little took the notes, wrapped them up in their protective plastic, and put them back in the cardboard box.

Then she stabbed an accusing finger toward my tape recorder.

"Is that thing switched on?"

I admitted that it was.

"Have you been taking down everything I said?"

I admitted that, too, mildly puzzled at the question. She had been perfectly well aware that I was recording the interview, and I wondered why she chose to make an issue of it now. I was not left wondering for long.

"I want to hear it," Mrs. Little said firmly. "Especially that bit at the beginning when I said I thought they were guilty."

Oh dear. I had been afraid that might happen. I played back the offending section. It was all there, clear as a bell. She was aghast. "But you can't use that," she said. "That sounds as if I believed my Bobby did it."

I agreed. That was exactly what it sounded like. Furthermore, though I did not say so, I suspected it was the truth. But now I was in a quandary. I had no wish to hurt Mrs. Little, whom I genuinely liked and admired. On the other hand, that slip of the tongue was too important to be ignored. I decided to try for a compromise. "How would you prefer to put it, now that you've had time to think about it?" I asked.

"You could say that I thought it was very fishy," she said after a moment's consideration. So I promised to do that, and I have. Without prejudice, as the lawyers say. I refrained from promising not to use the original version as well.

It took a lot more persuading before she would finally agree to let me borrow the Loewenstein notes. I had to leave my tape recorder and its precious contents behind as security, promising to return next day. Then I spent an anxious twenty-four hours wondering if Mrs. Little knew how to erase a tape and, if she did, whether she would do so.

But my fears were groundless. I returned to find everything intact, and Mrs. Little got her notes back, duly copied. Now all I had to do was to try and find out what Loewenstein was writing in his last moments on earth.

It was an exhausting business.

I began by deciphering each page, leaving gaps where Loewenstein's scrawl defeated me. They I spread out all the pages on the floor, trying to fit them together like a huge jigsaw puzzle. But with no beginning, and no obvious end, the task was next to impossible. There were, it was true, some familiar names to lend encouragement. Pam and Szarvasy cropped up; so did Frank Tiarks and the mysterious Mr. Fischer who was so much distrusted by Norbert Bogden. There was also a Victor Emanuel mentioned, which confused me more than a little. I thought at first that Loewenstein had been writing to the late king of Italy, which would have been perfectly in character, but later discovered that Victor Emanuel was a wealthy young American financier who shared Loewenstein's interest in racehorses and public utility companies. Emanuel's obituary in *The New York Times*, published on his death in November 1960 at the age of sixty-two, described him as "a man of mysterious intrigue." There seemed to be a lot of those about.

Still, nothing made much sense. It was going to be difficult, I knew, unless Loewenstein had been writing about a deal of which I had intimate knowledge, to get much understanding of what he was trying to say. But I hoped to salvage something comprehensible from the disconnected jottings. Where inspiration failed, perhaps science would have something to contribute: I put everything on to my word processor.

Using the cunning device that moves blocks of type around at will, I arranged and re-arranged the pages. Now that I no longer had to cope with Loewenstein's scrawl at the same time, they slowly began to make some sort of sense. I was looking for links—words at the beginning and end of each page that might conceivably fit to others to make coherent sentences.

Little by little, they came together. Not all of them—at the end of the day, I was still left with a few cryptic notes which bore no relation to anything else—but enough to indicate that Loewenstein in the last moments of his life was still setting up deals. There was certainly no hint of impending suicide. The last vestige of doubt that he might, after all, have forced open that door and jumped to his death had been removed.

I quickly realized that what I had was not one letter but several, interspersed with memoranda to remind the writer to contact this person or that.

Where to start? I ran through the pages until I found one, the only one, that seemed to have any kind of a heading. "Wednesday evening" was scrawled in the top right-hand corner. Well, that at least made sense. July 4, the day of Loewenstein's death, had been a Wednesday.

Then, infuriatingly, came the single word: "Re."

"Re" *what?* I wondered. The notes did not say. Loewenstein must have known the answer too well to need to jot it down. There followed six lines which I could read fairly clearly:

"As you know we have loans with Yale and Langley and another one, if smaller, with Spinks and Hazerton . . ." I was not sure about the proper names, making an inspired guess on the basis of Loewenstein's handwriting elsewhere in the notes. In the context, they were probably merchant banks and might still be in existence. It should be possible to check.

I ran through the notes on the glowing screen once again, trying to find some phrase that might follow in logical sequence. Halfway down there was a page that began with two words: "being called." That made sense, I thought. Loewenstein had borrowed money and was being asked to pay it back. It fitted with what I knew about his last and latest business problems.

———

THEN CAME AN UNCOMPLETED SENTENCE, which had been crossed out with a quick stroke of the pencil but was still quite legible. It read: *"Telephone to Fischer to ask Pam-Szarvasy why, if this telegram—"* Damn the man, I thought. If he was going to interrupt his own train of thought like that, what chance did I have? There was nothing more on that page. What I had to find now was a page that began with a fresh sentence that related to the borrowing of money.

I found two. The first read: "Of course I am rather anxious to be relieved of that responsibility, and I am awfully sorry to trouble you to obtain agreement of our other banker . . ."

"Banker" could have been "broker." Either way, it sounded as though Loewenstein was in trouble and was asking a favor of someone. The second page that could have fitted read as follows: "And we owe Schroder bank between 3 and 4 million dollars in all in case we don't enter into a contract with then for a contract for a loan we don't . . ." I had the feeling that this was probably two sentences run together, and badly phrased at that, but Loewenstein had not favored me with many punctuation marks.

Now I had a fresh problem because the trail had split in two. I made my best guess and chose the first, which seemed to follow more logically. To this I could add another page: "for a short period. Please enquire discreetly as we don't want to do anything that may hurt our credit in New York, and of course we . . ." And after that seemed to come: "much prefer either to issue our bonds, or even to have a loan from the investments of Mr. — [the name was indecipherable]. For your formal . . ."

The next few pages were relatively easy to find. When I stitched them together in the word processor, this is what I had:

Wednesday evening.

Re:

As you know, we have loans with Yale and Langley and another one, if smaller, with Spinks and Hazerton being called. Of course, I am rather anxious to be relieved of that responsibility, and I am awfully sorry to trouble you to obtain agreement of our other banker for a short period. Please enquire discreetly, as we don't want to do anything that may hurt our credit in New York, and of course we much prefer either to issue our bonds, or even to have a loan from the investments of Mr. —. For your formal and absolutely confidential information, we have got an offer for all the shares we have got in our treasury, but we are hesitating to accept it because we must have shares for our bond issue, and also we believe that our shares are undervalued.

It made sense. At least, I thought it made sense. But try as I might I could not find any remaining pages that fitted into the same context. I came to the conclusion that the letter ended there, and I would have to start again to find the beginning of the next one.

The heading this time seemed to be "Saty." An abbreviation for Saturday? A letter that he intended to post later in the week? Or perhaps that one scrawled word was something different, possibly a name. The aircraft must have been vibrating badly at that moment, because Loewenstein's writing had become more like the meanderings of a drunken spider than ever. I did my best to transcribe what followed: *"According to our conversation which we had with Tiarks today* [Loewenstein seemed to have an inclination toward the royal "we"] *all find strongly that we prefer to buy common stock rather than non-participating preference stock."*

That was all right, I thought. Aside from the Belgian's rather stilted use of English, it confirmed what I knew of his business habits. He liked the type of shares that could give him control of companies, which preference stock would not. I searched for the next likely page and found it. The letter went on:

And I agree that no further purchases should be made without consulting Pam and Szarvasy, and if you like your friends at Schroder bank could receive the same remuneration as before, same participation in profits, and I will find my own guarantee to them that are members of the syndicate. But I insist that you do, too, and obtain necessary authorisation. Of course, Rorke would keep you informed of any purchase made, so that I think that our syndicate agreement could be much more simplified.

In fact, I have financed all the purchases myself up to date, and we owe Schroder Bank between 3 and 4 million dollars in all. In case we don't enter into a contract with them for a loan, which we don't want, the syndicate bought by me would produce their shares at any moment if and when required. Schroders publish their balance sheet half-yearly, and it may be that it suits them that we repay them.

On the other hand, we have also to consider that the manager of the syndicate under Belgian law cannot vote for other people. This difficulty may be overcome, because we should sell by contract note for immediate delivery. We would sell the shares on the 22nd, or three days before the meeting, buying them back three days after the meeting.

Another clause to which some of the bankers have objection was that syndicate members could borrow against the shares. They prefer no borrowings of money when required . . .

It was here that I ran against a blank wall. None of the remaining pages seemed to relate to this sentence in any way, and I could assume only that a section of the notes was missing or, possibly, that this was the point at which

Loewenstein got up to make his last, short walk. Nor was there any indication of a new letter beginning on the seventeen pages that remained to be slotted into place, though one or two were clearly consecutive. I struggled for hours and then gave up, in imminent danger of word-blindness. No doubt others have a greater talent for this sort of thing than I have. They are more than welcome to try. The following are the balance of Loewenstein's notes:

> make our issue of bonds very quickly or we don't make a contract with the underwriters of this issue, we want however to . . .

> pay at least all the shares from Langley Hazerton and Spinks, specially in bad days we don't want to have shares . . .

> and we only took that pref stock to be agreeable to you, but it is not a question that we don't have full confidence in your undertakings . . .

> agreement, and to try for balance Commonwealth Edison. I told you before that I did not desire to trust your being in pref stock . . .

> to make your task easier I reduce option price to 325 for 1st third, 400 for second, 500 for third. If really this may help you I would . . .

> and his reply which meets with my approval. In fact, if there is any possibility of selling around par or even 99 we . . .

should sell and try to limit your organisation up to 10,000 Mid-West Common, which will have to zenith at a price to be fixed by mutual ...

prepared to accept these terms, but only if we could get very quick decisions because if not we may have to change all our plans ...

We can also give you 5 million in Railway shares like New York Central and Allied Chemicals. So that we have ...

American securities for any loan ...

and I will show him drafts . . . Telephone losses . . . Complete (illegible) of Holding to Szarvasy ...

Victor Emanuel's telegram ... Tiarks suggests this ...

Mrs. Maline Graham ... Mrs. Munnings ... how are the new offices ...

Fischer. What reply has he given to Hamill . . . Bull Fischer (indecipherable) to me your telegrams ...

Telegraph Hardy...

Tiarks. Speak about sellings ...

And that was all. Random jottings, meaningless now at this distance in time. Perhaps it was too much to expect that Loewenstein's last words would contain some momentous revelation. After all, when he scrawled these notes he could have had no knowledge that they *were* to be his last words. But the fact that he wrote them was important in itself, for it seemed to prove conclusively that he had not committed suicide. They portrayed a man still wheeling and dealing, a man in some difficulty, but certainly not at the end of his tether.

So why did Robert Little fail to hand them over to the authorities? He had two clear opportunities: when questioned initially by French police at Fort Mardyk, and again when called to the Brussels inquiry. He took neither, allowing the possibility of suicide to cloud the issue when there was clear evidence in his possession to prove otherwise. He certainly knew the significance of the notes; his widow had told me so. If there were no plot, if Little were truly innocent, surely the natural thing would have been to disclose every possible piece of evidence. But Little had deliberately withheld them.

Was it possible that he hoped to make some profit out of them at a future date? Julie Little had told me that some years later, her husband had contacted Madeleine Loewenstein, told her that he had the notes in his possession, and asked for permission to publish them. Madeleine had refused to give her consent.

I wondered about that.

If Loewenstein's grieving widow had been part of the conspiracy, which I thought unlikely but conceivable, could the notes have formed the basis of a blackmail attempt? After all, numerous experiments by that time had knocked the Brussels verdict of accidental death well and truly on the head, and evidence that ruled out suicide would presumably have been somewhat unwelcome. It might have led to some real inquiries being carried out. I also found it surprising, if Julie Little's version was true, that Madeleine had not asked for the return of the notes when she learned they were in Little's possession. They were, after all, her property and must have had some sentimental value. Come to that, why had Little not simply sent them to her, if he was the upright fellow that his widow insisted? Why had they lain in that cardboard box for more than half a century?

It was intriguing, and I knew that I would never find the answer for certain. But around Loewenstein's last words I was weaving in my mind the threads of a grim tapestry.

22

I WAS NOW FAIRLY certain that I knew the modus operandi of Loewenstein's death, which meant that those on board the aircraft must have been physically responsible. But I did not believe for a moment that they had acted on their own initiative. It was also possible, indeed probable, that not all of them would have been directly involved. Some might have been bribed into silence by the others and threatened with the dire consequences of being charged as accessories to murder if they opened their mouths. In England in 1928, the penalty for murder was hanging, and accessories before or after the crime were subject to the same dire consequences as those who committed it. Given the fact that they were all on board the aircraft, the guilt of one would become the guilt of all if it became suspected that Loewenstein had been murdered. The deed was done: Better to take the money and keep their mouths tightly closed.

To my mind, the real villains were those who inspired the killing, who planned it in the foreknowledge that there was a loophole in the law and who were able to ensure—

presumably by bribery at a high level in French officialdom —that the on-site investigation was abruptly terminated. This would have required three things: intelligence, influence, and a great deal of money.

And there was still the question of motive. Murder is most often committed for jealousy, revenge, or money. And the greatest of these is money—which is why I had been following the financial trail. So who gained from Loewenstein's death? There was Madeleine, of course: She and her son stood to inherit a very large fortune.

It could be argued, however, that Madeleine already had everything she could possibly want in the material sense. Whatever else he may have been, Loewenstein was certainly not niggardly. He enabled his wife to live in the utmost luxury. True, having money by the grace and favor of even the most generous husband is not quite the same as having it yourself, especially if the marriage is less than satisfactory in other ways, but does the difference amount to a motive for murder?

Supporters of the "Madeleine did it" theory, and they exist, point out that Loewenstein's assets, though great, were wasting. The size of his paper fortune had been halved in a matter of weeks, and things were not going well. One more catastrophic loss of confidence on the stock markets and even *his* bright star might be extinguished.

Looked at from this perspective, Madeleine Loewenstein could be seen to face a dilemma. Alive, her husband was a gamble. The splendid houses, the jewels and haute-couture dresses, the friends in high society, could vanish overnight through circumstances over which she had no control. Dead, on the other hand—dead at that very moment—his estate was still worth many millions.

But would any wife do such a thing without some other factor being involved? I had no evidence that Madeleine hated her husband, though there was every indication that she was sexually deprived within the marriage. She and Alfred had occupied separate bedrooms since at least 1926; there were frequent periods of separation; and her husband was so obsessed with his business and his horses that he can have had little time or inclination for sex, in or out of the marriage bed. The fact that they were devout Roman Catholics and yet had produced only one child was not proof positive that they rarely slept together, but it could suggest that the physical side of their marriage had been less than passionate for a long time.

So could there have been another man to provide the stimulus to turn frustration and greed into an act of murder? Was I looking at an eternal triangle, and was Donald Drew at its apex? Madeleine was certainly a beautiful woman, and Drew was known to be an incorrigible Don Juan. But socially they were miles apart, and I found it hard to see Madeleine as a latter-day Lady Chatterley. If they were having an affair, they were certainly being very discreet about it—there was not a breath of gossip on the subject in the village. Nor had I found any sign of a continued association between them after Loewenstein's death, apart from Drew's role in the sale of the aircraft. His actions immediately after Loewenstein's disappearance—hiring a tugboat to search for the body—did seem somewhat above the call of duty. But perhaps Donald Drew had simply been that kind of man. Perhaps.

A greater obstacle to the "eternal triangle" theory was Norbert Bogden's firm conviction that Madeleine had not been very interested in sex. And he had known the lady. There was also the constant presence of the enigmatic Didi in the Loewenstein household to suggest to someone with a nasty mind that Madeleine's sexual tastes may have been less conventional.

So what of jealousy or revenge? There was no shortage of people who disliked and feared Loewenstein for his ruthless business dealings. There may well have been many with old scores to settle. But if there were any who felt strongly enough to murder the man, my inquiries had failed to uncover them. With one possible exception: Henri Dreyfus hated Loewenstein with a passion. He faced a potentially ruinous libel action, and he was probably rich and influential enough to have engineered both crime and cover-up.

Yet somehow the nature of the affair did not jell with the character of Dreyfus. He was hot-blooded, bad-tempered, and outspoken, and one could certainly envisage him taking a revolver and pulling the trigger. But the cold calculation that must have gone into the plot that ended Loewenstein's life did not fit what I knew of Henri Dreyfus, blabbermouth extraordinary.

He might have danced on the Belgian's grave, but I did not believe he put him there.

I was left with the possibility that someone had made a great deal of money out of Loewenstein's death other than by inheritance. But how could that be? It was undeniable that the stock market had crashed when the news of his disappearance broke. Millions had been lost, not won.

There were two ways in which a profit might have been made out of the situation. The first would have been for anyone with prior knowledge of Loewenstein's demise to have sold shares in International Holdings the previous day, when they stood at $215, and to buy them back cheaply when panic struck the market. Since the company was basically sound and the share price could be expected to recover quite soon, a lot of money could be made that way. It was a feasible scenario, but had it happened? The only evidence that it might have done so came from *The Times of*

London for July 6, 1928, which recorded that although the price of International Holdings had fallen during the course of the previous day to $115, "a large block is reported to have changed hands as low as $100." This big purchase had driven the price back up again, and the stock had closed at $145.

Someone had made a killing, but who? At this distance in time, there seemed no way to find out.

The second method by which money might have been made was through insurance. On the same day, July 6, *The Times* published a story, FROM OUR INSURANCE CORRESPONDENT, which contained some interesting speculations:

> Large insurances are understood to have been placed in the London Market covering the risk of the premature death of Captain Loewenstein. These insurances are believed to have been effected in connection with companies with which he was closely associated, or to have been made by shareholders in his different enterprises. They are distinct from any ordinary life insurances that may have been placed with companies.
>
> A total of £100,000 was mentioned yesterday for the special policies, but enquiries suggested that this figure was probably an exaggeration and that a more reasonable sum would be about £50,000.

This was somewhat inconclusive. Even allowing for the forty-fold depreciation in the value of money between 1928 and the time of writing, I had great doubt that either of these sums, divided between several policies, would provide a sufficient motive for murder. However, there was more to come:

Some, at any rate, of the policies effected are known to have been of the ordinary accident type, and they are for the usual period of twelve months. The risk of aeronautics was, however, specifically included.

Rates of premium ranging from three to five per cent were quoted—high rates which took into account the fact that Captain Loewenstein was known to fly frequently. Some of the insurances are known to have been placed within the last few weeks.

Policies for considerable amounts have also been taken out to cover any loss which might be suffered through the depreciation of share values caused by the death of Captain Loewenstein. It appears that the precise wording of these policies varies, but that in certain cases any loss was to be arrived at by comparing the prices ruling on the day before his death and a week afterwards. (My italics.)

My interest quickened. I already knew that the difference in value of Loewenstein's shares on the day before his death, as compared with the prices ruling a week later, had been considerable. In fact, if one merely looked at the Stock Exchange prices, it was huge. International Holdings had come down from $215 to $13 per share, which seemed to indicate that the insurers would have to pay $202 for every share covered by the policies.

With 436,950 shares issued (220,000 of them owned by Loewenstein himself), the potential pay-out would have been a colossal $88,263,000. Then I remembered that there had been a ten-for-one subdivision of the shares during the same week. In order to compare like with like, which the insurers would certainly have done, the $13 figure would have to be multiplied by ten.

This brought the fall in value down to $85 per share, and the potential insurance claim to $37,140,750. If one excluded the shares owned by Loewenstein, which presumably would not have formed part of any such policy, the claim on the remaining 216,950 shares still amounted to a possible $18,440,000, or more than a billion dollars in terms of today's money. It was enough money to murder one's grandmother for, let alone a bumptious Belgian financier. Of course, one had to take into account the probability that only a proportion of the issued shares would have been in the control of those placing the insurance, but even so the potential was enormous. And I had not begun to figure the value of other shares, such as Hydro-Electric Securities, into the calculation. I began to search the cuttings for more references to these mysterious insurance policies.

The New York Times, in a report on July 6 originating from the Associated Press news agency, carried the matter a little further.

"The estimates of the total amount [of the insurance policies]," it said,

> run all the way from £40,000 to £500,000 [between $194,400 and $2,430,000 at the prevailing rate of exchange].

> It was stated that some of these policies specifically included suicide among the risks covered.

> There was no information as to who placed the policies, but in some quarters it was believed that persons holding stock in companies with which the financier was identified had placed them to cover possible losses in the event of his death.

Well, well, well. Just fancy that. Leaving aside the estimates, which were meaningless unless one knew the number of shares involved and their value a week after those stories were written, the inclusion of a suicide risk was fascinating.

No one who knew Loewenstein would have thought it likely that he would take his own life, which was presumably why the underwriters were prepared to accept such an unusual risk, and yet someone had considered it worthwhile to hedge his bet.

If all went according to plan, Loewenstein's death would be ascribed to an accident. If not, and there was a suicide verdict, they would still be covered.

And there was something else about these two accounts: I had the distinct impression, born of experience, that the reporters had known very well who placed the policies. Their phrasing suggested strongly that they, or more likely their editors, had decided it would be safer not to name names. I cursed their prudence. For me, half a century later, those names would have been gold dust.

In the yellowing files of the *Daily News and Westminster Gazette,* long extinct, I found another clue. The financial page for July 10, 1928, carried the following report:

> Captain Loewenstein's disappearance has created a difficult problem for certain British insurance offices which had accepted a number of large personal and accident policies taken out on the financier.
>
> The extent of the policy was so large that the risk was distributed among different companies by reinsurance. For the purpose of claiming on these insurances, the circumstances of the disappearance would have to be fully investigated.

Of course. Why had I not thought of that? The French police might be susceptible to brbes; influence might be brought to bear to prevent a close investigation by authorities elsewhere. But no insurance company was going to pay out thousands or millions of dollars without a very searching inquiry.

A period of intense frustration followed. I began my search with Lloyds of London, reasoning that either the original policies or the reinsurance may have been underwritten by one of their syndicates. And perhaps they were, but after I had spent several days being passed from office to office like a particularly undesirable musical parcel, it soon became clear that I was not going to find any answers at Lloyds.

It was all too long ago; syndicates came and went, and the volume of business was too vast and too ephemeral for any trace to be left. No one could remember anything at all about insurance policies on Alfred Loewenstein. The commercial companies were equally unforthcoming. I emerged with only one piece of information that might be significant: In England it was illegal, and had been since the 1860s, to insure the life of a third party. True, exceptions were sometimes made, as in the case of a company wishing to insure the life of its chief executive or, one broker told me, where the person taking out the insurance was personally known to the syndicate involved.

Suddenly, that unexplained profit of $13,226,137 in the accounts of International Holdings began to assume a vital significance. And Messrs. Pam and Szarvasy would certainly have had close acquaintances in the insurance world.

Having failed with the insurance companies and Lloyds syndicates, I decided to try the loss adjusters: firms whose sole object in life is to investigate the genuineness or otherwise of insurance claims. Surely, Loewenstein's death would have caused one or another of them to be brought in. Surely, a case of such notoriety would have been remembered.

But at the Chartered Institute of Loss Adjusters in the Strand, I drew a blank once again. They referred me to an old gentleman in the West Country, Cato Carter by name, who had worked as an investigator at the time and who had written a book on the history of the loss-adjusting business. It seemed a promising lead, but it came to nothing. Mr. Carter could remember no such investigation being carried out. He vaguely recalled the name of Loewenstein. That was all.

In the dusty cellars of the Chartered Institute of Insurers, in the heart of the City of London, I did discover one more newspaper article on the subject. It was in the *Insurance Spectator of London and Citizen*, dated July 8, 1928, and it was in some ways a little odd.

> The insurance world as well as the financial world, have been very much concerned with the mysterious disappearance of Captain Loewenstein. The Belgian financier, whose death has been legally established by a Belgian court, was heavily insured through the medium of British insurance companies against the risk of personal accident. The accident policy is stated to be for a very large sum in keeping with the scale on which he based his financial operations. It is stated on reliable authority that the amount was so large that the risk was spread between various companies by way of reinsurance.

I wondered where they had gotten their facts, for on July 8 Loewenstein's death had certainly *not* been established. The Brussels inquiry did not take place until July 9, and then it refused to issue a death certificate. Loewenstein was not officially declared dead until after the discovery and identification of his body on July 19. In talking to the *Insurance Spectator*, somebody had jumped the gun. Somebody with an interest in getting the matter disposed of quickly? Somebody who knew Loewenstein was dead? Was it possible that the reporter had been talking to those who took out the policies? I read on.

Naturally, in order to enable a claim to be made on this insurance, the circumstances of Captain Loewenstein's disappearance would have to be fully investigated. The investigation has (as stated above) been put forward in the Belgian court, with the result that he has legally been declared dead. [Again, the same mistake.]

In these circumstances, the presumption is that the policy money will be paid over to his beneficiaries. Doubtless the announcement of the fact will be made shortly. Captain Loewenstein is also said to have taken out a life policy, which is said to have been only for a small amount.

Apart from any personal policies taken out by the late Captain Loewenstein, it is known that a considerable number of insurance policies have been effected by persons who were interested in the shares of companies more or less controlled by him.

The majority of speculators in International Holdings and Hydro Electric Securities, etc., have for some time past recognised the fact that if anything happened to Captain Loewenstein the immediate effect would be a sharp drop in the price of the shares. To offset this, numerous insurances have been taken out, some on his life and others providing against any loss on the shares that might accrue from his death. The late millionaire's well-known fondness for flying, with its attendant risks, naturally made people more nervous—and incidentally added to the cost of the policies.

It is at present impossible to estimate the total loss incurred by the various companies, but although in aggregate the amount may be considerable, when compared with the companies' resources it will doubtless be found to be infinitesimal.

The paper carried an unctuous editorial that day reminding its readers that it had continually warned them to steer clear of investing in Loewenstein's stocks because of their "one man" character. Now they could see what had happened to those who had failed to heed the paper's advice.

For myself, I was beginning to see daylight. If the risk had been spread around in small parcels, rather than in one massive sum, there would presumably have been less inclination on the part of individual insurance companies or syndicates to launch an investigation. There would either have had to be cooperation among the insurers to instigate and finance an inquiry or one of them would have had to undertake the task for the benefit, if wrongdoing was exposed, of all the rest. In these circumstances, human nature would probably have inclined them to leave it to the other fellow, with the result that nothing was done. It might also have been thought cheaper and less embarrassing—especially if those concerned were men of high influence and impeccable reputation, as I was sure they were—to pay up and look cheerful.

Was that, in fact, what they had done? I could find no more press references to the insurance issue, and that seemed to support the theory. Had the insurers refused to pay out, the matter would surely have found its way into the courts, with attendant publicity. My problem was to find out how much had been paid, and to whom. The answer, had I but known it, was right under my nose.

It was concealed in the morass of financial detail that was beginning to clog my research files like some inexorable growth. Finally, the day came when I decided to wrap a wet towel around my head and try to make sense of it all.

At first, nothing seemed to fit. The investors had lost money, had they not? I came across a quote from Loewenstein's financier friend James Dunn complaining that the Belgian's death had cost him millions. But something nagged at the back of my mind, and I turned back to a chapter I had already written. Someone *had* made a profit at that time: the International Holdings Corporation, via Messrs. Pam and Szarvasy, had announced an additional profit "arising out of transactions of a special nature" of $13,266,137.

Could this, I wondered, be in any way connected with those mysterious insurance policies I had failed to track down?

The policies, I recalled, were supposed to be linked to the fall in the price of shares in the week following Loewenstein's death. That fall, discounting the fact that there had been a ten-for-one share issue in the same week, amounted to $85 per share. But I had no means of knowing how many shares had been insured or who had owned them.

Of the 436,950 shares issued by International Holdings at that time, 220,000 were owned by Alfred Loewenstein—a majority holding. That left on the open market 216,950 shares, many of which I knew had been owned by small investors. I made the unlikely assumption that all of them had been insured against loss and multiplied the total by 85. The answer came to 18,440,750. If I was on the right track, therefore, not all the shares had been insured—which would in any case have been virtually impossible. I did the arithmetic the other way, dividing the $13,266,127 that showed up on the company's balance sheet by 85. The calculator showed that on that basis, 155,601 shares had been involved. It was too many: I was certain from my study of some of the earlier share registers of International Holdings that no one person, apart from Loewenstein, had owned such a huge block. And, in any case, that profit had been made by *the company* and not any individual, and the company would hardly have had any interest in insuring shares it had already issued on behalf of individual shareholders. Was I on entirely the wrong track? I tightened the wet towel.

And then, quite suddenly, the penny dropped. I remembered that not all the shares had been issued at the time of Loewenstein's death. There was a block of 62,440 (to become 624,400 with the ten-for-one split) that was on the point of being put up for sale at that time.

No doubt Loewenstein, had he lived, would have bought all or most of them in order to maintain his majority holding. But Loewenstein died, and as a consequence, those shares had been bought at bargain-basement prices by a syndicate headed by Messrs. Pam and Szarvasy.

I felt myself getting closer. What could have been more natural, and more accepted business practice, than for the company to have insured those unissued shares against the possibility that Loewenstein should die before they reached the market? For if he did so, given the extent to which the value of the company depended on his personality and leadership, they would undoubtedly be worth far less. As indeed they had been. In these circumstances, the insurance payout would have accrued to the company and would have been shown on the books. I remembered, too, that the "profits arising out of transactions of a special nature" had not been published until after the discovery of Loewenstein's body, which would have been necessary before the insurance company would pay out. The statement issued while he was still merely missing had made no reference to it.

I got out the calculator again—62,440 multiplied by 85 was, damn it, only $5,307,400. Less than half the figure I needed to prove my theory. Perhaps I was barking up the wrong tree after all.

And yet, that unexplained profit, so far in excess of the normal earnings of the company, still niggled at my mind. I searched through all the records I could find, and there was no trace of any business coup by International Holdings that might account for it. With the death of Loewenstein, the company seemed to have stopped its headlong expansion, being now under the control of more conservative and prudent men. That money had come from somewhere, but where?

Suppose, just suppose, I thought then, that the press accounts at the time had not been quite correct about the terms of the insurance policy. Suppose the share issue had been insured for its *full value* on the day of Loewenstein's death, possibly coupled with an assurance from someone —and that "someone" had to be Pam and/or Szarvasy— that the shares would be purchased back from the insurers at whatever the ruling price was one week after the event. In that case, the sum payable would be $215 per share, times 62,440, and it would show on the balance sheet as clear profit.

I thumbed the calculator again and watched the figures jump up on the liquid crystal display: 13,424,600.

"Eureka," I said.

The match between the two figures was not exact. In fact the sum International Holdings declared represented a price of $212 a share rather than $215, but, given the fact that share prices invariably differed in different markets on the same day and that $215 was merely the closing price in London on July 4, 1928, I felt certain I had found the answer. The insurance company would presumably have insisted on taking an average price, or perhaps the lowest ruling price that day.

It would seem that Albert Pam and Frederick Szarvasy, by dint of a prudent piece of business management, had secured a very nice profit for International Holdings. They had also made money for themselves by arranging to buy cheaply a large parcel of shares in a company which, through their inside knowledge, they knew to have boosted its assets very considerably. Once news of the quadrupled profit got around, the value of the shares was bound to rise.

And none of this would have happened if Alfred Loewenstein had not taken a very high dive.

Coincidence? I found that rather hard to believe.

23

IT WAS A TIME FOR PIRATES. Loewenstein was not the only one to take advantage of the crazy surge in gambling on the stock exchanges of the 1920s—a forerunner of the current frenzy in .com shares—and the laxity of the financial laws of the time. He was merely the most ostentatious. It is ironic to think that had he lived another fifteen months, the crash of 1929 would almost certainly have pulled him down. As it was, he died rich.

But die he did, and before his time. And though he may not have been the most loveable of men, he was a man for all that. Among the grey-faced, whey-faced entrepreneurs who wheel and deal in the new millennium, we shall not find his equal. Some may be richer, some more ruthless, and probably a great many are more dishonest than Alfred Loewenstein. But none that I can think of possesses his charisma and sheer brazen effrontery.

"If you've got it, flaunt it," said the late Liberace. Alfred Loewenstein flaunted it, and the world—outside the financial coterie in which he lived—vastly enjoyed the spectacle. No man who buys Christmas presents for all the children of his village, who travels across England, as Loewenstein once did, to ask the mother of his army batman if his son can come and work for him again, is likely to be wholly bad. And, if his taste for conspicuous consumption seems an offense at a time when social conditions in England were even worse than they are now, at least he spread his wealth around.

He was, perhaps, inconsiderate of people. At least in his business life. He certainly neglected his family, except in the material sense, and he was choleric, impetuous, and demanding. On the other side of the coin, he was brave, generous, and, so far as one can judge, loyal to the few whom he could call friends. Those who attacked him for being tricky in his dealings were invariable those he had outsmarted, for Alfred Loewenstein was smarter than the average bear.

Did any of these qualities condemn him to an early grave? If one accepts the common view that Loewenstein died by accident, the point does not arise. It was a convenient solution at the time, avoiding embarrassment and scandal in high and respectable places. And, if Loewenstein had had any genuine friends, anyone who really cared, this view might never have gained the currency it did. As it was, inquiry was stifled, curiosity discouraged, and a spurious air of authenticity attached to a theory that had more holes in it than Loewenstein's broken body.

As far as I am aware, none of those who held to the "accident" theory ever looked at the whole picture, including the cast of characters surrounding the central figure, with their motives, weaknesses, and opportunities. Those who have come this far and not skipped to the final chapter (and if you have, please go back and start again) I hope will share my view that suicide can be ruled out and that death by accident was a physical impossibility. Which leaves us with cold-blooded murder as the only explanation for the untimely death of Alfred Loewenstein.

One question remains: Who did it?

There is no "smoking gun" solution. It would be convenient if there were, but history is rarely so tidy. Nonetheless, the clues are in place and the cast of suspects assembled. If this locked-door mystery were fiction instead of fact—the kind of tale beloved of Agatha Christie—this would be the moment to get them all together and confront the killer. But alas, they are all dead.

If they were not, what evidence could be assembled against each of them? First, let's take Fred Baxter, mouldering quietly in his Paris grave with a lump of lead inside his punctured skull. He was certainly on the aircraft, and the manner of his death was, to say the least, curious. Does a young man in the prime of life really commit suicide because he owes his employer, himself a young playboy, a paltry sum of money? And if that were so, why should that employer flee the country forthwith after a conversation with his mother, Alfred Loewenstein's widow, and urging the police to keep the affair quiet?

Poor Fred Baxter was a little man from a sleepy village who had traveled a long way and who drank and gambled more than a man in his position should have been able to afford. He was on the aircraft, he must have seen what happened, and he probably played at least some part in the murder—possibly, in view of his seating position, the detaching of the door hinges.

I believe that he confessed his secret to Bobby Loewenstein that day, when drink and his conscience overwhelmed his common sense. And that was why he died, shot to death in that bachelor apartment on rue Antoine Bourdelle.

As for the others on the aircraft that day, Arthur Hodgson, Loewenstein's secretary, remains a mystery. Save for Norbert Bogden, who met him briefly in Brussels during the days that followed, I was able to find no one who knew what happened to Hodgson after the death of Loewenstein or who knew him very well before it. To all intents and purposes, Arthur Hodgson vanished. As with Eileen Clarke and Paula Bidalon, the two stenographers, there were no statements, no follow-up interviews. Whatever they knew, whatever they did, vanished with them.

But Donald Drew did not vanish. The pilot went on, as we have seen, to live the rest of a short life doing the things he loved best: flying, making love to as many women as possible, and being the life and soul of the party. Living, incidentally, at an improbable level for someone on a mere pilot's salary. Did he already know, in July 1928, of the cancer growing in his stomach? And because of that did he accept a bribe to engineer the death of Loewenstein? Or was he involved in an affair with Madeleine, persuaded to do the deed, and then rejected (or merely paid off) after the event. This last seems to me the least likely solution. Drew's life was sardined with women; why put himself at risk for just one more?

Whatever the reason, something persuaded Donald Drew to land on a deserted beach when the airfield at St. Inglevert was in clear sight. Something induced him not to use his radio, to tell conflicting stories about whether he did or did not turn back to search, and to deceive the Brussels inquiry with a patently false tale about the ease of opening the Fokker's door in flight. What can Drew's thoughts have been while Major Cooper, the Ministry inspector, performed the test that proved his statement to be a lie? Even with his carefree nature, it must have caused a few sleepless nights. And yet he got away with it.

It has been suggested to me that an alternative method of ejecting Loewenstein's body would have been to induce a sideslip to starboard, thus deflecting the airflow from the door on the port side. This is possible, but I think unlikely. The forces generated in a sideslip would have made the task, if anything, more difficult. It would, in any case, increase rather than diminish the pilot's responsibility for the crime. There can really be no doubt that if Loewenstein was murdered, Drew must have had full knowledge of it and be a leading member of this cast of killers. But was he the moving force behind the assassination? I think not.

Robert Little, the co-pilot and mechanic, is in some ways an even more interesting case than Donald Drew. If only because we have the evidence of his widow, Julie, and the story that she says he told her. Which brings us to the strange absence of Loewenstein's jacket.

———

LITTLE, you will remember, recalled looking back from the cockpit and seeing the financier take off his jacket, plus his collar and tie. Loewenstein had stood at the window, as if gasping for breath, and Little told his wife later that he wondered if he had been drugged. That remains a distinct possibility, for the Belgian was a strong man and it might have simplified matters if he was incapacitated before being ejected from the aircraft. Since there was no official autopsy—only a private postmortem examination with its odd discovery of alcohol that should not have been there—the point remains moot. At all events, Loewenstein had apparently, according to Little's account, retired to the toilet without his jacket, his collar, or his tie.

If Little's account to his wife was true, these articles of clothing should have been found in the main cabin after the financier's disappearance, along with the notes Little picked up and kept from the authorities. They were not. The collar and tie were found, lying beneath the washbasin in the toilet compartment. But of the jacket there was no trace, and the body was almost nude when taken from the water.

It is possible to speculate that those who killed him stripped Loewenstein to delay or prevent identification of the body and that they threw the clothes out after him. They could hardly have known that he was carrying his name and address engraved on the strap of his wristwatch —which was the means by which identification was made.

Little's account differed radically from that of the passengers, who had been facing Loewenstein as he sat with his back to the cockpit and were well able to see what he was doing. Hodgson, et al., insisted that he had been reading a book (which he was hardly ever known to do), and made no mention of his standing up and gasping for air or taking off his jacket, collar, and tie.

One wonders why not, unless they were anxious to avoid any suspicion that he might have been drugged. Or unless Little was lying. As for the omission of Loewenstein's note-making from their account and the substitution of a book (which was also never found on board), we know that part of Little's story to be true because we have the notes. Did the others search for them after Little had picked them up and in the general confusion assume that they had blown out of the door after him?

Did they think that to tell the truth and mention the notes would arouse suspicion, because no notes could be found—not knowing, of course, that Little had picked them up?

There is a possibility that Little, separated from the others in the cockpit (though he had access to the cabin via a door behind the pilots' seats), was not party to the common story that Hodgson, Baxter, and the two women agreed to tell on landing. And that the authorities arrived on the scene with unexpected speed, leaving time to replace the door, but not to coordinate everyone's version of events.

The contradiction between Little's version of the incident and that of the others may well have been what aroused the initial suspicion of the French policeman who interviewed them. A suspicion, of course, that was never pursued.

Then again, Robert Little's account to his wife stopped oddly short. It stopped, in fact, at the moment, when he handed over the controls to Donald Drew and the pilot headed for the beach. There was no mention of the interview with Inspector Bonnot of the Sûreté, so quickly and so inexplicably taken off the case. Nor of the Brussels inquiry. Nor of that flight back over the Channel when he and Drew, or so they had said, had opened the door with such ease. The last, at any rate, he would surely have thought worth mentioning. After all, it was the peg on which the whole "accident" theory hung. Assuming, that is, that the experiment ever took place. Which I doubt.

Was Robert Little involved? He had to be. But was he the instigator of the murder? I think not.

The extent to which those on the aircraft benefited from Loewenstein's death is difficult to assess. It must be admitted that most of them lost their jobs (though Baxter did not). But Donald Drew certainly lived extremely well and probably above his income for the rest of his life. Robert Little was able to set up an independent aviation consultancy at a prestigious London address and had a splendid apartment in Paris. He had, it is true, married an American heiress, but her father's fortune had disappeared in the Wall Street crash of 1929. Baxter was said by his friends at the time of his death never to have been short of money. For the rest, I simply do not know.

It is easier to assess the gain made by those on the ground. Bobby, only eighteen at the time of his father's death, can almost certainly be acquitted of any complicity. Though he did eventually inherit his share of Loewenstein's fortune at the age of twenty-one, and after more than ten years of profligate expenditure still had almost £1 million in the bank at the moment of his own untimely death, there is not the slightest indication that he was involved. Indeed, if my theory about Fred Baxter is correct, he may even have attempted to avenge Alfred Loewenstein's murder.

Nor, for reasons explained earlier, can I find it in me to associate Madeleine with the plot. Yes, she inherited great wealth, but she had the use of that wealth already and her lifestyle appears to have gone on much as before. Would the mere possibility that her husband would suffer financial disaster if he lived turn her thoughts to murder? I seriously doubt that women think that way. It is true that the marriage seems to have been lacking in passion and, therefore, the idea of an affair with Donald Drew might seem attractive to readers of romance novels (and was to my original publishers). There is not the slightest evidence to support such a theory, at least none that I could discover. As for the fact that she failed to attend the funeral, seen by some as evidence of a guilty conscience, I tend to think the reverse. Had she been guilty, the last thing she would have done would be to draw attention to herself by such a callous omission. Perhaps the woman had a bad cold that day; who knows?

Let us review the rest of the cast. One can feel a degree of affection and sympathy for almost all the characters reviewed thus far, even the putative villains. For myself, no such warmth extends towards Henri Dreyfus, who seems to have been an impossible man and, in his manipulation of the dope scandal, a crook to boot. A thoroughly nasty piece of work. Dreyfus's war with Loewenstein was long and bitter, but it was fought with shuffling papers and with speeches in which the Swiss chemist could rarely bring himself to mention his adversary's name. For Dreyfus to have composed and circulated the anonymous memorandum on Loewenstein's activities that did him so much damage in the week before his death would have been wholly in character. For him to have plotted and executed the Belgian's murder, even to save himself from possible ruin in a libel action, seems altogether too bold an act. Had their positions been reversed, one can imagine Loewenstein doing such a thing without a qualm. But not Henri Dreyfus. For one thing, the man was so prolix and incoherent that whoever he hired would have had problems in understanding what he wanted done.

No, though it is tempting to fit a posthumous noose around the neck of Dr. Dreyfus, I cannot do it. You may read the evidence and reach a different conclusion, but for me he was, to quote Winston Churchill's apocryphal (and unjust) description of F. E. Smith: all wind and piss. Such men do not murder, even at arm's length.

But, as one runs down the list of Loewenstein's business associates, the trail becomes warmer. For there is little doubt that even to his friends, and I use the word loosely, the Belgian Croesus was becoming an embarrassment. And an expensive embarrassment as well. Times were changing, and the heyday of freebooting capitalists like F. S. Pearson, William Mackenzie, and James Dunn was on the wane.

They were being replaced by sober men with stiff collars who put collateral before adventure and respectability before display. Loewenstein, however, was not changing; he was still raiding companies, brewing wild schemes, celebrating victories, and absorbing defeats to fight again. To their eyes he was wild, unprincipled, and perhaps a little crazy.

Such things did not matter so much while he was winning more battles than he lost, and while their own personal interests were not threatened. For, like pilot fish following a shark, there were always pickings to be had from the last meal. And while the boom continued for International Holdings, those pickings were rich indeed.

All that changed when the slump began on the Brussels bourse after the *Neptune* article. Suddenly Loewenstein, like Lord Byron, had become mad, bad, and dangerous to know. He was costing them money, a lot of money, and who knew what the fellow might do next?

Looked at in this context, the death of Loewenstein became as inevitable as Greek tragedy. Had he been willing to moderate his excesses, to go away and lick his wounds and don a cloak of sober respectability (an unlikely thought), all might have been well. But his schemes were becoming more grandiose and more bizarre, not less. To attempt to take the Bank of Brussels, to merge it with the Société Générale and through the merger to subsume SOFINA, Brazilian Traction, and all the rest was, to the onlookers, the stuff of fantasy. And yet he might have succeeded. To some, at least, this was the most terrifying thought of all.

There were a few with a foot in both camps. The Holts, for instance. Though they have not featured largely in this story, Sir Herbert Holt and his son Andrew are figures of considerable interest. Sir Herbert, owner of the Montreal

Light and Power Company, banker and financial magnate, had recently been appointed by Loewenstein as chairman of International Holdings in Canada. He had apparently been unimpressed by the attempts of Brazilian Traction, of which his son was a director, to warn him off the Belgian. The alliance between the two was a constant threat.

Yet, as chairman of the company, Sir Herbert can hardly have been happy to see its shares decline so rapidly in the weeks before Loewenstein died. He must have been aware that the Belgian's tarnished reputation was responsible and fearful for what might happen next. It is worth noting that when Loewenstein telephoned him just before his last take-off, he made a dinner date with Sir Herbert for the following week (again, hardly the act of a man contemplating suicide). But if Holt ever meant to keep that appointment, he must have changed his mind very rapidly, for four days after Loewenstein disappeared he had left Liverpool by sea on his way back to Canada.

It is possible, of course, that he managed to book a passage at extremely short notice and saw no point in waiting in England to see what had happened to Loewenstein. Anything is possible.

As for Andrew Holt, his position on the board of Brazilian Traction made Loewenstein's latest scheme a direct threat. His whereabouts at the time are unknown, but in the months and even years ahead he was to become one of the more active exponents of the accident theory. Coincidentally, he himself acquired a Fokker F.VIIa/3m in July 1928—the fifth off the production line after Loewenstein's ill-fated machine—which he kept until October 1930.

Holt was in the habit of showing friends the door of the aircraft and explaining how easy it would have been for Loewenstein to fall out. Though as far as is known he only did so on the ground, never in flight. Was he protesting too much? I wonder. At least in a passive sense, both the Holts could be said to have benefited from Loewenstein's death, although there is no real evidence that they were involved in it.

And then there is Dannie Heineman. Mysterious Dannie Heineman, the man who shunned publicity. The man who first befriended Loewenstein and then changed sides and stabbed him in the back—at least metaphorically. The man who Loewenstein insisted had already tried to kill him.

Of all those involved, only Heineman—with the possible exception of Sir Alexander Mackenzie of Brazilian Traction—stood to lose everything if Loewenstein's plan to take over the Bank of Brussels succeeded. The others had widespread financial interests, but Heineman had spent his whole life building up SOFINA, and he knew he could expect no mercy if Loewenstein gained control.

Informed opinion at the time said that the Belgian's bid was doomed to failure, but informed opinion had been wrong about Loewenstein before, and the man himself was brimming with confidence.

Did Heineman decide to take no chances, to end the threat from Alfred Loewenstein once and for all? It is worth more than a passing thought, though possibly his habit of avoiding the limelight makes him seem a more suspicious character than he deserves to be. For all that, he did have a strong motive, and he certainly had money and influence. His views on the danger of Loewenstein were well known, and he was a man of considerable ambition—not to be casually thwarted.

Loewenstein was scarcely a popular figure among his peers, and if the rest of the financial community ever suspected that Dannie Heineman had done them all a favor, they could be relied on not to ask too many questions. Nor did they. They rested content in the knowledge that the wayward genius from Brussels would bother them no more.

So, did Heineman cause the broken body of Alfred Loewenstein to lie, unmarked and unmourned, in that remote corner of the cemetery at Evere?

The very elusiveness of the man makes it tempting to say so. But again, there is a lack of connection to Drew, and no evidence to show that he made a direct financial gain. In my self-appointed role as judge, I have to return a verdict of "not proven" on Danny Heineman. I do so with some reluctance, and only because I believe there is a better case to answer against my final suspects.

24

"FOLLOW THE MONEY," said Deep Throat when tipping off Woodward and Bernstein of the *Washington Post* to the Watergate scandal. It was excellent advice. And although in this case the money trail led in several directions, the clearest signpost pointed one way: to those pillars of society Major Albert Pam and Mr. Frederick Szarvasy.

Consider this: With Loewenstein's death, these two were left as the sole captains of International Holdings, now free to run the company without the danger of a loose cannon charging all over their quarter-deck. They enjoyed the rewards of a huge insurance payout and profited from many thousands of cheap shares. They had the twin motives of money and power, added to self-preservation— for Loewenstein could have dragged them both down with him if he failed.

Pam and Szarvasy certainly had the means to bribe the occupants of the Fokker to dispose of their employer and to keep their mouths shut subsequently. There are strong indications in the lives of Drew and Little, and possibly Baxter, that somebody did just that, and with the threat of capital punishment hanging over the heads of the actual perpetrators, the danger of blackmail would have been negligible.

As for the purchase of the insurance policy, with International Holdings as the beneficiary, this seems strong evidence of premeditation. Of course, it may have been sheer coincidence that the company insured Loewenstein's life in such a manner at such a time, and the alacrity with which Pam and Szarvasy assumed his death before it had been proved may have been no more than financial prudence. And pigs have been known to fly.

If one looks at the subsequent careers of these two highly respectable gentlemen, which is all that is on public display, it is admittedly hard to imagine them conniving at, indeed organizing, a murder. And yet, a peek behind the scenes at their South American activities in earlier years creates a strong impression of a streak of ruthlessness and a certain lack of scruple. I doubt if, at the time, anyone had the slightest suspicion that Pam and Szarvasy might be involved, for there is a human reluctance to look up instead of down when considering possible involvement in violent crime. In the socially stratified conditions of the 1920s, this would have been even more true than it is today.

But men of power and influence have committed high crimes and misdemeanors in the past, and no doubt will do so again. I will never be able to prove it in court, but just for the record, if the shades of Albert Pam and Frederick Szarvasy are listening, hear this, gentlemen: In the words of Émile Zola, *j'accuse*.

FOR FURTHER DISCUSSION

1. Does the author's evidence make you feel certain that Loewenstein was murdered? Do you agree with the author about the identity of the culprit?
2. Discuss the statement "Follow the money" and what it means in the context of Lowenstein's death.
3. Do the author's descriptions of aeronautics in the 1920s make you want to learn more? What specifically is interesting about the flying of airplanes during this time?
4. Do you feel that Loewenstein's extravagant life style and mysterious death is somewhat symptomatic of the "roaring twenties?"
5. What do you make of Madeleine Loewenstein's absence at her husband's funeral? Do you find her more or less innocent than the author does? What do you think about his reasoning that a beautiful woman is less likely to be guilty?
6. What do you think of the title of the book?

7. What do you think about the author's research? Was it easy to see where the author got his information? Were the sources credible? Is the author's overall account of the events credible?
8. Was there a specific section of the book that left an impression on you, good or bad? Share the passage and its effect.
9. Discuss how the mystery of Loewenstein's death compares to other mysterious deaths of the rich and famous.
10. Would this book make a good basis for a movie? Why (not)?

NOTES

Chapter 8

1. This refers to pre-decimal currency. There were 20 shillings in £1. A shilling was often called 'bob,' so 'ten bob' was 10/-.

ABOUT THE AUTHOR

William (Bill) Norris has been a professional writer since the age of 16, when he joined his local newspaper as an apprentice reporter. After ten years of working for various newspapers in England and Africa, Norris was appointed as Parliamentary Correspondent to the prestigious *Times* (of London). He is one of the youngest people to hold this position. He remained in this position for seven years, revolutionizing the art of the "parliamentary sketch" before transferring to become Africa Correspondent for *The Times*, covering political events and wars in Biafra, Nigeria, Angola, the Congo, Mozambique, Botswana, Zambia, Tanzania, and Zimbabwe. In 1968, he became ITN's Political Correspondent while also covering overseas stories, such as the Paris Riots happening that same year. He transitioned to freelance work in 1980 after moving to the United States. In 1997, Norris became the Associate Director of the PressWise Trust (a British media ethics charity) where he counseled young journalists to promote journalistic ethics. Along with being an experienced writer/journalist, he has a strong public speaking background. He has spoken to students at the University of London and was the keynote speaker at both the World Health Organization conference in Moscow and a European Union conference on journalistic ethics in Cyprus. He now resides in the South of France with his wife, Betty, two cats, and two exhausting dogs.

EXCERPT FROM A TALENT TO DECEIVE

It was, to quote a famous phrase, a dark and stormy night in the Sourland Mountains of New Jersey on March 1, 1932. It had rained heavily in the afternoon. By evening the rain had ceased, but there was a cold and blustery east wind. In the newly built Lindbergh house, still uncurtained, there were five people in addition to the baby: Charles and Anne Lindbergh; Ollie and Elsie Whately, the English butler and maid; and Betty Gow, the child's nursemaid. There was also a young fox terrier named Whagoosh, a notoriously noisy dog, whose name means "fox" in the Chippewa language.

Much of what happened that evening is open to doubt, but what follows—for what it is worth—is the officially accepted version.

Anne and Betty Gow began preparing the baby for bed at about 6:15 p.m. Young Charlie was recovering from a cold, but they rubbed his chest with Vicks VapoRub and decided to make him a flannelette shirt to wear beneath his night clothes. This was quickly sewn up by Betty, an accomplished seamstress, from a piece of scrap material. Over this the baby wore a sleeveless woollen shirt, which was pinned to his nappies under a pair of rubber pants. And on top of it all, Charlie wore a grey sleeping suit—size two, manufactured by the Dr. Denton company. His bedcovers were fastened to the mattress of his cot by two large safety pins, and on his hands he wore two shiny metal "thumb guards" to stop him sucking his thumbs. Charles Augustus Lindbergh Jr. was not going anywhere or doing anything, at least, not under his own volition. One of the thumb guards, which were attached to the baby's wrists by lengths of half-inch tape, was later to pose one of the unexplained puzzles of the kidnapping. It was discovered, still bright and shining, at the entrance to the property some twenty-nine days after the crime. The thumb guard lay in full view in the middle of the road; somewhat flattened—possibly run over—but not trodden into the mud. And yet none of the hundreds of people who had passed that way over the previous four weeks had noticed it until Betty Gow and Elsie Whateley picked it up. It was, to say the least, curious. Had it lain there all that time? Or had the perpetrator, finding it in his possession, casually dropped it when making a later visit to Hopewell? If the latter were true, a totally different list of suspects would be opened up. But the lead was never explored.

The two women tried to close the shutters of the window in the east wall, which lay directly over the window of Lindbergh's study, but they were warped and refused to latch. There was a second window in the south wall, away from the wind, and they left this slightly open to let in some air. The whole putting-to-bed process took more than an hour, and it was 7:30 before Anne left the room and went into the living room to await her husband's return. He had telephoned earlier to say he would be a little late. (In fact, he should have been much later because he was supposed to be speaking at a dinner given by New York

University at the Waldorf-Astoria that night, but there had been a secretarial mix-up over his calendar and he forgot the appointment.) Betty Gow stayed a few minutes longer; then she, too, put out the light and left the nursery. The baby was sleeping. If the accepted accounts of those in the house that night are correct, this was the last time any of them saw him alive.

Charles Lindbergh arrived home at about 8:25, parked his car in the large garage that lay beneath the Whateleys' quarters in the west wing, and entered the house through the connecting door into the kitchen. He joined his wife for dinner ten minutes later. A little after nine o'clock, while they were sitting by the fire in the ground-floor living room, Charles heard a sharp crack that he later described, rather oddly, as "like the top slats of an orange box falling off a chair." He thought the noise came from the kitchen. It has since been assumed that what Lindbergh said he heard was the kidnapper's ladder breaking outside the nursery window, but the kitchen was in the opposite direction. Anne apparently heard nothing. In any case, as we shall learn later, Lindbergh's hearing was not something to be relied upon.

The couple decided to have a bath before going to bed. Charles went first, using the upstairs bathroom, which was directly adjacent to the child's nursery. It was then about 9:15. He dressed again and went downstairs to the library to read, sitting next to the uncurtained window that was directly beneath the southeast window in the nursery. Anne drew her own bath, then discovered she had left her tooth powder in the baby's bathroom.

She went in without turning on the light, retrieved the powder, and returned to the main bathroom. Then she rang for Elsie Whateley and requested a hot lemonade. It was almost ten o'clock.

Betty Gow and the Whateleys, meanwhile, were in the servants' sitting room, which was on the ground floor at the western end of the house. Whagoosh the terrier, who had shown no sign of hearing the odd noise Lindbergh said he heard earlier, was with them. Ten o'clock was the regular hour when the baby would be lifted and invited to use his potty, and Betty Gow went upstairs, passing through the kitchen, the pantry, and the foyer en route and apparently noting nothing amiss. She thought of getting Anne Lindbergh to join her, but Anne was still in the bath, so she entered the nursery alone, first turning on the light in the adjacent bathroom.

Betty Gow, according to her own account, first went to close the south window, which had been left partly open when they put the child to bed. Then she turned on the electric heater before moving toward the cot. She could not hear the child breathing. "I thought that something had happened to him," she said later. "That perhaps the clothes were over his head. In the half light I saw that he wasn't there and felt all over the bed for him."

Panicking, the nursemaid ran down the corridor to the Lindberghs' bedroom and found Anne leaving the bathroom. "Do you have the baby, Mrs. Lindbergh?" she asked. Anne Lindbergh was puzzled. "No," she said, and went to look in the child's room while Betty Gow raced downstairs to the library to see, if by any chance, Lindbergh had him. The answer, of course, was no.

Ever the man of action, Lindbergh ran upstairs to the main bedroom, opened the closet, and loaded the rifle he kept there. Then he told his wife that the baby had been kidnapped. In the nursery, he discovered that the southeast corner window was open a crack, that the cold wind blowing through it, and that on top of the radiator case forming the sill was a white envelope. Assuming that it contained a ransom note and might bear fingerprints, he did not touch it. Instead, he took his rifle and ran out into the night, having first told Whateley, the butler, to telephone the sheriff at Hopewell.

Lacking a flashlight, Lindbergh could see nothing but the woods around the house. Whateley, having made the telephone call, brought the car round and shone the headlights on either side of the road. But it was clear that the kidnappers were long gone. Whateley was instructed to drive into Hopewell to buy a flashlight (though where he would find one at that hour was unclear), while Lindbergh returned to the house and telephoned the New Jersey State Police in Trenton and his lawyer, Colonel Henry Breckinridge, in New York.

The call to the State Police was made at 10:25 p.m. The delay of almost half an hour is interesting. The call was answered by Lieutenant Daniel Dunn, who was surprised to hear the voice at the other end say: "This is Charles Lindbergh. My son has just been kidnapped." Startled, Dunn asked what time the child had been taken. "Some time between 7:30 and 10 o'clock," Lindbergh replied. "He's twenty months old and wearing a one-piece sleeping suit." Then he hung up. This had to be a hoax call, thought Dunn, but on the advice of a colleague, he telephoned the Lindbergh house. The same voice answered him. "This is Lieutenant Dunn, sir," the policeman replied quickly. "Men are on their way."

The State Police reacted swiftly. At 10:46, a teletype alarm was sent out across the state, requesting that all cars be investigated by police patrols. By 11 o'clock, checkpoints had been established at the Holland Tunnel, the George Washington Bridge, and all ferry ports along the Hudson River. New Jersey streets had road blocks, and hospitals were alerted to report the admission of any children matching the Lindbergh baby's description. Police were notified in Pennsylvania, Delaware, and Connecticut.

The first police to arrive on the scene at the Lindbergh house were Harry Wolfe and Charles Williamson of the Hopewell force, who turned up at 10:35, ten minutes after the alarm had been raised. They made a quick inspection of the nursery, where they found small particles of yellow clay on the carpet and on a leather suitcase beneath the southeast window. The window itself was closed, the left-hand shutter also closed, and the right one open. Lindbergh, asserting an authority he was never to relinquish, ordered them not to touch anything. The policemen then went outside and discovered holes in the mud on the right-hand side of the study where a ladder had evidently been placed, and the ladder itself some seventy-five feet from the house. They left everything where it was and went back to the house.

The police were now beginning to gather in droves. There were State Troopers Wolf and Cain from Lambertville; State Troopers de Gaetano and Bornmann from the Training School at Wilburtha; State Trooper Kelly, the fingerprint expert from Morristown Barracks; Captain Lamb and Lieutenant Keaten; Major Schoeffel, deputy to Colonel Schwartzkopf, head of the New Jersey State Police, and, a little later, Col. Schwartzkopf himself. Wolf, who was one of the first to arrive, went out to look for footprints. And found some. "The kidnappers consisted apparently of a party of at least two or more persons," he reported. "Apparently two members of the party proceeded on foot to the east side of the Lindbergh residence and assembled a three-piece home-made extension ladder . . . Two sets of fresh footprints led off in a south-east direction . . . Kidnappers arrived in a car which was left parked some distance from the house, either in Lindbergh's private lane or in a rough road known as Featherbed Lane." Trooper de Gaetano reported: "We traced rubber boots or overshoe impressions from the ladder down an old road towards the chicken coop. The footprints went across the road and appeared to stop alongside impressions from an auto." There was one very clear print in the dirt beneath the nursery window, which measured 12 to 12-1/2 inches long by 4 to 4-1/2 inches wide. This discovery was never mentioned at the trial because, inconveniently, these measurements did not match the shoes of Bruno Richard Hauptmann. Nor, of course, did the existence of *two* sets of footprints conform to the prosecution theory that Hauptmann had acted alone. These were details best forgotten. More favorable for the ultimate prosecution was another find by the police: a Buck's chisel, about thirty years old, with a three-quarter-inch blade and a wooden handle, lying near the ladder. That was all right because Hauptmann was a carpenter.

At this time, kidnapping was not a federal crime but was dealt with at the state level (things were to change as a direct result of the Lindbergh case). This meant that the FBI, which had immense experience in the solving of complex crimes, had no authority in the case, though they could have been called in. Colonel Norman Schwartzkopf, on the other hand, had no experience in this field whatever. Nevertheless, persuaded by Lindbergh, he was determined to keep the FBI out of it. And did.

Schwartzkopf—the father of "Stormin' Norman" of first Gulf War fame—was thirty-seven years old at the time, a handsome man with a crewcut hairstyle and a waxed blond moustache. He was a veteran of the First World War and a graduate of West Point, who had once worked as a "floor walker" at Bamberger's department store in Newark. This meant that he was supposed to be watching out for shoplifters. He had never patrolled a beat or arrested a criminal in his life, but he was determined not to let this deter him.

Besides, he worshipped the ground Lindbergh walked on and was once quoted as saying that he would "break any oath for that man." In retrospect, he may have done just that.

At all events, there was no doubt about who was in charge of the investigation from very outset: It was not Colonel Norman Schwartzkopf; it was Charles Lindbergh.

With the arrival of fingerprint expert Trooper Frank Kelly soon after midnight, the ransom note could at last be opened. "I put on a pair of gloves," said Kelly later, "picked the letter up by the edges, and brought it over to a small table in the centre of the room where I conducted a latent print examination of the outside surface of the envelope. Black powder was used in an effort to obtain any possible prints, but without results. I then opened the letter with a nail file and powdered the note and the inside of the envelope for possible prints, but none were obtained."

The ransom note was written in pencil in a clearly disguised hand. It read:

```
Dear Sir!

Have 50.000 $ redy 25.000 $ in 20 $
bills 1.5000 $ in 10 $ bills and 1000
$ in 5 $ bills. After 204 days we will
inform you were to deliver the Mony.
We warn you for making anyding public
or for notify the Police the chld is
in  gute  care. Indication  for  all
letters are Singnature And 3 holds.
```

There was a symbol consisting of two interlocking circles, and within the interlock an oval. The circles were colored blue, the oval red, and at the centre of each in a horizontal line were square holes. What did it mean? This symbol has remained an unsolved mystery in this case. Was it intended to identify the kidnapper to Lindbergh? If so, he never disclosed the fact. Was it the recognition symbol of some secret society? This raises a possibility; no more. For it is known that certain college fraternities, rather like the Masons, employed such symbols on their correspondence. One such was Beta Theta Pi, which had (but no longer has) a chapter at Amherst College. Dwight W. Morrow was a member of Beta Theta Pi at Amherst. More to the point, so was his son, Dwight Jr., in 1932. The archivist at Beta Theta Pi's headquarters confirmed to the author that the fraternity employed a secret recognition symbol at the time of the kidnapping and still did so today. Asked to confirm or deny whether it matched the symbol found on the ransom note, he declined. "That's a secret," he said.

Not only did Trooper Kelly fail to find any fingerprints on the ransom note, he failed to detect any prints whatever in the entire nursery. Nothing on the window sill, nothing on the cot, nothing the various objects in the room. This seems rather extraordinary. It might be reasonably supposed that the kidnapper would be wearing gloves, but the nursery was frequented by Betty Gow, Anne Lindbergh, the Whateleys, possibly Lindbergh himself, and certainly the child. And it is unlikely that *they* were wearing gloves. How could it be possible that none of them, not one, had left a single fingerprint inside the nursery? Unless, of course, someone had wiped it clean before the police arrived. And who could that be? Not the kidnapper, in my opinion. He was working in the dark and under great stress, and would hardly have taken the time, with so many people in the house, to risk discovery by spending ten minutes or more to wipe off every single surface in the room. Besides, if he was wearing gloves, there would have been no need. I cannot come up with an answer other than this: The room was wiped clean by Lindbergh himself or by someone acting under his orders.

So why was it done? Did Lindbergh know the identity of the kidnapper perfectly well, or at least suspect it? Did he wish to prevent his or her identification in order to avoid scandal? And if that were so, who could that person possibly be? The most obvious candidate had to be a member of the prestigious and enormously wealthy Morrow family into which Lindbergh had married. I'd be hard pressed to think of any stranger who would inspire Lindbergh into launching an instant cover-up operation. Perhaps he thought that this was no more than a malicious prank, that the child would be returned unharmed very soon by the person he suspected. Perhaps he reasoned that to blurt out his suspicions now would bring needless shame on the family of which he had recently become the male head. It may well be that in the ensuing days and weeks, when the child was not returned, Lindbergh regretted his actions. But by then it was too late. He would have had to face some very awkward questions and possibly prosecution for obstruction of justice. The absence of fingerprints in that room remains one of the most mysterious and most significant aspects of the whole case. Even odder, perhaps, is the fact that, as far as is known, Charles Lindbergh was never questioned about it.

Perhaps Trooper Kelly had merely been incompetent? This was the thought of a former justice of the New Jersey Supreme Court, James F. Minturn, when he heard the news. Minturn contacted his friend Dr. Erastus Mead Hudson, an amateur fingerprint specialist who had been experimenting for years with a silver nitrate process that had proved very successful. Hudson was invited down to Hopewell to use his method and did succeed in revealing several of the child's fingerprints on his books and toys. But as far as adult prints were concerned, the room remained clean as a whistle. This was all the more extraordinary because Betty Gow had rubbed the child's chest with a vapor rub when putting him to bed and her fingers would have been greasy when she closed the window. Yet there were no prints on the window frame.

Hudson then inspected the ladder, on which Kelly had also failed to reveal prints, and found between thirty and forty examples other than those of the policemen known to have handled it. Ultimately, none of these proved to belong to Hauptmann. Hudson suggested that the prints should be sent to Washington for comparison with the FBI's huge fingerprint collection of known criminals, which was the most comprehensive in the country. Remarkably, Schwartzkopf refused to permit such a move. He also refused Hudson's offer to subject the ransom note to a special iodine-gas process he had invented.

Why should the New Jersey police chief turn down such an opportunity to clear up the case? Was he merely protective of his turf, or was he, as so often in later stages of the investigation, acting under the instructions of Charles Lindbergh?

The ladder turned out to be an extraordinary construction, crudely made in three sections and composed, according to one police report, of "old, nondescript lumber which has been lying around for some time." One officer suggested that it might have been made from timber left over from the building of Lindbergh's house, but this possibility was never explored. Perhaps it should have been.

Fully extended, the ladder was twenty feet long, tapering from a width of fourteen inches at the bottom to eleven inches at the top, with each section being joined by dowel pins. The rungs, which were merely nailed across the side pieces, were eighteen to nineteen inches apart, as opposed to the standard twelve inches, which would have made it much more difficult to climb and descend— especially when carrying a thirty-pound baby in a sack. When found, only the bottom two sections of the ladder were joined together, suggesting that only these had been used, and one of the lower rails was broken near the joint.

If the theory that the ladder was employed in the kidnapping is correct, the kidnapper must have had considerable athletic prowess. Placed as it was to the right of Lindbergh's study window—presumably to avoid being seen—the ladder would have been well to the side of the nursery window above, and, if only the bottom two sections were employed, some thirty inches below it. The kidnapper would have had to stand on the topmost rung, bridge the gap, balance on the narrow sill somehow as he manipulated the shutters and opened the window, and then climb through an opening which measured, at most, 30-1/2 by 26 inches. He would then have had to repeat the process in reverse, carrying a heavy and possibly struggling load, and contrive to close the window behind him. All of this in a howling gale—which, curiously, failed to dislodge the ransom note left propped upright on the interior windowsill. If, as was alleged at his trial, Hauptmann had managed to do all this single-handed (despite the evidence of dual foot marks), he must have had the nerve of a steeplejack, the agility of a circus performer, and the strength of a weightlifter. Tests on a duplicate ladder constructed by the New Jersey Police showed that it would not bear a weight of more than 155 pounds. The actual ladder was so flimsy that this is probably a very generous estimate. Hauptmann weighed rather more.

It was the contention of the prosecution that the ladder broke as the kidnapper descended, causing him to fall and/or drop the baby, which caused the latter's death. There was no sign of such a fall on the muddy ground, however; at least, none that was mentioned in the official reports. There is a much more likely explanation of what happened.

As anyone who has ever tried to erect a long ladder will know, it is an unwieldy object, and the high wind would have added greatly to the difficulty of putting it against the wall. This may have been why only two sections were used. Having put it up, however, the kidnapper(s) must then have seen that getting through the window was a near-impossible task and changed their plan. This would explain why the ladder was found some distance away (why bother to move it if the objective was to make a rapid getaway?). There was a much easier way to get in and snatch the baby: through the front door. This theory is supported by another oddity about the ladder: In spite of the mud that must have been adhering to the shoes of the kidnapper, there were no traces of mud on the rungs.

There was a staircase leading from the front foyer straight up to the child's nursery. It would have taken no more than a couple of minutes for the kidnapper to remove his boots, tiptoe up the stairs, pick up the sleeping baby, and escape by the same route. Assuming that the sound heard by Lindbergh was the ladder breaking as it was being taken down, this would put the time of the kidnapping at around 9:15, when Lindbergh was running his bath. Perfect (if fortuitous) cover for any strange noises. Even if the kidnapper had not been in the house before—which he may have been, even if he were not a family member who had been there before, because the Whateleys were in the habit of giving impromptu guided tours while the Lindberghs were not present. Also, the plans had been widely published in several newspapers.

———

Lindbergh lost no time in instructing Schwartzkopf that his priority should be the payment of the ransom and the return of his child. The identification and arrest of the kidnappers, he said, was of no immediate importance. Schwartzkopf, whose job was catching criminals, seemed powerless to resist. He was quoted as saying, "I would do anything he asked of me." Anne Lindbergh admitted to an interviewer many years later that her husband was not really a leader, but because of the awe in which everyone held him he was led to believe that he was. He never listened to advice, believing with some justification that if he had taken notice of what people advised him at the time of his Atlantic flight, he would never have flown to Paris.

Law enforcement duly fell into line, not only in New Jersey but across the United States. Instructions went out to all police forces that the objective of any search was to be the return of the baby. According to General Order No. 18 of the District of Columbia Police Department: "The arrest of the kidnappers is a subordinate consideration, and any member of the Force is authorized to enter into personal and confidential negotiations for the safe return of the infant without responsibility for the detection or arrest of the kidnappers."

The direction of the search was now in the hands of a "Committee of Four Colonels." In addition to Lindbergh himself, who took the chair, there were Schwartzkopf, Col. Breckinridge (Lindbergh's lawyer), and Col. "Wild Bill"

Donovan, who was then preparing to run for governor of New York. They began sitting on the day after the kidnapping, March 2, and met daily at Hopewell. Their first action was to issue instructions to the kidnappers on the baby's diet. He was to be given, they said, half a cup of orange juice on waking, the yolk of one egg daily, and half a cup of prune juice after his afternoon nap. Every newspaper in the country published the menu on its front page the next day.

On March 3, a further statement was issued in which Lindbergh declared that any representatives of his whom the kidnappers found suitable would be prepared to meet their representatives "at any time and in any place they may designate." He promised that all arrangements would be kept strictly confidential, "and we further pledge ourselves that we will not try to injure in any way those connected with the return of the child." Breckinridge took the responsibility of handing this statement to the press, adding that Lindbergh himself would be prepared to meet the kidnappers "under any conditions they may wish to lay down."

This did not go down well with New Jersey's then Attorney General William A. Stevens, who issued his own statement. Neither Lindbergh nor the New Jersey State Police, he said, had the authority to grant the kidnappers freedom from prosecution. If the Lindberghs were not prepared to prosecute, the State of New Jersey would.

Lindbergh and his committee now decided to seek the help of the criminal underworld. They were encouraged by a message from the notorious gangster Al Capone, then serving an eleven-year prison sentence for tax evasion, saying that if Lindbergh could arrange his release from jail, he would achieve the boy's release within days. In addition, he offered $10,000 for information that would lead to the recovery of the child and the capture of the kidnappers. The offer came to nothing, probably because not even Lindbergh could spring Capone, but it was a fact that various gangs in New York and other eastern cities were beginning to feel the heat from police engaging in the search and were as keen as anyone to see the baby returned. Kidnapping the Lindbergh baby was not something that any professional criminal would contemplate—they were making too much money by other means without excessive police attention—and one suspects that Lindbergh knew this perfectly well. However, even without Capone, he decided to go down this unorthodox route.

The chosen instrument was one Morris (Mickey) Rosner, a diminutive gangster said to have abundant contacts in the New York underworld, including "Legs" Diamond, Owney Madden, and Waxey Gordon. The committee had been urged to contact him by Congresswoman Ruth Pratt, and the arrangement was made through a partner in Wild Bill Donovan's law office, Robert Thayer. Thayer was a habitué of speakeasies and gambling joints, who had the good or ill fortune to have Rosner as a client.

Rosner duly turned up at Hopewell. He was prepared to help, but not without conditions. He laid down that he was to receive $2,500 for expenses; he was not to be followed by the police or Secret Service; and he was to be given a free hand, reporting only to Breckinridge or Thayer. Abjectly, the committee agreed to everything.

There followed what may have been Lindbergh's greatest blunder in the whole affair, or perhaps his greatest triumph of obfuscation. Rosner was given a copy of the ransom note to take to New York, and there he showed it to Owney Madden.

In any other kidnapping case, the exact content and format of the kidnapping note, let alone the handwriting, would have been a closely kept secret by the authorities. How else could they know whether subsequent demands were genuine or merely the products of enterprising extortionists? Lindbergh had now blown that strategy out of the water. When a second letter arrived two days later, on March 5, it bore the same symbol of interlocking circles and the syntax was similar, though both symbol and handwriting had some subtle differences. But did it come from the kidnappers, or from one of Rosner's friends who had copied these things? No one could now be sure. The letter read:

```
We have warned you note (sic) to make
anyding Public also notify the Police
now you have to take the consequences
 .  .  .
```

It was interesting that the writer, whoever he was, had made the same spelling mistakes with simple words as appeared in the original ransom note, but appeared to have no trouble with words like "consequences." This phenomenon was repeated in subsequent letters. Perhaps he was not as uneducated or as foreign as he wished to appear.

At all events, Lindbergh was told that they would now have to keep the baby until everything had quieted down, and the ransom payment would be increased to $70,000. The kidnappers (who always referred to themselves in the plural) said they would not accept any intermediary chosen by Lindbergh. The letter assured him the baby was in good health, was being cared for night and day, and would be given the prescribed diet. In a postscript, the writer said that the kidnapping had been in preparation "for years"—a somewhat surprising claim since the baby was only twenty months old and the Hopewell house only recently completed. Given all that time, it was surprising that they could not construct, or even buy, a better ladder!

Lindbergh now persisted in his policy of pursuing the underground route. He gave the second ransom note to Rosner, who took it to New York, where it was read by Col. Breckinridge and Owney Madden. Rosner then enlisted the aid of two more unsavory friends, Salvadore Spitale and Irving Bitz, and introduced them to Lindbergh.

These were top-flight gangsters, strongly suspected of the murder of Legs Diamond, for whom Spitale had organized and committed multiple killings in the 1920s. In late 1930, Spitale had approached Bitz on Diamond's behalf to raise $200,000 in seed money to finance a major drug purchase in Germany. The money was delivered, but Diamond never repaid the loan. Instead, he paid with his life.

Spitale, prior to his association with Legs Diamond, had been a bootlegger and speakeasy owner who had begun his career as a bouncer in a Williamsburg dance hall. Bitz, who owned several speakeasies, had been to jail ten times between 1922 and 1927 and had done time in Atlanta for peddling drugs. He had a reputation as a vicious criminal.

Incredibly, these were the people enlisted by Charles Lindbergh—rather than the police or FBI—to help recover his son. He issued a statement appointing them as go-betweens with the kidnappers. Soon after Lindbergh appointed them, both men were charged with landing a cargo of liquor at a beach in Brooklyn, but thanks to their newfound status, they were acquitted. There was widespread outrage at Lindbergh's decision, not least on the part of New York Police Commissioner Mulrooney. It also transpired that Rosner, who had described himself as "a former government agent," was under indictment for grand larceny in a stock-selling promotion in which the public had lost more than $2 million and was awaiting trial on bail of $20,000. (The charge was subsequently dismissed in April 1933, possibly due to Rosner's other occupation as a police informant.)

Rosner, Spitale, and Bitz got nowhere. Unhampered by surveillance, they followed up every underworld contact they could think of, but gangsterdom remained firmly in denial. Rosner said at one point that he knew with certainty that the baby was alive and would soon be returned to its parents, but he was whistling in the dark.

Finally, Spitale called a press conference to admit defeat. "If it was someone I knew," he said, "I'd be God-damned if I didn't name him. But I been in touch all round, and I come to the conclusion this one was pulled by an independent." That is, it was the work of an amateur, not a professional.

A third note was received on March 8, this time addressed to Col. Breckinridge at his office. Breckinridge was at Hopewell at the time and had an assistant bring the note to Princeton Junction, New Jersey, where he and Rosner read it.

The note advised that the kidnappers would not accept any intermediary appointed by the Lindberghs, but that they would arrange one. Lindbergh was instructed to insert the following advertisement in the *New York American* of March 9:

Letter received at new address. Will follow your instructions. I also received letter mailed to me March 4 and was ready since then. Please hurry on account of mother. Address me to the address you mentioned in your letter. Father.

That same day, while the underworld was still being churned fruitlessly, a new figure entered the scene: Dr. John F. Condon. From this point on, Condon was to become the pivotal character in the case. Bombast, chauvinist, sycophant, liar, egotist supreme: Condon was all of these and then some. This was the man who, according to the actress Rosalind Russell and numerous other correspondents (see Chapter 6), had been responsible for looking after the illegitimate son of Dwight W. Morrow. It was possible to believe anything of the good doctor (of pedagogy, not medicine).

But there was more to John Condon than all that, as the FBI was to discover when they borrowed two of his scrapbooks in the summer of 1934. There they found not only press cuttings giving laudatory accounts of his athletic prowess and abilities as a teacher, but also stories of considerable heroism. In 1886, Condon had saved a boy from drowning when he fell through the ice at Zeltner's Lake in the Bronx, an act for which he was awarded the Congressional Medal of Honor. Two years later, he saved another skater, this time on a lake in New York's Central Park, earning the award of a pair of silver ice skates. Then, in 1900, he rescued a nine-year-old boy, Walter Hoy, who had been ice skating in Crotona Park. It was becoming a habit, and he had not finished yet. Shortly afterwards, the *Bronx Home News* carried the following story:

There was great excitement at Lake Teednyiskung Tuesday of last week over the upsetting of a canoe. In the boat were Jessie, Lloyd and Ward Brown, sons and daughter of Mrs P. Brown of Brooklyn.

There were no swimmers in the party and the entire trio was in danger of drowning. Had it not been for the timely action of Mr John Condon of Morrisenia, who notwithstanding the fact he was heavily encumbered with clothing, swam to the rescue and succeeded in keeping the Browns above water until Dr. Tanner Hawley rendered able assistance, there would undoubtedly have been loss of life. It is needless to say that the heroic New Yorker won the gratitude of Mrs Brown and a just measure of praise from all the witnesses of his brave act.

Condon was becoming a veritable Superman, always on hand when a life needed to be saved. At Staten Island, on an unrecorded date, he jumped from Doyle's Pier and saved a boy after he sank beneath the surface for the third time. And in 1903, he rescued a teenager, David Lickefberg, when he fell through the ice at Van Cortland lake. It almost seemed that Condon had spent several years patrolling frozen lakes just in case an opportunity for life-saving should present itself. One wonders whether he pushed them in before saving them.

Age had undimmed his heroism, whatever else it might have done to him. In March 1934, he was among several hundred people in a Bronx theater when it caught fire. In the ensuing panic, with everyone rushing for the exits, Condon stood up on a seat, reasoned with the audience, and restored calm. He was given a testimonial by the theater management.

None of this made the FBI like Condon any better, but the cuttings did go a long way to explain why Charles Fay, Dwight Morrow's lawyer, might have selected him as a suitable candidate to look after his client's illegitimate son, if such a child existed. In the early 1900s, he was clearly seen as a person of courage, integrity, and ability.

Condon, according to his own account, had been incensed by the fact that Lindbergh, whom he idolized, should resort to criminals in order to retrieve his son. He decided to act and sent a letter to his local newspaper, the *Bronx Home News*, in which he offered to act as an intermediary between Lindbergh and the kidnappers, and even to add his savings of $1,000 to the ransom money. He also promised not to testify against them.

To the editor of the *Bronx Home News*, circulation 150,000, Condon was no stranger. He had been a regular contributor for many years, writing poems and occasional articles that were signed "P.A.Triot," "J.U.Stice," or "L.O.Nestar." The editor decided to print Condon's letter as a front-page article, though it seemed unlikely that anyone would take any notice.

Dr. John F. Condon Offers to Add One Thousand Dollars of His Savings Ransom Lindbergh Child.

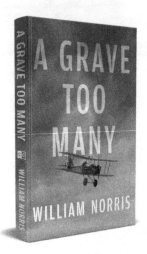

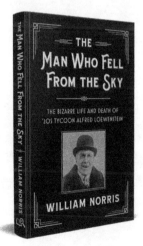
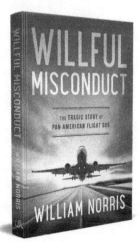

CamCat
Perspectives